The Financial Post

100

BEST

COMPANIES

TO WORK FOR IN

CANADA

EVA INNES, JIM LYON & JIM HARRIS

Harper Collins

TORONTO

First published 1986
This revised and updated edition
published 1990 by
Harper Collins Publishers Ltd.
Suite 2900, Hazelton Lanes
55 Avenue Road, Toronto, Ontario M5R 3L2

©   1990 by The Financial Post
     First printing

Canadian Cataloguing in Publication Data

Innes, Eva.
  The Financial post 100 best companies
to work for in Canada : 1990-1991 edition

2nd ed., rev.
ISBN 0-00-215673-3

1. Employee morale - Canada. 2. Corporations -
Canada. I. Lyon, Jim, 1935- . II. Harris, Jim
(James R.M.). III. Title. IV. Title: The 100 best
companies to work for in Canada : 1990-1991 edition.

HD2809.I66 1990   331.2'0971   C90-093086-1

Printed and bound in Canada by T.H. Best Printing Co.

ACKNOWLEDGMENTS

THIS SECOND edition of *The 100 Best Companies to Work for in Canada* is dedicated to Dalton Robertson, for many years the executive editor of The Financial Post. Without his support, encouragement and diligent, elegant editing, the first edition of this book would not have been nearly as successful.

The research and writing of this book would not have been possible without the assistance of the editors of The Financial Post, who provided us with the facilities needed.

Special thanks go to Shirley Golder, Kirsteen MacLeod, William Murray, Catherine Harris and Laura Fowlie for their editing and checking as we raced to meet the final deadline.

We're also grateful to Randall Litchfield, editor of The Small Business Magazine, who allowed us to share some of his research for his article on Canada's top bosses.

TABLE OF CONTENTS

CHALLENGERS   111

MAINSTREAM   176

CLASSICS   256

IN A CLASS OF THEIR OWN   319

LISTS   364

INTRODUCTION

FOUR YEARS have passed since we put together the first list of Canada's best employers. Re-examining that group of companies has been very instructive. Although we anticipated change, the amount we found came as a surprise.

Close to a third of the original 100 Best — 28 companies — are no longer in this select group. Without doubt, the single biggest external reason is the number of mergers and takeovers that have taken place in the brief interval between our first and second editions.

Mergers may make good business sense, but from the employee's point of view, most do not. In almost every case, the effects of the merger have had a negative impact on employee morale. Rank-and-file employees are all too often the victims of takeover mania.

In most mergers, events follow a depressingly similar pattern. The initial news creates anxiety among workers — what's going to happen to my job? Productivity goes down. The controlling organization restructures the acquired company, bringing in new managers, while dismissing, retiring or moving the previous managers. A fresh focus and a change in management style prompt some workers to leave.

During this period, the organization ceases to meet the criteria for high levels of employee satisfaction. Three or four years later, though, the new managers have moved the organization in a different direction and brought stability back to the company. Only then is it possible to re-establish a working environment that employees would characterize as excellent.

WHO'S OUT (DELETIONS FROM THE LIST)

Some companies have simply ceased to exist as separate corporate entities, and thus could not be included in our list. Wardair, for example, was taken over by Canadian Airlines International. Pemberton Houston Willoughby and Bell Gouinlock Inc. were absorbed by RBC Dominion Securities. Kidd Creek Mines went through two changes of ownership, first being taken over by Falconbridge, which in turn was gobbled up by Noranda.

Another kind of takeover occurred when National Life Assurance Co. of Canada was acquired by Industrial-Alliance Life Insurance Co. of Sillery, Que. National Life didn't lose its name, but restructuring soon undermined the company's people-oriented policies. In a major shuffle of senior management, National Life's president, Ross Johnson, architect of the people-oriented philosophy, took early retirement. No clearly defined corporate culture has replaced the former one at National, and the vacuum has taken its toll on employee morale.

Other forms of corporate restructuring also resulted in deletions from the list. C-I-L was reorganized by ICI, its British multinational parent. Famous Players Development Corp. lost much of its autonomy.

Internal restructuring within the Bentall Group changed the atmosphere in this formerly remarkable company. Another group of companies, also involved in restructuring of various kinds, withdrew from our survey voluntarily. Nova Corp., still struggling to absorb its takeover of Polysar, decided the present climate was not ideal for us to survey employee morale. After top management shuffles, two food companies, Peter Macgregor Ltd. and Farmer's Co-operative Dairies Ltd., declined to participate.

Several other organizations withdrew without explanation, and a few companies didn't respond to our repeated requests for updated information.

Two organizations have ceased to exist, most notably Principal Group Ltd. In 1985, we looked at Principal from an employee's viewpoint, not an investor's. We did point out that the company had an "aggressive, hustling, pressure-cooker" environment, where the pay was very good. We rated the atmosphere as "unsettled" and job security as "average."

The second shutdown was that of the phosphorus plant of Albright & Wilson Americas (formerly Erco Industries) at Long Harbour, Nfld. The plant was no longer cost-effective, and was being phased out by parent company Tenneco Canada Inc.

Then there's the group of formerly excellent employers that didn't make the grade this time. After checking and in some cases interviewing employees, it became clear these organizations had lost the superlative atmospheres they once had: the Blackburn Group, Develcon Electronics Ltd., the Edmonton Eskimos Football Club, Placer Development Ltd. (now Placer Dome Inc.), Thomson-Gordon Ltd., SNC Group Ltd. and the Toronto Transit Commission. However, these formerly excellent employers may well become candidates again.

WHO'S IN (ADDITIONS TO THE LIST)

There are some notable newcomers. In 1985, we suspected that oil and gas explorer Canadian Hunter was probably a winner, but it refused to participate then. Happily, the company changed its mind this time. Du Pont Canada, also reluctant in 1985, is on the new list. The Canadian McDonalds Restaurants joins the blue-ribbon group, as does the Hongkong Bank of Canada. Royal Trust, a high-powered financial services company, makes its debut this time.

Three retailers join the 100 Best this time: The Body Shop, Lipton's International and Weall & Cullen Nurseries. Two food companies made the grade: Jacobs Suchard and Pillsbury Canada. And two insurers are new on the list: The Prudential and Equitable Life.

We broadened the range of employers surveyed for the second edition, and two more Crown corporations make the list: Canada Mortgage & Housing Corp. and B.C. Building Corp. This time, the City of Waterloo, Ont., proves that government can provide an excellent working environment. A nursing home in Saskatchewan, the Parkridge Centre, is the first health care institution to join the list.

Eight of the newcomers are rooted in Western Canada, while the rest are based in Ontario and Quebec. There's not a single new entry from the Atlantic Provinces, which tells a lot about the lack of economic growth in the region.

We also discovered this time that if you want work for the single best type of company, then apply for a job at a *telephone company*. No fewer than three telephone companies are covered in this edition: British Columbia Telephone Co., Bell Canada and New Brunswick Telephone Co. The list also includes another four organizations involved in the manufacture or distribution of telecommunications equipment: Bell-Northern Research Ltd., Northern Telecom Canada Ltd., NovAtel Communications Ltd. and TSB International Ltd.

The number of media companies has shrunk. Only three make the grade this time: Canada Publishing Corp., Telemedia Inc. and the Toronto Sun.

NEW TRENDS

Certain trends became apparent as we analyzed the changes in the excellent workplace since 1985. In short, we found a number of differences in the way companies treat their workforces.

● **The concept of job security is rapidly changing.**

A few years ago there were still some traditional organizations where an employee could hope to get a job for life. That kind of paternalism has almost vanished now. There still exists many companies that pride themselves on their long-service employees, but it's because the workers are good performers, not because of tenure.

Job security now means job performance. An effective employee, prepared to learn new skills continually, needn't worry about job security at one of the excellent employers. And employers are increasingly linking compensation to effectiveness. Pay for performance is the rule, rather than the exception in today's top workplaces.

● **The general working environment has a harder edge to it today.**

The country club atmosphere is a thing of the past. The trend to bigger, more luxurious offices has given way to efficiency and ergonomics. For example, the Canadian division head office of Manufacturers Life in Waterloo, Ont., still provides a superior work environment in a beautiful building, but the offices are all smaller than in the firm's international headquarters in Toronto.

Extras and frills have given way to practicality and a down-to-earth, no-nonsense style. In 1985, almost every company the authors visited served us free muffins, doughnuts, coffee, tea and the like. Their absence in 1989 gives a new perspective to the term "lean and mean."

● **There's an even stronger emphasis on increasing productivity.**

Nearly every company on the list seems to be doing more business, but with fewer employees. Quality circles, gain sharing, suggestion plans and other productivity-boosting programs are common. This drive to do more with less stems from the prospect of increasingly fiercer competition, not only from the U.S. under free trade, but also from global competitors. Canadian companies are comparing their results with those of offshore competitors, and realizing they *must* do better.

● **The single biggest change from 1985 is the growing emphasis on training.**

Employers have realized that more training and personal development of employees leads to higher productivity. Training used to be limited to narrowly job-specific courses, but now companies are offering much broader training to a wider spectrum of employees. Many organizations have established full-time, in-house training centres that operate year round.

An average of five days of mandatory courses per year per employee has become the norm in many firms. Optional management courses are now being offered to employees on almost all levels. Ambitious workers take as many as they can fit in, knowing that these programs increase their chances for advancement. More companies also now subsidize external educational upgrading, even if it's not specifically job-related.

● **Change has affected the area of benefits.**

The most dramatic has been the shift toward flexible benefits, allowing employees to choose, cafeteria-style, the level and coverage most suited to their needs. This in many cases eliminates the duplication of benefits coverage now common in two-career families. Only five companies in the 100 Best offered flexible packages in 1989, but some other companies had plans to make the switch to flexible packages in 1990 or 1991. They include CMHC, Pillsbury Canada, Canadian Tire, Dupont of Canada and McDonalds Restaurants of Canada. Another half dozen have launched studies on possible future implementation. Still others provide partially flexible benefits. There's no doubt that flexibility is the trend for the future.

More interest in employee health shows up in the well-being

programs now common in benefits packages. They encourage employees to quit smoking, watch their weight and exercise themselves to fitness. Concern for the employee's psychological and emotional well-being has led to a dramatic increase in the number of employee assistance programs. More than two thirds of the 100 Best now have EAPs to deal confidentially with employees' difficulties in such areas as debt, alcohol, drugs and family.

● **Canadian business has started to develop a social conscience.**

Being an excellent employer often means setting high standards for every aspect of business conducted by the company. This translates into a concern for sensible waste management, recycling, energy efficiency and broader social issues.

The Body Shop, for example, exemplifies the new environmental consciousness. It built a worldwide business on its environmental philosophy, by manufacturing and retailing only naturally based, environmentally safe cosmetic and soap products for women.

Business scandals ranging from the revelation of questionable practices at the Principal Group to insider trading on Wall Street have underscored the need for superior standards of business behavior. Some Canadian companies, including Canada Trust, Royal Bank and Imperial Oil, have established corporate codes of ethics. Every new employee at these companies must not only read the code, but also sign an agreement to adhere to its principles.

For excellent companies, involvement in the community at large is part of good corporate behavior. Some organizations allocate specified percentages of their profits to support community events, charities and the arts.

● **An increase in the numbers of women in managerial positions is one of the most notable changes since 1985.**

Women presidents are still in short supply, but 20 of the 100 Best have more than 33% women managers. This leads to the hope that the coming years will see a big increase among executives as well.

METHODS

We picked the candidates for the second 100 Best much as we

did for the first. We talked to management consultants, business school professors and journalistic contacts, as well as searching library files. We again publicized our project in The Financial Post, urging readers to write and tell us about memorable and excellent employers.

Word-of-mouth recommendations played an important role. Many executives gave us the names of the companies they viewed as the competition in the good employer stakes. We tried to survey them all.

This time, we also tried to standardize our procedures by creating a questionnaire, which was sent to every company that wanted to participate. It asked detailed questions in 11 different areas: general corporate information, hiring practices, pay, benefits, promotion, job security, atmosphere, job satisfaction, communications, personal development and labor relations.

But what employees had to say about their place of work was still what mattered most to us — the make-or-break factor. In fact, some of the most impressive-looking corporate candidates on paper failed to measure up after we listened to their employees.

We interviewed employees of new corporate candidates in groups of different ages, departments, length of service and position. Seeking a balanced view of each company, we encouraged employees to speak frankly and assured them of confidentiality. (No company is perfect, and employees of the 100 Best companies always seemed to have a list of improvements in mind, things the company could do better.)

We also usually interviewed the head of human resources and the chief executive officer.

We didn't revisit personally all of the companies reappearing from the first 100 Best, but we did re-examine each through the questionaire and extensive telephone interviews.

CATEGORIES

We did not rate the companies on a scale of one to 100. Rather than attempting, in effect, to declare apples superior to oranges, or vice versa, we simply slotted the companies into five broad categories of management style. A corporation can be dynamic and innovative in a business sense, and yet still be classified as middle of the road or traditional in its corporate culture.

All of the 100 Best provide superior work environments, but some are more dynamic in the way they do things, while others remain cautious traditionalists. We categorized the innovative leaders as Pace Setters, while the next generation of up-and-comers are the Challengers. Mainstream represents the middle ground, while staunch traditionalists are Classics. The unique or hard-to-classify companies appear In a Class of Their Own.

The Toronto Sun, then a distant relative of The Financial Post through its corporate link with Maclean Hunter Ltd., qualified hands-down as one of the first 100 Best. Since then, by a quirk of fate, the Sun's parent, Toronto Sun Publishing Corp., has become the majority shareholder of The Post.

However, we reasoned that if the Sun made the list in 1985, it would be unfair to rule it out because of the corporate connection. We revisited the Sun, and found it still a fine place to work.

CRITERIA

What makes a company a good place to work? We applied the same eight criteria established for the first 100 Best. They fall into two distinct categories:

- Tangible, verifiable qualities — pay, benefits, job security and opportunities for advancement.
- Subjective, but equally important intangible elements — atmosphere, job satisfaction, communications and personal development.

We have tried to be scrupulously balanced in our assessments, but the judgments made by each of the three authors are journalistic and subjective. We do not claim to be scientific. We listened to employees, questioned them thoroughly on both the praiseworthy and criticial comments they made about their company, and made our assessments accordingly.

Our ratings on pay and benefits are based on information provided by the companies themselves. We tried to take regional variations into account, realizing that what counts as a good salary in Cape Breton wouldn't go very far in the superheated Toronto economy. We also paid attention to employees' own perceptions of their compensation.

Bread-and-butter issues such as pay and benefits are important considerations, but they're what the experts call "hygiene factors" — important mainly if they're not attended to. Generally speaking, employees seem to complain only when their pay and benefits are considerably below an average, competitive level.

Clearly, very few people choose a job or career simply because of pay. Once compensation is no longer an issue, other factors seem to be far more important. When asked why they like working for a particular company, employees' first response tends to be: "I like the family atmosphere here" or "I like the people I work with." Our research bears out earlier findings that intangible qualities are far more important considerations.

THE RATINGS

We decided to standardize the ratings for the second 100 Best. All rankings in all eight categories use the following words: poor, below average, average, good, very good and excellent. Any more subtle variations are discussed in the text.

CONCLUSIONS

Interviews with employees make it clear that certain characteristics are important in helping to create an excellent working environment.

• **Decision making:** Many workers value being brought into the process. Companies are making do with fewer managerial layers than in the past, and even those that used to rule by edict are finding it surprisingly easy to involve employees in more of the decisions.

Workers on assembly lines advise engineers on the placement of new machines. Office workers have a say in the selection of the office furniture they spend 35 hours a week using. And companies are discovering that increased productivity often results.

• **Communication:** Employees who make decisions need more information, so good communication is increasingly important. By sharing information, companies develop a sense of belonging among employees. Keeping workers informed about company policies, progress, upcoming ventures and so forth fosters teamwork, and lessens the risk of dissatisfaction. Excellent companies communicate all the time at all levels.

• **Recognition programs:** A pat on the back for a job well done goes a long way toward boosting morale, so excellent employers do it regularly, whether by formal awards or just sincere thank yous.

• **Career development:** First-class companies don't concern themselves with only the job an employee is doing today. They also plan for the long term. Succession and career planning pay dividends for both parties. The organization can chart a little more accurately its future manpower needs and at the same time help the individual employee make sensible career choices. An essential part of the process is training.

One purpose of this book is to demonstrate that such things as incentives, participative decision making, closer contacts between workers and senior managers, fewer rules and formal procedures, more flexibility in hours, an emphasis on continuing training, education and development are not mere kindnesses. They make good business sense.

There's a common misconception that spending on improvements to human resources is like flushing money down the drain. The reality is that most of the companies in this book have good bottom lines, better than many companies that don't rate highly as employers.

Another purpose of this book is to help job seekers who want to work for the best employers, and many do. Companies in the first 100 Best were inundated with applications. But a reputation as a fine employer carries an onus. A company with a quality working environment must be diligent about maintaining it. Employees are becoming increasingly knowledgable and more critical of their workplace, and not afraid to voice their views.

Job seekers should keep in mind that there's no one "right" type of organizational structure. Anything from the traditional rigid pyramid to a free-form matrix can be a fine place to work — if it suits the individuals in it. In other words, the same organization can "taste" different to different employees. Finding the right organization to work for depends as much on the would-be employee as it does on the corporate culture. Both have to complement each other.

THE
PACE SETTERS

These are the leaders — dynamic, trend-setting companies, always striving to be innovative in their management techniques.

Apple Canada Inc.

APPLE CANADA INC.

7495 Birchmount Road
Markham, Ontario
L3R 5G2
(416) 477-5800

Pay: **EXCELLENT**	Atmosphere: **EXCELLENT**
Benefits: **VERY GOOD**	Job Satisfaction: **VERY GOOD**
Promotion: **AVERAGE**	Communications: **VERY GOOD**
Job Security: **GOOD**	Personal Development: **EXCELLENT**

★ *Apple Canada is primarily a sales and marketing subsidiary of Apple Computer Inc. of Cupertino, Calif. The subsidiary has 396 employees in 11 offices across Canada. Apple Canada's 1989 sales were about $336 million.*

THE CORE of the environment found at Apple Canada is Apple values. "There's been a mention of Apple values at every meeting I've ever attended," one long-time employee says. "Everybody talks to us about them all the time," agrees another. enthusiastic worker.

So what are these sacred Apple values and what makes them so special? Put out by Apple headquarters in California's Silicon Valley, they are principles intended to create a challenging, exciting, entrepreneurial work environment. The emphasis is on aggressive achievement of goals, on innovative approaches, on high levels of teamwork, commitment and excellence. Individual rewards, both financial and psychological, are given for high performance.

The values are talked about so much that they seem to become guiding precepts. "We're not really a company," explained one fervent follower. "We're really a cult! You begin to believe in it like a religion."

This Californian enthusiasm is apparent immediately. People work with a shirt-sleeves informality, and everyone on a first-name basis. There is also a dearth of middle management — only four rungs separate President J. David Rae from the warehouse worker. When the need arises, everyone pitches in and helps out. One employee described Apple as the "company where the president dons jeans and ships product in the warehouse with everybody else."

This informality has persisted through Apple Canada's growth from 120 employees in the mid-1980s to 415 in 1990. "There's still that family atmosphere," says Peter Mason, human resources co-ordinator. But now there is more structure within the company, including formal job descriptions for all positions and more specialization. This means there is a clear path for career progression.

Growth also has meant a new approach to decision making. While at one time decisions were made by consensus, now decisions are made mainly by a six-member management team. "But there is still a lot of feedback from staff," Mason says. "There are many avenues for you to have your say."

One outlet is the quarterly communications day, when 250 staff from all Apple offices get together to exchange ideas and talk about the future of the company.

Despite the changes, Apple hasn't become hierarchical. "Everyone here works on the same floor; we don't have executives in the highest tower, " Mason says. And secretaries are a rare breed, because everyone does his or her own typing.

While long hours are the norm, a very good salary does compensate for the extra work. And so does the profit sharing plan, which pays out a quarterly cash payment based on operating profit.

Benefits are good, and getting better all the time. Extras include $200 a year toward a health club membership or purchase of exercise equipment, a $500 bonus for the birth of a child and a six week paid sabbatical (in addition to regular vacation) after each five years of employment. Generous educational assistance provides up to $2,500 a year for post-secondary courses successfully completed.

Another perk that Canadian Apple employees share with their

American counterparts is the right to take home an Apple computer on loan after two months on the job. A year later, the employee owns the machine outright.

To help in team building, some employees are sent on week-long Outward Bound trips in northern Ontario every summer. The result, enthusiastic converts say on their return from these gruelling outdoor tests, is a sense of teamwork and reliance on fellow workers.

Apple Canada has taken Apple values so much to heart that it seems to be outdoing its American parent. In both 1987 and 1988, the Canadian operation was chosen as Apple's country of the year by all its affiliated companies. In 1988, Rae was named manager of the year, and an Apple Canada sales representative won the sales rep of the year award.

Apple provides an excellent work environment for the innovative, hard-working, loyal team player who thrives on informality and change.

BELL-NORTHERN
RESEARCH LTD.

P.O. Box 3511, Station C
Ottawa, Ontario
K1Y 4H7
(613) 763-2211

Pay: **VERY GOOD**	Atmosphere: **EXCELLENT**
Benefits: **VERY GOOD**	Job Satisfaction: **EXCELLENT**
Promotion: **VERY GOOD**	Communications: **VERY GOOD**
Job Security: **EXCELLENT**	Personal Development: **EXCELLENT**

★ *Bell Northern Research (known as BNR) is the research and development subsidiary of Northern Telecom Ltd., while Bell Canada is also a shareholder. (Both owners also appear in this book.) BNR's operating budget of more than US$600 million operates six labs in Canada, the U.S. and Britain, staffed by nearly 6,000 full-time employees. The two Canadian labs, in Ottawa and Montreal, employ 4,300 people full time.*

BNR'S DRIVING force is its young employees, ranging in age from early 20s to late 30s. Ross Campbell, vice-president, human resources and administration, says they help to produce "an excitement you seldom see in a large organization."

The opportunity to work in the global arena adds to the excitement. In the past, parent company Northern Telecom was primarily a supplier of telecommunications equipment to the North American market, but it is rapidly becoming a world class organization. BNR designs and develops technology with this in mind. The drive is now on to develop products that can be put into any country, rather than being modified for international

15

use.

Campbell says this situation "gives the employees a lot more challenges and more opportunity," including travel. Northern Telecom operates in more than 100 countries, and an employee can be called on at any time to do "field work."

"We're in one of the highest growth businesses, certainly over the past couple of decades, and by all wisdom and suggestion, into the next two decades as well," says Tony Marsh, assistant vice-president, human resources. "This leads to a tremendous amount of ongoing change and activity. The challenge never stops."

The next challenge involves the recent announcement of "fibre world," meaning an expansion of all BNR product lines. Northern Telecom is committed to an end-to-end fibre-optic telecommunications network based on an international standard. Fibre optics will replace the old copper wires in the network, resulting in increased capacity and capability. "We always have something to rally around," Marsh says. "This gives employees a direction of purpose, a forward motion. Employees have pride in what they're doing, and pride in what BNR is achieving."

This vision of the future is not blind. BNR's Vision 2000 program asks, "Where do we want to be in the year 2000?" Employees across the country get together to share their views on where the company is heading, how it can get there and why the company does what it does.

Training is an essential part of the process. It's a reflection of the fact that BNR employees work with fast-growing technology. The company spends more than $20 million annually on in-house training. In addition, it will pay for relevant education pursued by employees at outside institutions. There are several competition-based rewards for employees returning to post-graduate studies.

Of the 800 people hired annually, about 50% are recent graduates. BNR is concerned with technical excellence, and while "we don't restrict ourselves to the top 10% of each class, we ask more questions of the others," Marsh says. About 1,000 students are hired each year in three- or four-month co-op programs.

"What we really want are people who are going to respond well to challenge, who can cope with pressure and who enjoy teamwork," Marsh says, adding, "We get our fair share of female graduates in the science and technology field but we aren't satisfied with the numbers." Women make up approximately 23% of BNR's work force. Many female employees visit schools not only to discuss career options but also to provide the students with role models.

Communication is excellent. "Lab Councils" meet in each division and on a corporate basis. Employees are free to raise concerns with senior management. The president attends the corporate council, which is held every few of months.

There is a "show and tell" held among different departments. Managers with new projects use the auditorium to put on demonstrations and displays. A lot of employee interest is generated this way, and it encourages workers to move among departments.

Computers have been demystified for BNR employees. Almost every desk has a terminal. There is an on-line job-posting program that allows employees to "check the want ads" each morning when they log onto their terminals.

A grassroots emphasis on fitness permeates the organization. A running trail winds through the greenbelt grounds. There are baseball diamonds, soccer fields and a company-owned fitness centre. Employees pay $50 annually for a membership. Interest is high, and currently there is a waiting list.

Other benefits include a stop-smoking program provided by the company's medical department, and additional payments on top of UIC maternity benefits to 75% of the employee's salary. Part-time employees are covered by a reduced benefits package, including life insurance, medical coverage, drug plan and travel-accident insurance.

The enthusiasm is discernible. "People don't ever take advantage of [things like flexible hours] because everybody is so dedicated to what they're doing," says a female software designer in her first job. "They're here for their work, not because of the money. And this is why I'm here,"

A building called Lab Three, described as "a monster computer room surrounded by people" and designed for 24-hour access, seven days a week, has coffee and food machines on every floor. Some BNR people prefer to work nights and weekends, when more computer power is available.

If you are a young, ambitious, team player who thrives on challenge, and interested in working in the global high-technology field, BNR is the place for you.

17

BOMBARDIER INC.
Mass Transit Division

350 Nobel Street
Boucherville, Quebec
J4B 1A1
(514) 655-3830

Pay: **VERY GOOD**	Atmosphere: **VERY GOOD**
Benefits: **VERY GOOD**	Job Satisfaction: **EXCELLENT**
Promotion: **GOOD**	Communications: **VERY GOOD**
Job Security: **GOOD**	Personal Development: **VERY GOOD**

★ *This autonomous division of Bombardier Inc. designs and manufactures rail passenger cars for an international market. In the 1988/89 fiscal year, this division manufactured more than 60% of all new U.S. rail transit vehicles. MTD has 1,050 workers in four locations, half of them unionized in the Confederation of National Trade Unions.*

IN 1974, when the Montreal Transit Authority awarded Bombardier a contract to build 423 subway cars, the company committed itself to something it had never done before, then hired an executive to do it at La Pocatière, Que. And so began a remarkable industrial success story.

La Pocatière, on the south shore of the St. Lawrence east of Quebec City, was a rural town of 5,000 with few technical skills. When Bombardier announced its plans to build subway cars in the snowmobile plant there, the workers shook their heads and said they could never learn to do such jobs.

With some government financial assistance, the division bought a school building and trained an entire workforce from scratch. Two years later, cheering and applauding themselves, the employees streamed out of the plant to watch the first finished cars move off to Montreal.

The new division has gone on to become an international leader. Adding to its front-runner status in North America, Bombardier recently won an $800-million contract to provide railway cars for the British/French channel tunnel. Other giant contract bids are in the offing as well, confirming MTD's global pre-eminence.

"There's not a mass transit company in the world that has an order book as filled as Bombardier's," a project manager boasts. "It's something to be part of a team [that can accomplish such a thing]. This is a very important point for me. I don't work for just anybody. I work for Bombardier."

When a purchasing man joined the division in 1979, he marveled at the fact that the operation had succeeded without experienced people. He soon came to understand why.

"The company could succeed and did succeed just by its way of doing things," he explains. "I think one of our major strengths is the ability to solve our problems. There's a strong desire to help one another. The atmosphere — [created by] people who want to help each other and are not afraid to discuss their problems to find solutions — sets this company apart."

Raymond Royer had an opportunity few men get — the challenge of building a large organization from the ground up. The proof of his success was his swift rise to his current position — president and chief operating officer of the parent corporation.

Armed with the knowledge that "a company cannot be better than the people who work for it," Royer began by drawing up the MTD's first organization chart, establishing 21 top management jobs, 18 of which would have to be filled from outside the company.

To attract people to La Pocatière, Royer set forth some alluring management principles. His first was that the new entity would operate on teamwork. The second: managers would face no impediment to their personal development or "growing up." (Royer's goal in his own working life was "to grow up, to become better at what I was doing.")

With the basic principles in mind, Royer drafted the hiring criteria for his senior managers. "Teamwork meant I needed people who would respect people. I wanted people with high principles and integrity. I wanted people with creativity — we needed ideas — and perseverance. To execute a mass-transit contract takes from three to five years."

Royer's prime rule was that all manufacturing problems affecting more than one department would be discussed in a group, but the department with the problem would have full responsibility for implementing the decisions. And the rule went into effect immediately.

The first financial objectives of the new division had been set by the terms of the Montreal contract. Once Royer and his department heads had decided in general how the goals could be met, each department was given the responsibility for its own planning.

"The people in the different departments felt involved. They felt that we were not putting any restraint on their growing up," Royer says. "Finally, I tied everybody [in top management] to a bonus plan, but a group bonus plan. If the division were successful, they would be successful. If the division were to fail, everybody would get nothing." So the amount of the individual bonus, paid in cash, was directly in line with the achievements of the whole group.

To promote quality and efficiency, Royer started a program in which he met all employees personally in groups of about 50, called technical councils. It took 21 sessions, but by mid-1985 he had managed to talk with every employee at La Pocatière.

The councils don't exist now, but management seeks feedback through regular all-employee discussions about the company's future. Gaetan Tessier, vice-president of human resources, says these meetings are valuable to the company. Recently, for example, when employees were consulted about how to lay out the plant for a new contract, "they told us where the best places were for the machines, and saved a lot of time and money."

The result of Royer's groundwork is a youthful, aggressive, friendly organization with a minimum of written rules. In the MTD, as an employee puts it, "there's a deep respect for everyone." Workers describe a "family" in which letters and memos are signed with first names, in which top management has a self-confidence that makes employees feel free to express themselves. And the pride is almost tangible.

People dissatisfied with decisions can take their complaints as high in the hierarchy as necessary, even right to the top.

On three occasions, in fact, employees used the open door to ask Royer for help, and and he gave it.

A plant training supervisor says: "Decisions you make are backed up. You can make a mistake, and there's no finger-pointing. If you have an idea, you can put it forward and be sure it will be pursued. Nobody really holds all the truth. It's a team effort."

A plant man who has left and returned to Bombardier three times: "You're not just numbers here. You're people. I think what makes the company a success is that management considers everybody on the same level all the way down to the workers. I think that here, if you're asked to do something, you'll do it and you'll do a little more. It's that little more that makes the difference."

"You're left alone to do the job," a male program director says. "They give you the basic guidelines and the goal to achieve. How you get there is your problem. For me, it's very important not to have somebody looking over my shoulder all the time."

"I've got a feeling of real involvement and real participation," a production planner says. He's proud of managers "who really care about people, who try to reach goals through people. Those goals are not small goals. They are large goals. And this company lets you make a choice of the route you're going to follow to reach the goals."

"Where I used to work, you used to run equipment instead of running people," a production manager says. "Here it's more human. They get you involved. You participate in most of the de-cisions taken. It's a big family. You get all the help you need. What amazes me the most here is the human way it's run. You al-ways have a certain [sense of] belonging. They make you feel it, and it goes right down to the workers. Everybody belongs to the company. It's not, 'You're paid to do such and such a job. Do it and shut up.' Here, if you have an idea, you always let it out and somebody will listen to you."

"It's one of the few companies where you start working and after a short period you're not nervous. Everybody is willing to help you," a purchasing man says. "Each individual is given a chance to express himself, to contribute to the overall success of the company. The goals and objectives are very well defined. We all share these goals."

A man in production engineering: "Everyone is a part of the

company, with the same objectives. Everyone is young, and has the energy to do a little bit more when it's important."

Not surprisingly in such an environment, employees take full advantage of Bombardier's stock-purchase program, in which the company makes newly issued shares available at a price below the market average of the previous month. "The price formula isn't what makes everybody jump at it," an employee explains. "If you don't have the money, the company will arrange a loan through a banking organization at prime rate. It's very convenient."

Tessier adds that if employees buy, they get a 10% bonus per year for two years on their investment.

In fact, the spirit of the Mass Transit Division even extends into formal labor relations. Other areas of Bombardier are not unionized, but it is important to remember that the various divisions function as autonomous companies. And the bargaining unit at La Pacatière is a legacy from pre-Bombadier days. It had been organized before Bombardier purchased the plant in 1972.

Many consider the CNTU to be Quebec's most militant union, but it has posed no problems at La Pocatière. The bargaining in 1981, when management and the union reopened the contract a year early to reassure a large customer, tells something about the nature of the relationship. Tessier says this friendly, accommodating tone has been maintained since.

The spirit of involvement and participation is so strong at MTD that in the company's recent employee opinion survey more than 80% of the employees said they were satisfied specifically with "the behavior and attitudes of superiors, the organization of work and the opportunity for making suggestions." A broader question, dealing with the degree of general satisfaction of each employee with the entire work situation received the overwhelming positive rating of 92%. This company offers a model in harmonious labor relations.

BURNS FRY LIMITED

BURNS FRY LTD.

P.O. Box 150
1 First Canadian Place
Toronto, Ontario
M5X 1H3
(416) 365-4000

Pay: **VERY GOOD**	Atmosphere: **EXCELLENT**
Benefits: **AVERAGE**	Job Satisfaction: **VERY GOOD**
Promotion: **GOOD**	Communications: **GOOD**
Job Security: **VERY GOOD**	Personal Development: **EXCELLENT**

★ *Burns Fry is one of the five largest Canadian brokerages, with 1,507 employees scattered in 18 cities in Canada, as well as in the U.S., Britain, Switzerland, West Germany, France and Hong Kong. More than half of the workers are located at head office in Toronto. Burns Fry is owned 51% by an employee holding company and 49% by Security Pacific Corp., the fifth largest U.S. bank holding company.*

"WHEN PEOPLE ask me what I do, I don't say, 'I'm a stockbroker.' I just say, 'I work for Burns Fry.' " This sort of pride, commonplace at Burns Fry, sets the employees apart from most workers in the financial arena.

Toronto's Bay Street is not normally spoken of in the same breath as quality of working life or devotion to people. It's more usually linked with "burn-out." The performance-oriented working life creates pressures and stresses that are not always balanced by potentially high monetary rewards.

People at Burns seem to work just as hard as anyone else on the "Street," but they give the impression of enjoying it more and suffering from fewer of the disadvantages.

One of the reasons is the firm's genuine attempt to live by its corporate philosophy, which the company prides itself on, and believes sets it apart from its competitors:

● We wish to be a well-balanced, full-service, diversified financial service organization where the integrated whole is greater than the sum of the individual parts.

● The broad distribution of the company shares owned by the staff should provide a wide base of ownership, as well as long-term financial incentive for the employees.

● We want to provide a working environment which is challenging and rewards initiative. At the same time, the working goals should recognize the need for the work to be enjoyable. To have fun!

As Chief Executive Officer Jack Lawrence explains it: "We encourage entrepreneurial talent. We also encourage people to be creative, and give them great freedom to do so. We spend a great deal of time and trouble creating an environment that attracts the right kind of people."

And the right kind of people are "professionals, with high standards of integrity and ethics, balanced by a sense of humor; hard working, entrepreneurial types who are also team-players."

Entrepreneurial spirit extends even to the entry level. "There is always the chance to do the job more effectively or efficiently. We encourage people to make improvements. They are told that right from the time they are a candidate," says human resources generalist Doug Hennessy.

"When someone makes a mistake, we look at what went wrong and how things could have been done differently," says Colleen Watson, director of human resources. "People are not raked over the coals. As a result, people are encouraged to take risks, if they feel the quality of service to our clients will be improved. We all make mistake, but it takes mistakes to grow."

Most of the turnover is in administrative and clerical positions, mainly in the competitive Toronto market. In these positions, salaries are competitive with other brokerage firms, and also include the possibility of earning bonuses by making quality-improvement or money-saving suggestions.

Getting maximum performance from its employees meant Burns showed a profit in 1988, while the industry as a whole experienced a $100-million after-tax loss.

"There is recognition on the street that we are the most

professional firm," Vice-Chairman Don Johnson says. "Therefore we do tend to attract the best people." And they also work actively to bring new people to the company.

Burns Fry's Career Day, introduced in 1989, attracted more than 300 people interested in working in the industry. Managers described the industry and company and answered questions. Some 25-30 attendees were hired, and the company plans to initiate an annual recruitment drive.

What keeps people at Burns is a combination of factors, including prestige, reputation and concern for people, but also pay. As one salesperson candidly admitted: "Let's face it, money is a big motivating factor for everyone."

The October, 1987, crash didn't result in any drastic cuts in staff. Salaries and commission plans stayed the same. "We try to avoid cyclical hiring. After the market downturn, we relied on normal attrition to decrease staff numbers. There were no across-the-board cuts. Some people did leave on their own because industry turned down," Watson says.

The norm in the brokerage industry is low base salaries for sales and professional staff, augmented by performance-based bonuses. At Burns, though, unlike the norm, there's no ceiling on pay. As an employees explains, "Annual renumeration is above average. It's called incentive. Anyone can double their salary here."

This concern with money has its negative side, too. One Burns Fry employee complains that "we're too cash-reward oriented here." He feels that more effort should be made to provide alternative forms of recognition for performance, such as more time off, for example.

Benefits are comprehensive at Burns Fry, but employees carry more of the costs than at many other companies. For example, employees earning more than $27,000 pay their own provincial health plan costs. The company pays 80% of the dental plan fees; the employees, 20%. Additional benefits include educational assistance for job-related courses, with cash bonuses for successful completion, and a physical fitness subsidy. Employees have the option of joining a company pension plan or participating in a deferred profit-sharing plan.

Broad employee ownership of the firm also helps to ensure loyalty. More than 500 employees own company shares, allocated by position and length of service. "Employee ownership and control are an important part of our culture," says Chief Financial Officer Fred Troop.

In 1989, Security Pacific increased its holding in Burns Fry from 30% to 49%, but left the controlling interest with employees. There are no provisions for Security Pacific to increase its stake further. "Employee ownership is key, because it is a strong motivator," Watson says.

Problems are few at Burns Fry, but are most apparent in three areas: women, promotion and stress. Some employees are concerned that there are only two women among the 84 directors and only 25 women among 430 stockbrokers within the firm. The relative youth of senior managers at Burns Fry (the average age on the executive committee is only 49) creates worry in junior ranks about the possibilities for promotion.

And the stressful pace of life in the fast track inevitably causes strains and pressures. Some workers believe not enough attention is paid to the question of "burn-out" and how to avoid it. Performance is a god, and tolerance is not high for nonperformers in this highly competitive industry.

Watson has a response: "Physical fitness is a pivotal factor in controlling stress, we want people to participate in cardiovascular acitivities. The productivity increase [of people who exercise] is incredible."

This answer, of course, is not for everyone. But if it interests you, you should know the company has 200 corporate memberships in a fitness club in the basement of the head office building. Burns pays the initiation fees and reimburses employees for half of the $600 annual fee — as long as they use the club two to three times a week.

Employees at other offices can join any other club under the same arrangement, as long as the club has a qualified fitness instructor. Only 20% of staff take advantage of this benefit — perhaps because they have to pay the annual fee up front and wait a year to be reimbursed.

The quality that stands out about Burns Fry is its determination not only to make money, but to have fun doing it. Employees stress this repeatedly: "The concept of fun has always been fostered here. The job is so complex you have to have fun."

"You can have fun here and still be professional."

"Fun is a strange thing. It's not just partying, but doing the deal. Fun is doing and being challenged."

CAE
ELECTRONICS LTD.

8585 Côte de Liesse Road
Saint-Laurent, Quebec
H4T 1G6
(514) 341-6780

Pay: **GOOD**	Atmosphere: **VERY GOOD**
Benefits: **GOOD**	Job Satisfaction: **EXCELLENT**
Promotion: **GOOD**	Communications: **VERY GOOD**
Job Security: **VERY GOOD**	Personal Development: **EXCELLENT**

★ *CAE Electronics (CAE), based in Montreal, is the founding company of CAE Industries Ltd. (a family of 12 diversified, highly autonomous subsidiaries with a consolidated, after-tax net income of $43 million 1988-1989). CAE develops and manufactures sophisticated electronic systems, including flight and power-plant simulators, as well as marine and air traffic control systems. Roughly half of the 3,200 employees are scientists, engineers and technicians. Employees unionized in the Communications Workers of Canada are approximately 1,000 in number.*

CAE IS A world leader in glamorous, high-profile products, and the employees enjoy the international reputation. "Our successes tend to be widely recognized, and there's nothing like belonging to a successful company," an engineer comments.

CAE Electronics can be described as a remarkable place to work — from top to bottom — regardless of one's rank, experience or function. In fact, the company has many attributes of an ideal employer, with one glaring exception.

Almost everyone we met there thinks the compensation could

be better. The company did not provide specific information, but employees describe their pay as ranging from "adequate" and "not too bad" to "slightly above" the regional high-tech average. The benefits package (with an optional pension plan) rates as "only average."

Not surprisingly then, many CAE employees have moved to other high-tech industries in the area for financial betterment. The fascinating point is that a substantial number have taken salary cuts to return to CAE's welcoming fold.

People return to CAE, employees say, because of pluses that can't be deposited in a bank account. The most prized qualities can't even be measured in numbers.

"Although the work is highly professional, it is not formal," says a new employee. "It is not a high-stress environment, but a very relaxed, open atmosphere. I have never seen anything like it before. I can see myself staying here for the rest of my life."

"There's a certain electricity in the air," a marketing man explains. "You can feel it walking in from outside. It's the nicest atmosphere I've ever worked in."

Success and growth themselves imply reliable employment, but the strong sense of job security at CAE stems as much from the organization's attitude as from its bottom line. Even during down cycles, the company strives to avoid layoffs and dismissals.

When orders decline in one area CAE will juggle the work force as much as possible to hold on to its people. "Even if they had to eliminate a whole division, they would try to fit everybody in somewhere else," an employee comments.

CAE people enjoy themselves. They describe their environment as universally warm, personal and open — a family of responsible adults (without "second-rate citizens," "robots" or interdepartmental feuding) in which "everybody helps everybody."

There are job descriptions, but they're only a beginning, because one's responsibilities grow with one's self. A veteran manager says: "I don't think I can ever remember hearing someone tell me, 'That's not my job. Go see someone else.' That's something I deplore in most other places."

Snobbery simply doesn't exist on the job or off. Even identification badges give no hint of anyone's rank or duties.

"There's not one person I can't talk to in this company," says a veteran female plant-floor inspector. "I came here temporarily to send my husband through school. Today he's an engineer, and he makes three times my salary. I don't have to work now, but I like to work here. When people ask me how long I'm going to work, I say: 'Until 65, I think.' "

The word "recognition" crops up frequently at CAE. People also talk about responsibility, flexibility, mobility, job rotation, meritocracy, self-development and freedom. They speak of "the freedom to do things and in how you do things" and "the freedom for me to talk to any manager up to the president." There is also the freedom for women to take maternity leave of up to nine months.

"I think this place exists more in spite of the management structure than because of it," a professional employee says. A colleague adds: "The place really runs on individual enthusiasm. Responsibility goes down to quite a low level."

Buzz words such as "participation" have had real meaning at CAE for many years. As a senior engineer states it: "Any individual at any point in the organization can have impact. People listen. People pay attention."

According to William Booth, vice-president, human resources, "Our world position and reputation in our industry and the marketplace is the true reflection of the qualities of our employees. They are essentially 'the company.' "

A man in engineering has "the feeling that I'm growing daily. There are some things I've done that I didn't know I had the capability of doing. It's a superb learning environment. It forces you to expand your own horizons."

A foreman: "When it comes to promotion, it's the only company I know where they ask, 'Can he do the job?' Not: 'Does he have a BA? Does he have a CA?' "

In short, CAE provides a fascinating vehicle for continuing personal development. At the same time, the organization offers unique opportunities for the right kind of newcomers.

"If someone comes in with a talent we didn't have in the group before, he's suddenly an expert," a young engineer explains. "If he's a self-starter, he'll become an expert at a lot of things. These people seem to find their way. In fact, before they know it they find work and responsibility heaped onto them, and they sort of wonder how they got there."

CANADA MORTAGE & HOUSING CORP.

National Office
682 Montreal Road
Ottawa, Ontario
K1A 0P7
(613) 748-2000

Pay: **AVERAGE**	Atmosphere: **VERY GOOD**
Benefits: **VERY GOOD**	Job Satisfaction: **VERY GOOD**
Promotion: **GOOD**	Communications: **GOOD**
Job Security: **GOOD**	Personal Development: **GOOD**

★ *CMHC is a federal Crown corporation responsible for federal housing programs, often in conjunction with the provinces. At the end of 1988, the corporation had outstanding loans and investments totaling $9.2 billion and $44.9 billion of mortage insurance in force. CMHC has 3,011 employees (less than 2% of them unionized) in offices right across Canada.*

A TRADITION of social purpose, family ties and a caring attitude toward employees is what characterizes CMHC. CMHC employees feel good about and take pride in what they do.

"When I was looking for a new job, I wanted a corporation that had a good cause. CMHC works to help house Canadians. That's a noble objective and CMHC is a clean organization. For instance, we don't pollute," a new employee says.

What makes CMHC stand out is its sensitive attitude toward employees. "At CMHC we are dealing with a whole family, not with just an employee," says President George Anderson. "We recognize that employees have a life outside the company. He or she has a spouse who has a job, and they probably have kids."

Employees can take up to five days a year of family related leave. Work hours are flexible around the core hours of 9:30 a.m. and 3:30 p.m. There is also the opportunity for part-time work and job-sharing. Video display terminal operators are taken off their computers and given other responsibilities during pregnancy. And a well-used confidential employee assistance program was introduced in all regions in 1989.

CMHC is not a typical quasi-government organization. "We are not public servants and we're proud of it," says one CMHC employee with conviction.

"We operate like a private business, not a federal government institution. It makes my work a lot easier," adds another.

CMHC is a leader among Crown corporations in introducing progressive policies. Women on maternity leave receive 93% of their salary for 17 weeks. The corporation pays for the first two weeks before UIC benefits begin, and raises the UIC's 75%-of-salary benefit to 93%. In addition, employees (both men and women) can take an unpaid parental leave of up to 50 weeks with their job guaranteed on return.

CMHC's social purpose, its proud history and people-oriented philosophy evoke a strong sense of loyalty. "A girlfriend of mine told me about another job that was open at her company that paid more money. I told her I couldn't think of leaving. My baseball team was in the finals," a secretary says. (The head office baseball league has 16 teams of 15 to 20 people each.)

Family involvement is an old tradition at CMHC. "My grandfather worked for CMHC, so I grew up going to the picnics and hearing about CMHC and being proud of what he did," says a manager. Many current employees have a relative who does or did work for the corporation.

And the ties to CMHC last long after the age of 65. CMHC "alumni" keep in touch with former colleagues through the annual United Way fund-raising drive, at the annual summer picnic and other social events.

In his 1988 report to Parliament, Auditor General Kenneth Dye identified CMHC as one of the eight best-performing government organizations. "CMHC derives its strength from its focus on people, both clients and employees," he wrote.

For Dye, the characteristics of excellence common to all eight were: emphasis on people, participative leadership, innovative working styles, strong client orientation, and a mindset that seeks optimum performance. Anderson sent a copy of the CMHC chapter to each employee, with a note saying: "In recognition of your contribution in helping to make CMHC one of Canada's most efficient federal government agencies."

Such a commendation is impressive, considering CMHC had to eliminate 900 jobs in 1985 and 1986. "We did it by being open and honest with employees," Anderson recalls. "Second, we had to have a tangible way of demonstrating concern. We set up employees' committees throughout the organization and said, 'We have to downsize, but you can help by devising strategies on how to deal with it. If there are things we can do to soften the blow, tell us.' "

Normal attrition reduced staff by 326; 223 employees took early retirement; 149 chose to take a severance settlement; 97 were immediately redeployed and 105 were put on the priority list. All employees had the chance to be on the priority list. For some — say, in a small office being closed — redeployment would have meant relocating and they opted out. "But all employees had the option of being redeployed," says a representative of the human resources department.

Vacant positions at CMHC were then filled by the first person on the list who was qualified or could be trained for the job. There was no external hiring.

Anderson adds: "We offered an attractive early retirement package. We offered a generous severance package. We put a lot of effort into redeploying people."

Even today, with the job situation stabilized, hiring comes first from the priority list. If this search doesn't produce a candidate, then the job gets posted, first internally, and only after that externally.

CMHC already has taken the plunge in introducing pay equity, as required by the federal government. The pay levels of all positions were evaluated on the basis of job responsibility. The study found 1,800 jobs were underpaid; 700 were in the proper range; and 500 were overpaid. The study favored clerical staff, who have traditionally been women, and field office staff.

For those who were negatively affected, the corporation has guaranteed current pay levels for 27 months, a move not required by the legislation, but which will cost the corporation more than $1 million.

There are numerous training program and job exchanges. The temporary vacancies created by employees on maternity and parental leave are often filled by people from other departments wanting to enrich their experience. Each year CMHC also hires 10 university graduates under a two-year training program that exposes them to 10 or 12 departments. "It is the most wonderful program. You are basically being paid to learn," says one program participant.

Being tied to the federal government has advantages and disadvantages. On the positive side, CMHC must always be seen to be fair on issues of pay equity, bilingualism and women in the workforce, thus giving it an impetus to be a leader in progressive work practices. On the negative side, given more emphasis on financial constraints, future Treasury Board regulations may decrease the corporation's autonomy.

But as in all companies, the demographic profile of employees shows that promotions will not be as readily available in future as they have been in the past. So the corporation has set up a task force to recommend ways of dealing with the problem.

CMHC is a heavy user of task forces to solve problems. Staff from all affected departments are drawn in to wrestle with issues and propose solutions. "The vast majority of recommendations are accepted by management," says one veteran of 12 task forces. The only criticism employees have is the need for more lower-level input.

Union organizing drives usually begin in workplaces that have gone through staff cuts, but Anderson points out that one of CMHC's unions actually was decertified after the downsizing, because members of the union were not eligible for performance pay increases. Employee performance is reviewed annually and pay increases range from 3% to 5%, based on performance. Employees who achieve more than what's expected of them receive an additional 3% to 5% performance bonus, while outstanding performers get an extra 8%-10%.

CMHC has plans to get even better. Anderson proposes to introduce flexible benefits in 1991. It is a corporation prepared for the future. Says one employee of 15 years: "We don't know where we'll be in 10 years. What we rely on is that we can adapt."

canadian hunter
noranda group

CANADIAN HUNTER
EXPLORATION LTD.

435-4th Avenue S.W.
Calgary, Alberta
T2P 3A8
(403) 260-1000

Pay: **EXCELLENT**	Atmosphere: **EXCELLENT**
Benefits: **VERY GOOD**	Job Satisfaction: **EXCELLENT**
Promotion: **AVERAGE**	Communications: **VERY GOOD**
Job Security: **GOOD**	Personal Development: **EXCELLENT**

★ *Canadian Hunter, a wholly owned subsidiary of Noranda Inc., is involved in the exploration and production of oil and gas, primarily in Western Canada. It has been remarkably successful in its search for hydrocarbons, and its numerous discoveries include Elmworth, which it claims to be Canada's largest natural gas field. The company was consistently profitable from its founding in 1973 until 1987. In 1988, however, Noranda had to take a $76-million writedown of Hunter assets, since much of its value lies in its probable and potential reserves, which are ignored for accounting purposes. As a result, Hunter reported a 1988 loss of $46 million. In 1989, it still had an ambitious $200-million capital spending program. It has 330 non-unionized employees.*

CLOCKS, PROMINENT in the lobby at Canadian Hunter's office, hint at attitudes within. One (set normally) is labeled "Calgary Time." Alongside it, another (five minutes fast) is identified as "Canadian Hunter Time." A sign tells employees: "Stay Ahead."

Canadian Hunter thinks of itself as being smarter than the competition. It hires the best people and rewards them handsomely. Pay is outstanding even by the historically generous standards of the oil patch, and some of the benefits have a surreal quality to them.

President John Masters boasts so proudly about the excellence of his workforce that he provokes a question about encouraging elitism. His response is quick: Certainly he encourages elitism — he even preaches it. And if outsiders sometimes think he hypes the capabilities of his people too much, he is not apologetic.

He quotes the Roman poet Virgil who wrote 2,000 years ago: "They can because they think they can."

The employee handbook sets a rather self-satisfied tone: "You have been hired to find and produce oil and gas fields. Nothing is more essential to our lives. We welcome you into an exciting company which has a different style than you may be accustomed to.

"We have chosen you because, from the many who apply to us, we think you are outstanding. We hire only the best. We want you to work with us and we want you to join our family. At Canadian Hunter you will feel an atmosphere of accomplishment. We are doing a big job developing energy, and we are serious about it.

"Every day, all of us are trying to make real progress. We help each other and we'll help you. We are all friends. Many of us are highly skilled and we have great respect for each others' talents and experience. . . When someone asks you where you work, you may be forgiven a little inner smile when you say 'Canadian Hunter.' "

Hunter is decidedly different. Masters and Executive Vice-President Jim Gray, both geologists, who founded the company, have put their personal stamp on it to a degree rarely encountered in Canadian business. Their free-wheeling, entrepreneurial style isn't what one would expect to find in a wholly owned subsidiary of a multinational resource giant.

The two men are given great freedom to run their own show and they thank Noranda for it. The names of the two senior executives crop up endlessly in conversations with employees: "John and Jim like to do this. . . John and Jim believe. . . " Employees said they find it hard to imagine what Canadian Hunter would be like without these two very strong personalities at the helm. Some even worry about it a bit.

Hunter is remarkably free of bureaucracy, and individual initiative is encouraged, even expected. Says one junior employee: "We are expected to think." For many who have spent time in regimented, hierarchical companies, being expected to think and offer suggestions is unexpectedly refreshing. Even better is that their ideas are actually listened to and acted upon.

Many employees said they were performing duties that normally would be reserved for people much higher up the command ladder in other oil companies. There's a small staff turnover (3.3% in 1989), resulting in limited opportunities for promotion. This doesn't seem to trouble employees, however, who find a flat management structure to their liking.

Managers said their job satisfaction and rewards came in the opportunity to work closely in teams with other professional disciplines and to champion projects. The chance to seek professional excellence was in itself a major reward.

There are more tangible rewards, too, in the high pay scales. Clerical/secretarial staff are being paid at about the 80th or 85th percentile for the industry, which Masters feels comfortable with. Some professional salaries are over the 140th percentile. A "soft landing" is currently in progress to bring them down a little — perhaps to the 120th percentile.

Exceptional effort is recognized in several ways. Department managers can provide small dinner parties or time off for their workers. Senior officials may authorize trips for an employee and spouse, or up to a month's bonus pay. High achievers among the lower salaried employees sometimes get a leather pouch with 50 gold dollars. More significant achievements — such as the discovery of a new oil field — are rewarded by a net profit interest in the field, which could reach a value exceeding $1 million.

Masters and Gray have a personal arrangement with Noranda under which they share 12.5% of the net profit from Hunter's oil and gas fields once exploration and development costs have been repaid. This share of earnings ranges from $10 million to $15 million a year.

The two top executives give away half of this to about 75 people in the company to reward them for the part they have played in hydrocarbon discoveries. These rewards are structured to keep top talent at Hunter. To ensure this, there is a delay before entitlements are vested, and anyone leaving Hunter forfeits half the award.

Masters says the scheme has been very effective in sharing the wealth of the company with a lot of people. "I'd say we probably have more millionaires in Canadian Hunter than any other company in town."

Masters says he believes Hunter employees perform at perhaps 95% of their potential, compared with 40% to 50% of potential achieved by workers in big oil companies around Calgary. His own staff also feels this is an accurate statement.

New employees, no matter how junior, are taken around and introduced to everybody. They will already have had about half a dozen interviews before they were hired, and will have met Masters who sees all newcomers. He reserves, and occasionally exercises, the right of veto on new hirings.

The atmosphere at Canadian Hunter is open and friendly. Employees feel free to walk up to Masters and Gray and chat casually about business and social activities, and everyone is expected to know the names of all their co-workers. This was easy a few years ago when Hunter was smaller, but today it requires effort. New employees are advised to learn the name of 50 fellow workers a week until they have got them all down pat.

Hunter places great emphasis on team work, and it reinforces team building with a range of outside social and sporting activities, fully paid or generously subsidized by the company. Not surprisingly for a company in the high-risk oil and gas exploration business, these include such hazardous activities as kayaking, ice climbing, rock climbing, mountain biking and so on.

Vacations are generous. Most professionals get six weeks off after five years. In addition, employees get six Fridays off each year, and the company closes down between Christmas and New Year. Plus there's a sports day and the annual skiing trip.

The benefits seem endless: subsidized YMCA membership, an annual $100 allowance for meals and accomodation in nearby national parks, education assistance, a $38-a-month transportation allowance, and kitchens stocked with tea, coffee, bread for toast, jam, and muffins. Hunter also offers a stock savings plan, to which it adds 30¢ for every $1 invested by employees in Noranda shares.

No wonder Hunter employees smile a lot.

digital ™

DIGITAL EQUIPMENT OF CANADA LTD.

100 Hertzberg Road
P.O. Box 13000
Kanata, Ontario
K2K 2A6
(613) 592-5111

Pay: **GOOD**	Atmosphere: **VERY GOOD**
Benefits: **GOOD**	Job Satisfaction: **VERY GOOD**
Promotion: **VERY GOOD**	Communications: **VERY GOOD**
Job Security: **VERY GOOD**	Personal Development: **VERY GOOD**

★ *Digital Canada (a subsidiary of Digital Equipment Corp., Maynard, Mass.) manufactures, sells and services computers, peripheral equipment and software. With 3,400 employees in 40 sales and service offices across Canada, the company had revenues of $826 million in the fiscal year ended mid-1989.*

"BEING A PART OF Digital means giving a great deal of yourself in terms of effort, creativity and responsibility," new employees at Digital are told. "Digital is proud of the initiative of the many employees who have embraced our corporate business philosophy with enthusiasm, dedication and hard work. Teamwork is central to reaching our corporate objectives, and with your co-operation, Digital will continue to be one of the industry's leaders. In return, Digital provides meaningful jobs, career opportunities, and competitive compensation and benefits programs."

Digital is clearly a force in computers in Canada, having taken an aggressive approach to business and a humane attitude toward its employees, who enjoy being part of the electronic revolution.

As a subsidiary of an American corporation, Digital Canada is proud of its roots north of the border. In 1963, the Canadian operation started as a two-man sales outfit in Ottawa and opened its first Canadian manufacturing operation in an old woolen mill with a staff of 10.

While its Canadian headquarters remain in Kanata, just outside Ottawa, its presence is felt throughout the country.

The move of a large number of staff to Toronto from Kanata between 1985 and 1989, part of a new and aggressive marketing approach, illustrates to what extent Digital cares for its employees.

The company helped those affected by the move by sending them and their spouses on a two-day, all-expenses-paid trip to Toronto to see the city. For those who chose to move, there were additional company-paid trips for orientation and house-hunting. To help spouses find work in Toronto, Digital not only engaged a placement agency but also financed a series of special job-hunting trips.

In addition to moving expenses, Digital absorbed other costs, including real estate commissions and lease cancellation fees. There was a one-time general relocation grant of $2,000 to $2,500 per family. The company also provided special payments to help offset higher housing and rental costs in Toronto.

To top it off, the company paid a temporary resettlement allowance "to recognize the disruption of the family unit and the potential for short-term increased costs." The allowance began at 5% of salary (with a $5,000 maximum) and was to drop by one third a year for three years. About 160 people made the move from Kanata to Toronto.

Digital helped about 40 employees who chose not to move by transferring them to other jobs within the company.

The care given to the employees involved doesn't surprise anyone because decent treatment is a fundamental, day-to-day aspect of every job at Digital. For example, flexible hours are offered at the plant and the program works on the honor system. There are no time clocks, "no bell, no whip, no pressure of that kind whatsoever," one plant worker says.

The company strives to be egalitarian. There is only one benefits package for all ranks. There are no reserved executive

39

parking spaces, and everyone stands in line at the cafeteria.

"We are always looking at our benefits," says Brian Coll, vice-president of external relations. Digital's maternity leave is one of the most progressive in Canada. The company supplements UIC benefits to the maximum allowable level of 95% of salary for the full 17 weeks. The benefit is also available to men who are adopting a child, once the adoption is approved by UIC.

Employees can take up to a year unpaid leave for any reason, with guaranteed employment upon return.

The final statement in the summary of Digital Canada's corporate philosophy is paradoxically known as the first rule: "When dealing with a customer, a vendor or an employee, do what is 'right' to do in each situation."

That mandate means a great deal to employees. Insiders say doing the "right" thing has cost the company short-term revenue on several occasions. It hasn't happened often, but the company has been known not to make a sale if it felt its system was not appropriate for a client.

Digital doesn't believe in layoffs in tough times. "It's a stated premise that if we end up with too many people, we in management have screwed up," explains Peter Richardson, vice-president of personnel. "So we're not going to make the employees pay the price."

Rapid expansion at Digital has meant the recruitment of 800 employees since 1986.

Individual initiative is encouraged. "People take responsibility for things," Coll says. In the fast-moving field of high tech "people have to be flexible," since a rigid, unchanging job description "would be obsolete in a few months."

Most employees realize the road to self-development and advancement (even in Digital's worldwide multinational family) is open, limited only by personal ability and ambition, not by where one starts out. Full support is given to employees continuing their education by offering leaves of absence.

"We have a new focus on management training in order to deal with the competitive business environment," Coll says. Starting in 1990, every manager will be given at least a week's general training each year. Managers also receive training specific to their jobs. "We are budgeting a million dollars a year on management training," says Frank Rambeau, manager of management development.

"You just want to get in the door at Digital and then work yourself from there," one employee states. "I think it's wide open," another adds. "I know I would have 100% backing if I chose to go into line management."

"The management style is very open door," Coll says. "It is part of our philosophy. People should be able to come in and chat about anything at any time. And they do. It is a way of resolving problems before they become earth shattering. As managers, we should always have time for a cup of coffee with somebody."

Digital uses a "matrix" management system, meaning that "while you're reporting to one person, you also have dotted-line responsibilities to others, which makes your day pretty interesting," one employee says.

"If people work for me, I like to think they would call me when they need help; not for permission," one manager says. "That implies people may make some mistakes, but that's how they learn."

Pay is good. Some administrative workers are ahead of national, all-industry averages. "I have the edge on them in both benefits and salary," one clerical employee says, referring to friends in similar jobs elsewhere. Salaries and benefits for technical people are in the middle to top range of the high-tech industry.

Digital is a company for people who enjoy the challenge of a fast-paced, changing environment.

DMR GROUP INC.

1200 McGill College Avenue
Montreal, Quebec
H3B 4G7
(514) 866-3301

Pay: **GOOD**	Atmosphere: **EXCELLENT**
Benefits: **AVERAGE**	Job Satisfaction: **EXCELLENT**
Promotion: **VERY GOOD**	Communications: **EXCELLENT**
Job Security: **VERY GOOD**	Personal Development: **EXCELLENT**

★ *DMR Group is a specialized information-systems consulting firm, based in Montreal, with 21 regional offices across Canada and subsidiaries in the U.S., Australia, Britain, the Netherlands, Belgium, West Germany and Switzerland. DMR has 2,000 employees and handles jobs ranging in value from $10,000 to $10 million. Billings for the year ending mid-1989 were $127.8 million, an increase of 27% over the previous year. Some 70% of the company's shares (publicly traded since 1987) are owned by 420 employees.*

"THERE IS a willingness to contribute and a sense of urgency here that I have never seen at any other company," says Pierre Robitaille, vice-president of human resources.

"Employees are excited by the corporation. We want to be one of the top 10 computer consultants by 2000. We are a developing company that will have 12,000 to 20,000 people by 2000," says Robitaille. "Employees feel they are part of something that is growing. And they know we are offering a product that will be in greater and greater demand."

Salaries are competitive, and profit-based bonuses awarded by each local office boost compensation to the top third scales in the

42

industry. "But people don't join us for the compensation," says Robitaille. "Of course it enhances our ability to attract someone, but people come to us because of our reputation, the opportunity for growth and work in other countries." (Some 60 Canadian employees work abroad.)

"We offer the freedom for growth. People join us because of this latitude," Robitaille says. The company's philosophy is to make the work so challenging, stimulating and rewarding that people will be attracted.

Employees describe DMR as an off-beat, fun place to work, with equal opportunity for women, and all the flexibility and mobility anyone could ask for. It's not uncommon for DMR people to be working on three or four projects at once.

A woman who joined in 1979 has been a project manager, a resource manager and a consultant. She's in marketing now, but she believes DMR offers the opportunity for her to return to any of the other fields or even to start up something entirely new.

"It's a very friendly place to work," she says. "People are encouraged to develop relationships at all levels and across all levels. There is a structure of a kind, but it's a very loose structure. People work in a variety of fields despite where they may fit on the organization chart."

Another woman now working in administration adds: "We don't have job descriptions for the administrative staff, because they would just go on forever. We're looking for people with flexibility there, as we are in our consulting staff. The more you can do, the more you'll get."

Pierre Ducros, Serge Meilleur and Alain Roy resigned from IBM to found DMR in 1973. They visualized a new organization very different from IBM, with office-by-office autonomy, close contact with the customer and no internal politics. The principle of autonomy is so firm that the DMR head office and the Montreal regional office are on separate floors of the same building and furnished quite differently.

DMR gives responsibility to those who have earned it. Ducros explains that the person sent to open an office "is as good as you are. He is as competent as you are." It sometimes takes a while to convince people that the company really will give them autonomy, he adds, but when convinced they take the responsibility and run.

For a similar reason, the DMR executive committee reaches

its decisions by consensus, he says. "I don't think we have ever voted. If you vote and some guy loses the vote, you don't get the commitment. Intellectually, it has not reached his guts. And I think that the 12 inches from the intellectual level to the guts are very long inches."

In such a decentralized company, communication and corporate continuity could be a problem, but managers' meetings — held monthly in each region and Canada-wide twice a year — keep information flowing between the autonomous offices. And a worldwide newsletter provides detailed information about key contracts. New consultants are introduced to company culture through week-long seminars run four times a year.

The benefits package for all employees is based on industry standards prevalent in corporations such as IBM. The one exception is the absence of a pension plan. DMR plans to introduce one by the end of 1991. The company covers the full cost of all plans, including provincial health-insurance premiums. In an unusual move designed to attract senior people, DMR determines vacation time on the basis of an employee's years of experience in the information-systems industry, not with the company.

At the outset DMR attracted mainly former IBM people. By 1989, though, only 5% of new hirees were IBM alumni, Robitaille says. DMR does have a preference for people with certain characteristics. Intelligence, drive and self-motivation are the key attributes the company looks for in a new employee. DMR has found it can train people in technical areas, but has run into difficulty training them in business and human relations. "It's much easier to train a generalist to become a specialist than the reverse," Ducros says.

Before technical background even enters the hiring scene, the company looks for integrity and then for what Ducros calls the "the spark in the eye" — visible enthusiasm and interest. The third yardstick is competence in the field.

"It's a 'je ne sais quois' that we are looking for — something a little extra that a candidate will bring to the company," says Robitaille. "We want employees to have fun in the professional sense, and have the opportunity to grow, push, probe and enjoy themselves."

DU PONT CANADA INC.

Box 2200
Streetsville
Mississauga, Ontario
L5M 2H3
(416) 821-3300

Pay: **VERY GOOD**	Atmosphere: **GOOD**
Benefits: **GOOD**	Job Satisfaction: **VERY GOOD**
Promotion: **GOOD**	Communications: **AVERAGE**
Job Security: **EXCELLENT**	Personal Development: **EXCELLENT**

★ *Du Pont Canada manufactures synthetic fibres, chemicals and plastics. The company operates plants at Saskatoon and, in Ontario, at Ajax, Whitby, Sarnia and Maitland. The company has 4,100 employees, of whom 39% are unionized. In 1988, sales exceeded $1.3 billion. E. I. du Pont de Nemours & Co. of Deleware owns 75% of Du Pont Canada — the remaining shares are held by Canadian investors.*

"DU PONT offers employees as much opportunity for growth as any other company in Canada," says Gerry Fox, vice-president of human resources. "And we are paying more attention to human resources than any other company I am aware of." Fox points to the fact that more than 30% of CEO Ted Newall's 1990 objectives are focused in this area.

Du Pont's strategy heavily emphasizes education, training and development. Fox says Du Pont benefits from the increased productivity a well-trained staff provides. In 1988, Du Pont won the gold Canada Award for Business Excellence for productivity improvement.

45

By conservative estimates, Du Pont annually spends 3.5% of payroll on education (excluding salaries paid to employees attending courses). That comes to $1,707 per employee.

Courses are interactive — employees use work experiences as case studies, so instructors and the company learn with the employees.

"There are so many interesting courses that the hard part is figuring out how many I can take and when," one employee says. Employees say the emphasis on their development allows the company to take full advantage of their energy and intelligence. "The company wants us to feel good about ourselves and equip ourselves for the 1990s, mentally and physically," one manager says. (There is a subsidized fitness centre — membership costs $10 a month — at head office in Mississauga.)

The emphasis on education "is going to pay dividends over time, because we are suffering from the same problem every other company is: traditional movement up the corporate ladder isn't there," another manager says. "Downsizing and reducing layers of management have limited the opportunities. The crew ahead of me are all in their forties, and they are not going anywhere. So I have to start looking at moving laterally. We have the culture to do that. Moving and investing in people will give us long-term advantages."

In 1990, Du Pont is launching a career-planning program to which any employee can have access. The program will identify the skills needed for jobs in different departments, and list the courses employees can take to develop skills they lack.

At Du Pont, education goes hand in hand with self-management. Employees annually set their objectives. Their managers must agree on what the objectives are but not how they are to be achieved.

The company has reduced its once top-heavy management. One manager used to supervise every three or four staff, but now the optimum number is 15. As a result, Du Pont has only five levels between the CEO and the non-supervisory employees.

The only limitation placed on employees is that they are expected to work within Du Pont's general operating principles. "We want to avoid setting down rules and regulations," Fox says, "and instead set down policies and principles that can guide people through any problem they may face."

One employee recalls his manager saying: "Please don't ask

me permission to do something. I would rather you do it, then ask me to back you up later. Otherwise, it is my decision and not yours."

As a result of self-management, "the first thing you do is throw away your job description because you have exceeded it," one employee says.

"The boundary within which you work is defined by you," another agrees. "A manager doesn't draw it for you. That is tremendous freedom. There are a lot of people who work long hours, but a good part of that is by choice because we are interested in what we do."

Self-management, however, has not been entirely successful. Some employees accustomed to the old style find it difficult to adjust, and in some of the plants the concept has not taken off. "The self-managing teams at the manufacturing sites have run into a lot of problems because of removing the traditional foreman," one manager says.

Atmosphere can vary significantly among plants. "I worked at Ajax and my husband at Whitby, and we thought we were working for different companies," another manager says. Three of Du Pont's plants are unionized. In unionized shops "promotion is strictly by seniority, unless you are in management."

With the advent of self-management, communication has improved. "There used to be the attitude of 'need to know,' " one employee says. "Now it's more 'entitled to know.' Openness promotes better understanding."

Employees say the company is compassionate and will bend over backward to meet personal needs. "We are very conscious of the family aspect. If you don't have harmony at home, you bring your problems to work," co-ordinator of the employee assistance program says. A new mother who wanted to spend more time with her baby had no problem rearranging her hours. Du Pont has had a flex-time program for years.

Du Pont's benefits are comprehensive, but certain elements lag behind leading-edge companies. And the company's policy of hiring employees' children as summer students first is very popular.

Starting in 1990, 4% of employees' salaries will be tied to company performance. If Du Pont's return on equity falls to 11% or less, employees lose the 4%. But if ROE reaches 28%, they get 10%. Employees can take it all in cash or invest half in company stock. For every $100 invested, the company will add $200 every year for five years.

"What first comes to mind when talking about Du Pont as a good employer is security," a manager with the company 24 years says. His division had been sold the week before, but he knew that there was still a place for him within Du Pont.

Another employee from the same former division adds: "The business wasn't making money, but we did not lack resources. Some other companies in the red stop training, don't give salary increases, and even tell people to stop taking holidays."

Du Pont's turnover is a very low 4.7%, but those who do leave land "solidly on their feet," an employee of 30 years says. "The Du Pont experience and reputation open doors."

"We want to redesign our compensation system so that it is motivational," Fox concludes. "We are trying to design our education system so that every employee will want to continuously improve his or her abilities and will have the opportunity to do so. And we are trying to create an atmosphere that will leave everyone happy to work here."

With its strong emphasis on personal development, Du Pont is already a secure, rewarding and friendly place to work.

ESSO RESOURCES CANADA LTD.

Esso Plaza
237 4th Avenue South West
Calgary, Alberta
T2P 0H6
(403) 237-3737

Pay: **EXCELLENT**	Atmosphere: **POOR**
Benefits: **VERY GOOD**	Job Satisfaction: **VERY GOOD**
Promotion: **VERY GOOD**	Communications: **VERY GOOD**
Job Security: **VERY GOOD**	Personal Development: **VERY GOOD**

★ *Esso Resources is the exploration and production subsidiary of Imperial Oil Ltd., itself a subsidiary of Exxon Corp. in the U.S. Its employees work at corporate headquarters in Calgary and throughout Western Canada. In April, 1989, it began a merger with the upstream (exploration and production) arm of Texaco Canada Resources that was to be completed Jan. 1, 1990, pending approval of the Competition Tribunal. The result would be a much larger company, with 4,700 employees (3,600 from Esso, the remainder from Texaco). The combined company would have assets of $8 billion and aims to earn $1 billion annually by the year 2000.*

ESSO RESOURCES WAS featured enthusiastically in the first edition of this book. It was described as "a Cadillac of a company — with rhinestone wheels;" that is, its dedication to excellence was taintedby some unexpectedly cornball management practices.

For instance, at Cold Lake in northern Alberta, where Esso began full-scale commercial extraction of heavy oil in June, 1985, informality acquired an eccentric edge. Handling rapid expansion became a preoccupation and senior managers took to meeting regularly wearing T-shirts with the legend "Swamp Management Team" — inspired by the expression: "When you are up to your ass in alligators, you can't worry about draining the swamp." Late arrivals at meetings were fined $2. Those improperly dressed (that is, without T-shirts) had to pay $5. One senior manager commented the Cold Lake group was "deliberately trying to cultivate a little insanity. The whole object up here is to have fun while we are growing."

Having fun while the company was growing became much more difficult in 1989, following the proposal by parent Imperial Oil to take over Texaco. Employees of both companies experienced months of uncertainty and apprehension while an intense effort was made to identify the best elements of both organizations and create a progeny superior to the sum of the parts. The effort even had its own "corpspeak." Adding two and two and hoping the result would make five became known as "breakthrough thinking."

Much agonizing occurred as joint committees scrutinized functions from top to bottom of the two companies, organizational realignments were recommended, job functions reassessed and individual skills and aptitudes examined to decide who would fit where in the emerging organization. About 300 employees, drawn equally from both companies, worked on "synergy" teams, planning the merger. The approach was egalitarian; senior management permitted all employees to help define the structure and function of entire departments.

The immense energy expended in this exercise is testimony to the seriousness with which Esso tackles its business. One example is a joint communications team that visited 30 companies throughout North America, among them the Big Three Detroit automakers, to pick their hosts' brains. From the team's recommendations emerged a new department that combined the functions of four previous ones. Three managers, whose jobs disappeared, had to be reassigned.

While Esso had given an assurance no layoffs would result of the merger, everybody's job was up for grabs — with the exception of Esso President Doug Baldwin and former Texaco senior vice-president Howard Agnew, who became executive vice-president of Esso Resources. The company asked employees where they wanted to work in the new organization, but there was no assurance their preferences would be met when the final organization emerged.

At time of writing, employees were still uncertain about the successful outcome of the entire exercise and its impact on their careers.

However, a survey in the summer of 1989 (to which 2,175 employees responded) showed 80% believed they were well informed about the merger and that management was trying hard to keep them informed. Just over 50% believed their ideas for the merged company would be listened to and the merger would benefit their careers. More than 75% believed both Esso and Texaco employees would receive fair and equitable treatment in the new company, while the remainder thought the merger could cause some of the best people to leave. In the meantime, more than two thirds said they believed the merger was causing problems in running the business day-to-day.

When the dust settles, Esso will undoubtedly retain its crown as one of Canada's superior employers. Its record to date shows an integrity and respect for its employees that should earn it a continued ranking among Canada's Top 100 Companies.

Esso, like its parent Imperial, has always placed much emphasis on recruiting career employees, and workers say they can make career switches while remaining in the corporate family. For instance, Esso has many technical and professional people — engineers, accountants, tool pushers — on loan for two- or three-year tours of duty to Exxon international operations.

When workers are moved around, Esso treats them royally. If an employee owns a home, the company will pay all bills — such as lawyers' fees, brokerage commissions — plus a relocation allowance of about 10% of the employee's salary to cover expenses such as new drapes or a dishwasher. "Even if your plants die they will come in and give you a cheque," one employee says. "There is virtually no cost out of your pocket."

The company still maintains an attractive savings plan under which workers can contribute up to 30% of their earnings through payroll deduction and Esso matches 5%. Esso's benefits seem endless: It pays university costs for employees' children (providing they keep up grades) and gives them preferential hiring for summer work; it offers generous rewards for cost-savings ideas (one employee collected $25,000); and it has a non-contributory pension plan.

One female employee said: "How many people, starting at my age in their 40s, would get a pension plan? My husband spent 25 years in the military; he joined up at 18 and got out at 43. I will make a higher pension after I have worked here for only 16 years. For a woman, there are a lot of jobs where you are never offered a pension plan."

The jury's still out as Esso strives mightily for something extra, but the future holds promise.

GENNUM CORP.

P.O. Box 489
Station A
Burlington, Ontario
L7R 3Y3
(416) 632-2996

Pay: **AVERAGE**	Atmosphere: **VERY GOOD**
Benefits: **AVERAGE**	Job Satisfaction: **VERY GOOD**
Promotion: **GOOD**	Communications: **VERY GOOD**
Job Security: **GOOD**	Personal Development: **VERY GOOD**

★ *Gennum designs, manufactures and markets miniature integrated circuits for special applications. Roughly half of the hearing aids produced in the non-communist world use Gennum amplifiers. Sales (almost entirely exports) were $18.5 million in fiscal 1988. The company has 215 employees (about 40% professionals and highly skilled technicians) in offices and two plants at Burlington, Ont. Gennum is a subsidiary of Linear Technology Inc. (LTI), a Canadian-based holding company.*

GENNUM'S BASIC philosophy is summarized in its mission statement: "Serve the customer; respect people; pursue excellence." Significantly, employees see the goals as the legs of a stool, which must have all three to stand.

"It works," a Gennum engineer states emphatically. "If you put something on paper and it doesn't work, then people don't believe in it. With us, people believe in it."

When President Doug Barber, LTI Chairman Wally Pieczonka and a small group founded Gennum in 1974, they decided the new high-tech organization would have some basic qualities not yet common in Canadian industry:

• An atmosphere of constant innovation and challenge. "We try to instill innovation. There's always a better way to skin the cat. You've got to have that kind of atmosphere [in a high-tech company]," is Pieczonka's attitude.

• A deliberately fostered egalitarianism, to open the lines of communication. "We believe that people, no matter what their position in the company, are to a large extent equal," Pieczonka says. "That isn't quite the case, because people make different salaries, but what we're trying to say is that everybody is important."

• A profit-sharing plan for every employee in the company to generate a commitment to its success.

As far as innovation and flexibility go, says John Griffiths, manager of human resources, the company measures the momentum and career potential of all employees "by how easily you assimilate and take on new jobs and develop new jobs. If you don't do that, you'll stand still. And if you stand still, then you're a passenger."

A male mechanical engineer: "I've only been a short period in the company, but I exercise all my ideas without any barriers. In some other places, they say, 'Do it this way,' even if you don't believe it's going to work. Here, you have a free hand. Whenever you do a good job, you hear about it."

Another engineer adds: "One of the ways you can judge a company is how you feel in the morning. I was working for a company before where I hated every day. When I left it, I felt relief. Here, I come in in the morning and I feel good. It's teamwork. It's a very good atmosphere. Everybody really does his best. And you feel this rapport with your colleagues."

Salaries for most positions are at the industry average, but for technical people Gennum is competitive with large firms such as Bell Northern Research, which pays above the industry norm. "In terms of long-term income potential, we are ahead of any company of our size," Griffiths says. "On immediate renumeration we are competitive. We make annual market adjustments. In 1988, total salary additions came to 6.5%, for performance and market. In terms of working conditions, we're probably ahead of them."

While pay may differ, all benefits are equal. The perks for the president are the same as those for the production-floor operator. The president walks around in shirt sleeves and takes his chances on winding up in the far end of the parking lot with everyone else.

Furthermore, there are no hourly rated workers. Everyone is salaried. Employees keep track of their own time on an honor system. Absenteeism and turnover are extremely low. Rather than management pressure, there's peer pressure.

"We deliberately try to keep people mixing. We encourage people to ask others over to see what they are doing. We encourage interdisciplinary team problem solving. We also have a fairly active social committee," Barber says.

"We try to cloud over the lines of authority," Griffiths explains. "We don't want people to be inhibited about speaking up because they're low on the totem pole."

A woman, who as executive assistant to a senior executive has wide contact with the entire organization, looks at her work life this way: "The majority of the employees feel that it's 'our' company. The upper management is very free with information."

Not only are employees kept well informed, she says, but "we're made to feel that what we do count. Our shares are going up in the stock market. We have a profit-sharing plan. Everybody is a part of it. If an employee is dissatisfied with the work he's doing, they will try to give him different work that's more challenging. Because we're growing so fast, there's something new every day."

Her job has changed greatly since she started, mainly because of her own initiatives. If an employee sees a better way to do a job, "you suggest it. Fine. It's your idea. Do it. If it doesn't work, that's fine. If you try something and it doesn't work, it's not held against you. People in this company are treated like adults. Management is not looking over your shoulder."

Instead of a pension plan, there is a deferred profit sharing plan for eligible employees. After six months, new employees receive a half share of the profit payments and a full share after one year of service. Six per cent of pre-tax profits are shared, a significant percentage considering that profit in 1988 was $7.5 million on gross revenues of $18.5 million.

In 1988, a total of $450,000 was shared, 60% on a pro rated basis according to salary, 40% in equal payments to all employees, so lower salaried employees received a higher percentage of salary. On average, the plan delivers 8% of salary.

The company's stock-option plan is open to all employees after six months' service. Employees can contribute up to 5% of their salary through payroll deductions, and for each 1$ employees contribute, the company adds 50¢. The stock is immediately vested. Over 95% of the employees participate, most at the 5% limit.

Equally important, in the eyes of a woman who has had three promotions, "there's a lot of advancement. If you have the initiative, it's definitely there, because we're expanding so much."

Gennum strives to hire from outside the company only at the entry level. "It's a very ambitious program, and it's not a rule, but a goal," Griffiths explains. "Since the policy was introduced in 1988, 70% of all external hiring has been at the entry level. We want to develop management resources from within the company."

Some young people in their first jobs have left Gennum, employees say, and more will undoubtedly follow. Maybe they'll make bigger salaries somewhere else, but they'll also learn some lessons about working life.

"The company really is its people," Barber says. "Our slogan is: excellence through people and technology. Increasingly, it is clear that we need not just the hands and bodies, but the minds and ideas of everyone. We believe in teamwork and interdependence. It's important that everyone feels they are playing a significant role, and that they personally have opportunities to develop. We like to challenge people to take on new responsibility to develop them to their fullest potential."

Great-West Life

ASSURANCE ⊙━━ COMPANY

THE GREAT-WEST LIFE ASSURANCE CO.

100 Osborne Street North
P.O. Box 6000
Winnipeg, Manitoba
R3C 3A5
(204) 946-1190

Pay: **GOOD**	Atmosphere: **GOOD**
Benefits: **EXCELLENT**	Job Satisfaction: **GOOD**
Promotion: **GOOD**	Communications: **GOOD**
Job Security: **VERY GOOD**	Personal Development: **GOOD**

★ *Great-West plays in the major leagues of the North American life insurance industry. In 1988, the company's life insurance business reached $139.2 billion, and annuity business (the value of funds held) was worth $11.8 billion. Today, it has offices in all 10 Canadian provinces and 48 states of the U.S. Corporate control has remained in Winnipeg, where it is one of the major employers with a nonunionized workforce of about 2,300. Its total Canadian employees number 3,178, but including agency sales people (considered by GWL to be part of the corporate family), the roster rises to more than 4,000.*

EMPLOYEES AT the Great-West Life Centre in Winnipeg don't use cash to pay for their subsidized meals. Instead, magnetized ID cards are fed through a computer terminal, and lunch bills are automatically deducted from twice-monthly paycheques. The computer also helps track the cafeteria's inventory and spots the most popular dishes.

GWL attends to its own business and the welfare of its employees with exhaustive attention to detail. It offers coaching for executives who are likely to face the rigors of a television interview (express a preference for your best camera profile) and it rents out antitheft locks to those who cycle to work.

There can be few working environments with more amenities than the GWL Centre. A 20,000-volume library housed in an attractive atrium offers not only technical publications, but the the staff club's collection of novels and biographies. Or you can visit the corporate art collection, valued at about $800,000.

There are large comfortable lounges — both smoking and non-smoking — a well-used fitness club, a 240-seat theatre than can be subdivided into four smaller rooms, and a fully equipped studio where a staff of four produce training films and audio-visual productions in English and French.

There is also a bank on the premises, and employees can buy bus passes and postage stamps without having to venture outside.

An employee attitude survey conducted among head office staff by an outside consultant in June, 1989, produced some remarkable findings, quite beyond the expectations of senior management. Among them: 98% approval of the company's overall image; 97% approval of both GWL's reputation in the industry and in the comunity.

About 95% of staff said GWL is a good place to work, and the overall benefits package won a 95% rating. In addition, 87% said they believed the company is run efficiently; 93% expressed satisfaction working for the company; and 90% believed the company tries its best to provide a good place to work.

The benefits package is certainly comprehensive. In addition to the usual array of medical, dental, pension and long-term disability plans, for example, GWL also offers a vision care scheme, which pays $150 every two years for lenses and frames or contact lenses and a one-time benefit of up to $450 for visual training and remedial therapy. For insulin-dependent diabetics, the health plan covers up to $700 a year for supplies and a one-time maximum of $350 for equipment.

GWL offers mortgages at 80% of current interest rates, and it contributes $1 for each $3 a worker saves in an employee savings plan. Staff can also get half a percentage point over the going rate on registered retirement savings plans and buy the company's life insurance policies free of commission.

Workers get time off to take work-related courses, and GWL

pays the cost of tuition. The company even throws in rewards of up to $500 for successful "graduates."

If you are concerned about your health, a staff nurse will check your blood pressure or give you an eye examination. If you are worried about financial planning, there's a free counseling service. And if your marriage is falling apart or your kids are on drugs, there's a confidential referral service to city agencies that can help.

In 1987, the Canadian Mental Health Association honored the company with a Work and Well-Being Award, which recognized its "impressive array of integrated programs, services and policies designed to look after employees' health and personal needs as well as motivate them with satisfying work and workplaces."

Not only does the company encourage an active staff club, it also pays a full-time coordinator, who organizes everything from Red Cross blood donor clinics, tickets for Winnipeg Jets hockey games, a Weight Watchers group, an assault prevention program for women, baseball, softball, curling, hockey teams to dinners, picnics and parties.

GWL is clearly a mature corporation that has given much thought to ensuring a high level of staff morale.

Group Benefits Manager Ed Nickerson, a 25-year employee, says his friends have difficulty believing him when he tells them of the company's social functions. For instance, the annual curling bonspiel is one of the largest in the world, attracting up to 120 four-person rinks, all GWL employees, to compete over three or four days.

A company as large as GWL offers lots of diversity and employees have the chance to move around within the organization.

A number of people, including the vice-president of corporate systems and the vice-president of individual systems, have made their way up the ranks from the bottom.

Bob Best, vice-president, human resources, describes the company's attitude toward career advancement this way: "We are not the kind of organization that tries to push people in one direction or another. We focus more on considering the needs of the individual and fitting people in where they are comfortable." There are formal, written job descriptions and evaluation procedures. And the company encourages employee education, whether it be learning French or supervisory management. For certain industry related courses, employees write their exams on company computers and get their results immediately.

It is a recognized fact in the industry that people don't go out to buy insurance — it is sold to them. The distinction means an effective sales force is crucial to GWL's success. Salesmen credit the company with good training and excellent support.

Barry Adams, who has been associated with GWL for 24 years, variously as a salesman, supervisor, manager, consultant and now as an independent agent, says it is very hard to get a start as a salesman. "The company has a good training program, but perhaps more importantly they are very fair and very tolerant and very open. We are very competitive in our portfolio of product. Right now if I wanted to go up and see the president he would be approachable."

The average gross commission income of salesmen in the Winnipeg office with more than three years' experience is $67,000. Says Adams: "The president of this company is not the highest paid employee of the company." A handful of salesmen probably earn $200,000-plus, and perhaps a couple earn twice that, he says.

Like all sales-oriented organizations, GWL places much emphasis on motivation and on the ego-massaging recognition important to those who hustle its products. Every two years, GWL hosts a sales convention, attended by 700-900 of its top sales people (including spouses) at a luxury resort (such as the Princess Hotel in Bermuda and the Weston Kauai in Hawaii) where there is golf, tennis, swimming and much hype. Top performers are given "high recognition."

And things are done in style. One year at Palm Beach, Florida, the company staged an elaborate black-and-white ball. The ballroom was filled with black and white balloons, the women were asked to wear black and white formal gowns and GWL rented nearly 300 tuxedos for the men. In 1989, the company jetted about 650 people to Cannes on the French Riviera for a lavish session.

GWL is a great employer — if you can stomach the hype.

Hewitt Associates

HEWITT ASSOCIATES

4110 Yonge Street
Toronto, Ontario
M2P 2B7
(416) 225-5001

Pay: **VERY GOOD**	Atmosphere: **VERY GOOD**
Benefits: **VERY GOOD**	Job Satisfaction: **EXCELLENT**
Promotion: **GOOD**	Communications: **VERY GOOD**
Job Security: **GOOD**	Personal Development: **EXCELLENT**

★ *Hewitt Associates is an international firm of consultants and actuaries, specializing in designing, financing, communicating and administering employee benefit and compensation programs. With 80 employees in Toronto, this Canadian company is a subsidiary of Hewitt Associates, Lincolnshire, Ill.*

IT'S TOUGH to get a job at Hewitt. In hiring, Hewitt looks for SWANs — people who are Smart, Work hard, are Ambitious and Nice. Candidates are interviewed by different associates, and may be flown to Lincolnshire to meet more associates and spend half a day with a psychologist. Human resources consultant Anne Burrows can't estimate how much the company spends on hiring but it is significant — the psychologist's session alone costs $700. Bill Scott, managing partner of the Canadian office, feels the money and effort are well spent. "We want to make sure it is a good fit. If we do our recruiting properly, it reduces turnover." At 8% annually, Hewitt's turnover is less than half the industry average.

Salary is not an issue, Scott says. "We couldn't recruit the quality of people we have unless we paid top wages. It would be a surprise if anyone left because they weren't being paid well enough."

Associates are taught to use "we" in place of "I" when making presentations. "In any business, unless you are a one-person shop, someone else helped you," a lawyer at the firm says. The firm emphasizes collective responsibility and encourages new consultants to take risks. "There are always three people who check what you do," the lawyer says. "As a new associate, the expertise in the firm is daunting. You have to be fairly secure and not be offended by red ink. But that's how you learn."

It's not only partners who have contact with clients, sign proposals and reports or make presentations. All consultants do. "I didn't have the title necessary to give a breakfast seminar to clients, and it was something I wanted to do," says a lawyer, commenting on a former employer. "After a few weeks of joining Hewitt, I was asked if I wanted to give a breakfast seminar. I was overjoyed. People are allowed to grow here."

The firm stresses teamwork, and traditional status symbols are noticeably absent. All offices are the same size, there are no titles on business cards and all employees are called associates. "There is tremendous egalitarianism and participative democracy here," a new associate says. And a receptionist adds: "I get the highest amount of respect, just like everyone else in this office."

Teamwork extends worldwide, and includes profit sharing. Employees receive a share each year. In 1988, the average profit share represented 11% of base salary.

"A client is the firm's client, not the office's client," an associate points out. "There is no competition among offices." As a result, a consultant in Toronto may spend a lot of time researching a problem for the West German office. Associates say Hewitt provides the best consultants possible, regardless of where they're located.

Electronic mail links all of Hewitt's offices, scattered throughout 18 countries. An associate with an urgent problem can ask for help using E-mail and can expect several responses within hours. "Such a quick exchange of ideas is like standing around the electronic water cooler," one associate says. "There are tremendous resources to back you up," another adds. "We are 80 employees in Toronto, but we are actually part of 2,800 worldwide." Associates say this is one of the reasons Hewitt has been able to grow so fast in Canada.

Associates are recognized for their efforts. A member of the support staff tells how, after staying late one night to finish a report, she got a call the next day from Scott to thank her for a job well done. "People catch you doing things right here," another agrees.

Hewitt makes it easy for employees to work long hours. The company covers any child-care, taxi or evening meal expenses because of working late. Employees say senior people often put in 70 hours a week. For many consultants, 50- to 55-hour weeks are commonplace.

Employees feel the company's growth is positive. "It means there will be new opportunities in the future," one associate says. But a manager points out: "It is hard to bring people in and keep the culture" when growth stands at 30% to 40% a year. "We don't want to be the largest consulting firm, but the best," he says. Hewitt will not grow through takeovers because acquisitions bring "another culture with it and people you don't want."

Benefits are flexible; not surprising considering Hewitt conceived and implemented the first flex-benefits plan for U.S. clients in the 1970s. Associates receive credits based on length of service and the level of medical and disability coverage they select. With their credits, associates can buy additional health-care coverage, different types of insurance or take days off. They can also deposit the money in an RRSP, deferred profit-sharing plan or receive cash.

In addition to an employee assistance plan, there is a cancer consulting service and adoption assistance of up to $2,500 per child. The company pays 75% of stop-smoking courses for employees or their family members and the balance if the treatment is successful for 12 months. Hewitt pays 90% of tuition fees and books for up to two courses a year. The company pays for the care of a child or for an ill or elderly family member when an associate is away on business or working late. Hewitt also pays for care of a dependent for five days a year. Employees who travel receive leather briefcases and they choose their own Christmas gifts from a catalog. Even couriers and cleaning staff who are not employees receive gifts.

At the subsidized cafeteria, associates can choose from

muffins, fresh fruit, yogurt, coffee and juices for breakfast. At lunch, there are hot dishes, salads and sandwiches prepared by a full-time chef.

Hewitt is a firm of young, ambitious people who thrive on challenge, learning and responsibility. "The firm seizes people who have potential," one employee says. If you are willing to meet the demands, it is a great place to work and grow.

HEWLETT-PACKARD (CANADA) LTD.

6877 Goreway Drive
Mississauga, Ontario
L4V 1M8
(416) 678-9430

Pay: **VERY GOOD**	Atmosphere: **VERY GOOD**
Benefits: **EXCELLENT**	Job Satisfaction: **GOOD**
Promotion: **GOOD**	Communications: **VERY GOOD**
Job Security: **VERY GOOD**	Personal Development: **GOOD**

★ *Hewlett-Packard (Canada), a wholly owned subsidiary of the California-based computer company, manufactures, sells and services data acquisition and control equipment. In 1988, its 1,308 employees in 26 offices across Canada generated sales of $364 million.*

"THE PRESIDENT doesn't drive a Lincoln Continental; he drives the same car as a 23-year-old sales rep," says John Cross, director of human resources. "Actually, he drives a Mercury Sable. Sales reps drive Tauruses."

Employees describe Hewlett-Packard as egalitarian. There are few walls and even fewer titles to interfere with communication. Shirt sleeves and first names are the norm, and even the employee benefits are standardized.

This is all part of what employees at Hewlett-Packard call the "HP way." Everyone is proud of the distinctive corporate culture at this company. And it is evident from the moment you scan the rows and rows of desks that characterize all of HP's offices. People walk around a lot and meet in small groups. There's an informality about the place, and an energy too.

Many employees attribute that energy to the freedom HP offers. "Working here is closer to being an independent business person than working anywhere else," one manager says.

Tasks are described and the deadline determined, but it is up to the employee to determine how to do the job. This is no place for those who like a structured environment. "But it's a great place for extroverts, over-achievers and perfectionists," says one self-styled example of these traits.

One negative side of this culture is the long hours. They seem to be the norm rather than the exception among this very competitive lot. Indeed, employees feel responsible for their compulsiveness in the name of fulfillment and potential advancement rather than peer pressure or corporate expectation.

In addition to driving themselves hard, HP employees have an obsession with communication. The open office plan helps make this exchange of information possible. So does the mandatory morning coffee break, where coffee and muffins are free and managers rub shoulders with clerks.

Once a month, President George Cobbe discusses sales, company performance and makes announcements over a public address system that reaches every Canadian office. Cobbe also meets and has lunch with new employees once a month. And new employees at head office are introduced at monthly meetings, where Cobbe also announces the employee birthdays that fall in the month.

Bimonthly newsletters and a semi-annual magazine also keep employees informed. Every three years, a company-wide survey seeks out areas that need improvement, and HP conducts surveys on specific issues, when needed.

"It's one thing to say that you have an open-door policy. It's another to install the checks and balances like this to ensure people aren't autocratic," says a sales representative.

"We have high quality formal communication and publications for specialty areas," says Michael Van Dusen, executive director of public relations. "But internal company surveys show the most satisfied employees are those who are satisfied with the communication with their managers. So we stress the importance of open employee-manager relations."

There is an emphasis on job training. All managers and sales staff undergo mandatory training, while others can choose to take courses for personal and professional development.

Each employee's performance is reviewed annually. Salary increases are based on pay for performance, with the highest increases going to exceptional performers at the bottom of their salary range.

The importance of people in this organization also can be seen in the benefits package. It is comprehensive and equal for everyone. There's a profit-sharing plan (for employees with the company more than six months) and a stock-purchase plan that allows employees to buy shares quarterly at a subsidized price.

All the usual benefits, including a pension plan, are provided at the company's expense. There is also a confidential employee assistance program that provides professional counseling to those in need of help with family, emotional, alcohol or drug problems.

Part-time employees working more than 20 hours a week receive full benefits except for vacations, which are pro-rated. Workers get free parking; 70% off on computer software; 50% off on calculators; 30% off on computer hardware; and the free use of vacation sites (including one in the French Alps).

These benefits more than make up for pay, which is considered competitive, but not tops. "I'm comfortable with the pay because the benefits are so good," says one middle manager. For five years in a row, the profit sharing plan paid employees cash bonuses averaging 5.2% of their salaries.

At HP, employees like to have fun. In addition to the annual Christmas party and summer picnic, there are three or four beer bashes a year. On beer-bash days, work stops at 4 p.m. and as many as 400 employees get together to live it up.

"Last year [1988] at Halloween was around the time Malcolm Gissing, our president for 12 years, was retiring and George Cobbe our new president was taking over," recalls Van Dusen. "Everyone came in to work dressed in a costume. Malcolm came dressed as a dragon and George as Saint George. All day George was chasing Malcolm around with a sword. It's corny but it means we don't take ourselves too seriously all the time."

The feature that inspires the most employee commitment, however, is the company's caring attitude. "We have a good reputation. Most people who come to work for HP have heard good things about it beforehand. Our people are our public relations," Van Dusen says.

HUSKY INJECTION MOLDING SYSTEMS LTD.

P.O. Box 1000
Bolton, Ontario
L7E 5S5
(416) 857-3240

Pay: **VERY GOOD**	Atmosphere: **VERY GOOD**
Benefits: **EXCELLENT**	Job Satisfaction: **GOOD**
Promotion: **VERY GOOD**	Communications: **VERY GOOD**
Job Security: **GOOD**	Personal Development: **VERY GOOD**

★ *Husky designs, manufactures and sells high-tech plastic injection-molding systems. The systems turn out products ranging from plastic soft-drink bottles to cassette holders. In addition to the head office and plant at Bolton, Ont., Husky has plants in the U.S., West Germany, Luxembourg and Japan. There are 900 employees in Canada. Founder Robert Schad controls the private company, whose annual sales in 1988 were $157 million. Employees own 21% of stock either directly or through the profit-sharing plan. Subject to Investment Canada's approval, Komatsu Ltd. of Tokyo, a Japanese industrial manufacturer, will become a partner in 1990 when it purchases 26% of the shares. In 1994, Komatsu will have the option to acquire an additional 24%, with employees holding the balance.*

HUSKY'S continued success depends on maintaining its technological advantage. "There's been a shake out in the market — a number of our competitors are no longer there," says Robert Schad, who founded the company in 1964. "The reason we are still here is our technological base."

"The product is the most important thing," he says. "We put a

68

lot of effort into research and market analysis to make sure we have a better product [than our competitors]. We don't ever compromise on quality. Quality must be maintained in every part of the operation."

This drive for quality and the atmosphere in this unusual company are closely connected to Schad's strong personality. He is committed to success through high performance, and the spectacular growth of his company, both nationally and internationally, suggests he is doing a lot of things right. The company's statement of corporate goals is short and to the point.

"We measure our success against uncompromising goals:

● To provide our customers with the technology they need to be industry leaders.

● To encourage our own people to shape goals — not just to follow.

● To be totally dedicated to quality and to be the best in whatever we do."

Husky emphasizes education, and it shows. Its workforce is highly skilled. The company offers internal college-credit courses for the technical disciplines and a five-week training program on injection-molding technology for non-technical employees.

"I'm in charge of designing our largest injection unit now — a $2-million machine," an employee just three years out of university says. "It is quite a challenge and responsibility that perhaps I would not have been able to have at another company." A new graduate agrees: "Husky really is on the leading edge of technology. I have learned more in the two years I have been here than in the previous 20."

"Mr. Schad always claims that Husky is probably the best university for tool makers and plastics," one long-time employee says. More than 50 employees have left the company over the years to start their own businesses, either using husky technology or supplying Husky.

Technical expertise determines how far an employee will advance in the company. "If you don't have a technical education, you are limited in your selection of promotion — but that is the nature of the business," one administrator points out. With the proper background, promotion opportunities are very good, but it is up to the individual to target a job and then work toward it. If you make the firm's grade, job security is not a concern.

One employee describes the atmosphere as "one of total commitment, excitement, pressure and drive. This is not a nine-to-five company." Another worker adds: "You have to be aggressive, dynamic and have fire in your belly to work here."

The exacting standards, however, have resulted in a high turnover. David Alcock, vice-president of personnel, says 33% of all employees hired are recent university or college graduates — people not known for staying at their first job for long.

For those who make the grade and survive the atmosphere, the rewards are significant. Salaries are high and there's a profit-sharing/equity-participation plan. Employees may contribute 5% of earnings, to which the company will add 10% of pre-tax profits. Up to two thirds of the company's contribution may be used to buy company stock. Between 1980 and 1989, the company on average contributed $1.01 for every $1 employees contributed to the plan.

"Profit sharing doesn't cost a thing, as far as I'm concerned," Schad says. "The company just makes more money if you have such a plan, because you get better people and better performance. But you have to communicate the point of the plan clearly to your employees."

Schad regularly communicates with workers through an employee council that meets once a month. Members serve on a rotating basis, so everyone gets a chance to participate. "There are no secrets here," Schad says. "I always answer questions when they're put to me. We try hard to communicate effectively."

Husky also has a quality and productivity program, loosely patterned on quality circles, that encourages employees to make suggestions to improve product quality or increase productivity. "The company is very innovative," one machine operator says. "Everyone is open minded," another says. "It's easy to get ideas accepted. That keeps us on the leading edge." The program has been successful. Sales increased about 20% in 1987, 1988 and 1989, and the number of employees grew 10% each year.

Employees are proud of their company. "We're the Rolls Royce of the plastic injection-molding industry," one worker says. "The plant is a place where you can eat your dinner off the floor, it's so clean," another says.

And they like their tough-minded boss too. "Schad is demanding but fair, more than fair" one buyer says. "He's not afraid to invest money to make things better."

"He's a top-of-the-line person who tells us, 'If you can't do a thing well, don't do it at all,'" one plant worker explains. Another of Schad's maxims is, "There is no such thing as 'can't.' There is always a better way. If you can't find it, invent it."

There are no divisions between employees and management at Husky — no executive washrooms or reserved parking spaces. When Schad sees a piece of garbage, he picks it up.

Employees are worried about the deal with Komatsu. They're unfamiliar with the company, its management style and plans for the future, and therefore worried about what effect the strategic partnership will have on Husky. Investment Canada is expected to approve Komatsu's 26% purchase of the company and its option to buy up to 50% of the shares by 1994. Komatsu was the only company in a long list of suitors committed to the principle of quality, Schad says. "With the fluctuations among Europe, America and the Pacific, you really have to be in all three markets," and Komatsu will help Husky secure new business. Under these conditions, the strategic partnership makes sense.

Husky is not for everyone. But for high performers who like a challenging environment, it offers substantial financial rewards and excellent opportunities to get ahead.

Lavalin

THE LAVALIN GROUP

1100 René-Lévesque Boulevard West
Montreal, Quebec
H3B 4P3
(514) 876-4455

Pay: **VERY GOOD**	Atmosphere: **GOOD**
Benefits: **AVERAGE**	Job Satisfaction: **VERY GOOD**
Promotion: **GOOD**	Communications: **AVERAGE**
Job Security: **POOR**	Personal Development: **EXCELLENT**

★ *A privately owned, global organization based in Montreal, The Lavalin Group is Canada's largest consulting engineering firm (with 7,500 employees in 1989, based in both French- and English-speaking Canada). It specializes in construction and construction management, but also has interests in urban transportation, health, communications and real estate. It lists the huge James Bay hydroelectric project among its accomplishments. Revenue in 1988 was $520 million.*

LAVALIN PURCHASED a transit vehicle manufacturer, Urban Transportation Development Corp., from the Ontario government in 1986. By 1989, the atmosphere at UTDC had changed considerably.

For one thing, UTDC employees find that management now actually listens to them. "You have a better chance of expressing new ideas and getting them through," one explains. A shop-floor supervisor: "They are starting to implement a lot of recommendations that came from the floor. It impressed us that management would come and admit that they needed help."

And not surprisingly, the UTDC organization is a lot less bureaucratic than before. "People used to write a lot of memos to cover their asses, and send copies to half a dozen people so everyone knew their position," recalls Rod Halstead, UTDC's director of human resources. Halstead tells how after the acquisition a Lavalin executive, Pierre Ranger, called two memo-trading employees into his office and introduced them to each other.

"But we know each other," one of them said. "We've been working together for years."

Ranger replied: "I was sure you hadn't met. Next time you have a problem, talk to each other and don't waste any more time with these memos."

The executive's brief instruction reflected an important aspect of the new style. At Lavalin, you know your stuff; you get the job done well, on time, on budget; you communicate freely and effectively.

In Lavalin's core business — construction engineering and management — that style has made the company enormously sucessful. The success, in turn, lures employees in droves. (Lavalin's head office receives about 500 applications a week for jobs at all levels, professional and otherwise.)

For professional engineers, success means an excellent track record in winning big contracts. This is particularly important in a field heavily dependent on the level of capital spending and where job security is scarce.

In Lavalin's kind of engineering (recent projects include the Vancouver Sky Train, the Regina Trade & Convention Centre and a rapid transit system in Thailand), most employees work on a per-project basis. The company lands a contract then assembles a project staff, mainly hired only for the duration of the project.

Outstanding per-project employees may be asked to go on the permanent payroll, but even then a downturn in capital spending can put juniors on the street. However, because it wins so many major jobs, Lavalin can and does transfer employees from project to project.

Professional staff think Lavalin is a fine place to work. They take pride in the company's reputation for being able to do just about *anything.* You name it and Lavalin can do it, employees will tell you.

The diversity of Lavalin's projects also has a very practical side. Coupled with open communication and a general willingness to share information, it enables professionals to grow. Any Lavalin division may tap the expertise of any other, freely, at any time.

All employees, both core and project, get the same benefits package. And there's a pension plan for those firmly established in the organization. About 250-300 senior managers also share in the profits.

In addition, the core company in Quebec offers what must be one of the most unusual fringe-benefit programs in Canada, called simply "Yannick et Benoît," the surnames of the first employees to receive the benefits.

Prix Benoît is a straight bonus of $600 per child paid to a male or female employee's family at the birth of a baby. Prix Yannick is a grant of $2,200 to female employees to supplement unemployment insurance payments while on maternity leave.

And there's no limit on Benôit. A female employee who bears twins, for example, gets $600 for each for a total benefit of $3,400.

Lavalin has been offering head-office employees day care for years. In 1989, the company operated two high-quality child-care centres in Montreal — one for 20 toddlers under 18 months and one for 60 children over 18 months — and parents paid only $15 a day. (Given Yannick and Benoît, it wasn't startling to find the two centres had a combined waiting list of 50 children.)

"We are miles ahead of other companies in developing employment equity," says John Penny, director of human resources at head office. More than 6% of Lavalin's engineers are women, double the proportion in the profession as a whole.

In short, Lavalin is an expanding and well-managed company. It offers both male and female engineers what may be a unique opportunity for professional development, if they're not looking for job security.

McDONALD'S
RESTAURANTS
OF CANADA LTD.

McDonald's Place
Toronto, Ontario
M3C 3L4
(416) 443-1000

Pay: **GOOD**	Atmosphere: **EXCELLENT**
Benefits: **VERY GOOD**	Job Satisfaction: **VERY GOOD**
Promotion: **VERY GOOD**	Communications: **EXCELLENT**
Job Security: **GOOD**	Personal Development: **VERY GOOD**

★ *McDonald's operates 570 company-owned and franchised quick service restaurants across Canada. The chain is the seventh largest employer in Canada, with 7,000 full-time and 50,000 part-time employees, all non-unionized. Sales in 1988 topped $1.2 billion. The publicly traded company is a subsidiary of McDonald's Corp. of Oak Brook, Ill.*

"IF YOU have the ambition, McDonald's has the position," says Beth Anderson, an enterprising first assistant manager at a McDonald's restaurant in suburban Hamilton, Ont. She has worked in the company for three years, and aspires to the higher managerial ranks of the world's biggest hamburger chain.

In fact, if you get past the lowest and poorest paid positions, promotional opportunities within the fast-growing corporation appear impressive. A fast-tracker like Anderson can move quickly through the ranks to become a restaurant manager or an area supervisor while still in her 20s. In her mind, it's a small sacrifice to work 45-50-hour weeks, often on weekends and holidays, because the potential rewards are high.

Pay levels are competitive, and include a bonus system that can see a manager earn as much as $6,000 more a year, plus a company car after two years on the job. In addition, McDonald's puts a substantial 18% of every full-time employee's annual earnings into a deferred profit sharing program that substitutes for a pension plan.

Other perks include a 12-week paid sabbatical after 10 years' service, and a quality benefits package that is currently being upgraded to a cafeteria-style selection plan. McDonald's also recognizes hard work in a number of other ways. In addition to the possibility of winning a $25 employee-of-the-month award, or a recognition prize of a radio or a camera, outstanding workers are occasionally sent on trips, such as Anderson's recent nine-day jaunt to West Germany to attend an international McDonald's convention.

McDonald's corporate headquarters in Metro Toronto's Don Mills area is full of employees who are proof of the promotional opportunities available to ambitious individuals. Roy Ellis, assistant vice-president and director of personnel, started flipping hamburgers in 1970 at a McDonald's in Brantford, Ont. He became corporate director of personnel at age 26.

The 300 people at head office work in state-of-the-art offices, decorated with colorful pop art sculptures. There are no walls — not even for President and CEO George Cohon. Instead, curving, pastel-colored, free-form partitions separate the cubicles, creating a unique environment. A subsidized cafeteria and in-house fitness centre complete the more-than-generous physical amenities.

The majority of McDonald's part-time employees are drawn from two groups: students and senior citizens. Starting salaries are quite low, beginning at $4 an hour for students, but there are hidden advantages. McDonald's tries to encourage its junior employee group with additional perks.

Student employees may pick their own flexible hours, up to a maximum of 15 hours during school weeks, but often full-time hours in the summer months. One year and two salary reviews after starting, a superlative student employee could be earning $4.70 an hour. Free uniforms and soft drinks, plus half-price food, also go with the job.

McDonald's demonstrates its commitment to student workers through its scholarship program. Most of the restaurants award a $400 scholarship annually to one of their employees, a program that amounts to a payout of more than $140,000 for the corporation. There also are a raft of team-spirit-generating social events, including picnics, parties and sporting events, plus regular meetings to discuss policies, procedures and problems.

In spite of all these incentives, student turnover rates at McDonald's outlets range from 85% to 98%, and restaurant managers admit that recruiting and retaining staff remain their biggest headache. Some managers believe a higher starting salary might alleviate the problem.

"McMasters," the name the corporation gives to its mature employee group, get the same advantages as students: flexible working hours, free uniforms and food discounts. The policy allows retired individuals the opportunity to re-enter the labor force on their own terms, for as many hours as they wish.

McDonald's prides itself on good corporate citizenship. In addition to its chain of 11 Ronald McDonald houses, assisting the families of children with cancer, the corporation sponsors a wide range of community activities and charities. McDonald's also offers employment to hundreds of disabled individuals.

Career opportunities at McDonald's often open new, unexpected vistas. The Canadian operation has sent workers to start up new operations in West Germany, France, Spain and now the U.S.S.R. The largest McDonald's in the world opened in Moscow in January, 1990, with seating for 900 (700 indoors). It is the first of 20 restaurants planned under a joint-venture agreement with the city.

The company is hiring and training Russian students to work in the new restaurants. As down-to-earth CEO Cohon says wryly, "For sure, we're going to be one of the 100 best companies to work for in the U.S.S.R."

Perhaps the clue to this company's success lies in its continual striving to be the best. Cohon explains matter-of-factly that the company doesn't allow itself to be taken in by its own promotional material: "Because you're number one in the industry doesn't mean you're the best. You're only the best because you work hard at it, and deliver the best quality, service, cleanliness and value."

NORTHERN TELECOM
CANADA LTD.

2920 Matheson Boulevard East
Mississauga, Ontario
L4W 4M7
(416) 238-7000

Pay: **VERY GOOD**	Atmosphere: **GOOD**
Benefits: **EXCELLENT**	Job Satisfaction: **VERY GOOD**
Promotion: **GOOD**	Communications: **VERY GOOD**
Job Security: **AVERAGE**	Personal Development: **VERY GOOD**

★ *Northern Telecom Canada (NTC) is the country's leading communications equipment designer and manufacturer, with 24 plants in nine provinces. They employ 17,000 people, of whom 58% are unionized. Revenues in 1988 were close to US$2 billion (NTC reports in U.S. dollars). NTC is a wholly owned subsidiary of Northern Telecom Ltd., which in turn is controlled by BCE Inc.*

TURBULENCE, AGGRESSION, conflict, challenge, stimulus: the same qualities that characterized Northern Telecom in 1985, but the emphasis has shifted slightly.

The one constant is still change, and anyone working for this dynamic company had better be prepared to deal with change on a daily basis. Change has become almost institutionalized within the organization. "We're so accustomed to change here that we don't even notice it anymore," says one NTC worker.

As Joanne Henderson, director of human resources, explains, "Not all change is comfortable or pleasant. Not all growth is painless, but having learned to deal happily with these factors is the most valuable 'benefit' the company has provided me over my 15 years as an employee."

Today, in its drive to achieve Vision 2000, NTC's goal of being the world's leading telecommunications supplier by the year 2000, the organization is putting more emphasis on teamwork and development of its people. The company demands tremendous results from its employees.

It expects nothing less than excellence, but provides more backup to achieve that result. There's continual training and upgrading, better employee recognition and reward programs, and a holistic approach to health and fitness. As one secretary puts it: "The company seems to realize that it's the employees who drive the company." The result is perhaps a slightly more balanced organization, aware that to get the best from its people it must earn their co-operation, rather than demand it.

"It's a more enjoyable place to work today," explains a manager. "We play hard, but we work hard too. The organization demands more of you if you're a manager. Lots of people refuse managerial positions because of the stresses and pressures."

However, some NTC workers remain skeptical about this change in culture. One critic says: "There's a lot of talk about people orientation, but when it comes down to the crunch, you're still rewarded for making the numbers. A strict bottom-line orientation."

Stress remains a daily part of the routine within this demanding company, but there are more ways of dealing with it. There are superbly equipped fitness centres at nearly every plant, and workers are encouraged to make use of them. In addition, a well-used employee assistance program helps people to get their worries off their chest. "It's like having a friend's support when you're having a bad time," one user says.

Northern Telecom's drive to increase both growth and competitiveness has meant shrinking its workforce several times in the past couple of years, and worry about job security is very real within the organization. After one recent purge, people started coming to work wearing T-shirts emblazoned with the motto "I survived!"

While it makes unusually strenuous demands on people, the company tries to compensate by eliminating financial worry. It pays near the top of the scale, although workers have noticed "a general competitive erosion over the past five years." As a result, the consensus is that pay has slipped from excellent to very good.

But the benefits package is still tops, containing an excellent medical/dental plan, an unusually generous noncontributory pension plan (partially indexed now) and maternity benefits that supplement unemployment insurance payments to 75% of salary for 15 weeks.

In addition, the firm's investment plan allows non-unionized workers to participate in the company's success through share ownership. For every $1 an employee contributes to the plan, the company contributes 50¢ (in the form of company shares) up to a limit of 6% of base salary. There are optional investment vehicles, including a registered retirement savings plan and a deferred profit sharing plan.

Another interesting perk for those who survive at NTC is the transitional retirement allowance, a significant amount based on years of service and salary level, paid to each employee on retirement. This noncontributory bonus can be taken as a lump sum or in equal installments over a period of time.

Internal communications, once a problem, have improved dramatically. A host of devices including voice mail, a telephone news hotline, senior management dialogues and newsletters, all contribute to keeping workers well informed about the company. In addition, groups of employees are sent regularly on fact-finding and communications-enhancing tours of other Northern Telecom facilities, both in Canada and abroad.

Employees still express concern about office politics and too much red tape in the organization. One employee believes stress levels could be reduced "through greater teamwork. There's still too much of the cowboys and Apaches syndrome here." When he was a newcomer, everybody kept warning him to " 'watch out for the Apaches. They're always lurking out there, just out of sight.' Most of the time that can be exciting, but sometimes it's just wearing."

In the leaner and meaner NTC, promotions are harder to come by and you need top qualifications to earn the upward move. And it's still tough to break out of the clerical ranks if you're ambitious to move up, according to one former secretary who made the big jump. "You must have a university degree and a mentor in the company," she says.

As Joanne Henderson says, "Northern's unique culture provides satisfaction for creative risk-takers who thrive on a challenge and enjoy the churn of never-ending change, while providing the opportunity and support to attain their personal and professional aspirations."

This is a company for high achievers. Top performance is the minimum requirement.

OMARK CANADA, LTD.
A BLOUNT, INC. COMPANY

OMARK CANADA LTD.

505 Edinburgh Road North
Guelph, Ontario
N1H 6L4
(519) 822-6870

Pay: **GOOD**	Atmosphere: **EXCELLENT**
Benefits: **EXCELLENT**	Job Satisfaction: **VERY GOOD**
Promotion: **AVERAGE**	Communications: **VERY GOOD**
Job Security: **VERY GOOD**	Personal Development: **VERY GOOD**

★ *Omark manufactures Oregon brand cutting chains, bars and sprockets for chain saws. Sales, mainly exports, total about $60 million annually. The firm's 750 employees work at the company's one plant in Guelph, Ont. The company is a subsidiary of a large U.S. construction conglomerate, Blount Inc., based in Montgomery, Ala.*

WHAT MAKES OMARK special is the high level of participation by employees and managers in making their plant a superior working environment. Omark employees are justified in their pride in the company. It is a remarkable workplace, recognized as an industrial pioneer.

Many of the innovations developed at Omark Canada have been adopted by the U.S. parent. In the latter 1980s, for example, Omark Canada introduced a zero inventory production system that dramatically increased productivity and was implemented in other Blount-owned plants.

It used to take workers six hours to replace the heavy dies in a machine press. Now one man can do the job in 35 seconds, thanks to participatory management. Workers meet in committees regularly to talk about how improvements can be made. The new die-changing technique stemmed from their recommendations.

Omark Canada is committed to participatory management, and clearly says so in its mission statememt: "We believe our people should be involved in decision making and problem solving, particularly regarding issues affecting their areas of interest and responsibility. A climate which consistently encourages the free and open flow of information and ideas is vital to employee involvement."

Omark has adopted a "philosophy of continual improvement in a problem solving format." This is a total commitment to satisfying customer needs through a formal problem solving approach. According to Eleanor Wickham, human resources manager, "this definitely unfolded a new world." Although it's still young, the program appears successful.

Employees say they "love to come to work." As one bookkeeper explained, "You can say what you think here, and not get fired. We're really allowed to express ourselves freely." Another long-term worker added: "Management is really willing to listen to what you have to say. There's no we-they attitude here."

Communication is good and fairly informal. All written company news gets mailed to the employees' homes to brief the whole family.

Omark also believes that employees deserve a positive work environment. Although noisy, the plant is spotlessly clean. And as a compensation for the noise, the employee lunchroom borders on an atrium filled with trees, plants and even a small stream, where employees can totally escape the industrial environment. The company provides free coffee, doughnuts, soft drinks, fruit, soups and salads.

Benefits also help to explain wny Omark workers love their jobs. In addition to the usual health and pension plans, Omark has some unusual benefits. For example, each worker can have one free consultation a year with the company's lawyers to deal with any personal legal business. The same goes for tax questions, which are referred to the firm's tax consultants.

The savings and investment plan is generous. The company pays 50¢ for every $1 contributed by workers, up to a maximum of 6% of earnings. Employees become eligible after three years of service, and company contributions are vested immediately.

The Omark Canada contributions are invested in the parent firm's stock, while those of the employee are put into a registered retirement savings plan. "This plan is a great incentive," explains one employee. "We want to do a better job, and sell more product, so that the stock will go up, and we'll get greater dividends."

The pay is good, particularly at the middle and upper levels, and increases are awarded on the basis of performance. The company is generous with tuition aid, and runs many in-house courses (computer training, for example) to foster personal development.

The company's mission statement says: "We attach a high value to people and believe they are the most important long-term asset of the company. . . Individual respect, mutual trust and a spirit of co-operation are a way of life at Omark."

And that's not just another idle slogan. This company really practices what it preaches.

To succeed in this dynamic workplace, you have to be flexible, adapt well to change and be strongly people-oriented. The rewards for those characteristics seem very worthwhile.

PILLSBURY CANADA LTD.

243 Consumers Road
Willowdale, Ontario
M2J 4Z5
(416) 494-2500

Pay: **GOOD**	Atmosphere: **GOOD**
Benefits: **VERY GOOD**	Job Satisfaction: **VERY GOOD**
Promotion: **VERY GOOD**	Communications: **GOOD**
Job Security: **GOOD**	Personal Development: **EXCELLENT**

★ *Pillsbury Canada, the processor of such nationally known food brands as Green Giant, Pillsbury and Clark, has 1,200 employees. Half the employees are unionized, mainly by the United Food & Commercial Worker's Union. The company — owned by Grand Metropolitan PLC, a British food, liquor and retail conglomerate — had sales in 1988 of $230 million.*

"WE WANT to be the best food company in Canada," says Jim Grossett, Pillsbury's vice-president, human resources. The company has some way to go to achieve that goal, but management appears sincerely determined to get there.

"If you can't stand in front of a group of employees and justify why you are doing something, then you should re-evaluate it," Grossett says.

Pillsbury has not always been an innovative, dynamic company open to new ideas. It used to be a very sleepy organization. The new dynamic atmosphere began with the issuance of the company's formal mission principles in 1985:

- Goal: to be the best food company in the world.
- People make a difference.

- Quality is essential.
- Excellence must be a way of life.

The change was dramatic. In 1988, Pillsbury introduced 71 new products, compared with half a dozen a few years earlier. The mission statement's values have become a focal point for employees, who now refer to them regularly.

Pillsbury has been improving itself by listening to its employees. The company conducted its first survey of all employees in 1985, intending to make it an annual process, but feeding the results back to employees and acting on the suggestions took a year and a half.

Communications have been greatly improved since the first attitude survey. The whole company works on management by objectives, set annually and communicated to everyone. Departments and then individuals set their own objectives to support the corporate goals.

A second survey was completed in 1988. Its recommendations — including flexible hours, longer vacations, career planning, benefits for part-timers, flexible benefits and a formal employee assistance program — are still being implemented. In total, 20 issues are being acted on.

Continuous improvement applies not only to the company and the human resources department, but to employees themselves. Workers take between 30 and 80 hours of job-specific and career-oriented training courses a year. Time- and stress-management courses are mandatory for all employees.

Emphasizing personal development and being the best has meant "the water level is rising," with respect to performance, Chief Executive Officer Richard Peddie told us. For two years, sales increased by 11% a year, while profits rose by 50% a year.

Pillsbury has a remarkably low staff turnover rate of 3%, achieved by moving employees to different jobs as often as once a year. The more diverse experience an employee gains, the greater the chance for promotion.

And people do rise quickly. Peddie was a vice-president at 30 and president at 35. But with young junior managers pushing up against young senior management, continually challenging employees is seen as essential. In hiring, as well, the company looks for candidates with varied backgrounds.

Employees feel their compensation is good and their benefits are superior. The planned introduction of flexible benefits will allow employees to tailor what Grossett calls a"hidden pay package" to their personal needs. Another longer-term goal: to make part of everyone's income incentive-driven, through a profit sharing program.

Peddie explained why the changes have taken so long: "Too many other companies have a flavor of the month. This month is such and such theme, and then it's in the sewer. At Pillsbury, we are committed to our policies. Everything is consistently building on our mission and values."

In the acquisition of Fraser Valley Foods, near Vancouver, Pillsbury inherited a history of antagonistic labor-management relations. Six months later, though, an employee survey showed 90% thought Fraser Valley was a better place to work under Pillsbury. One sign of the improving relationship is that union contracts have been negotiated for three-year periods, as opposed to two.

Many Fraser Valley employees gave Pillsbury high marks for opening up communications, listening to and (sometimes) acting on employee suggestions, making it easier for women to move into non-traditional jobs and improving marketing and quality control. An active and enthusiastic employee social committee now runs a program of activities, paid for by the company.

Another indicator of improving morale was the pride taken in a major cost reduction program started by Pillsbury in response to strong competition from New Zealand asparagus packers. Fraser Valley's plant at Sardis, B.C., is the world's largest exporter of canned green asparagus.

The company told its employees it needed cost reductions of $1.50 a case in 1988 and $1 a case in 1989. Declining production costs were posted in the plant daily, so employees could keep track of their performance. In both years, the workers exceeded the targets by a wide margin.

All of which may mean Pillsbury workers take to heart the message that flashes across the screen whenever anyone logs on to the company-wide computer system: "Keep an open mind to new ideas and encourage innovation and risk-taking with the knowledge that sometimes we fail."

Or as Peddie put it: "People make mistakes. Mistakes give you experience, and experience gives you wisdom."

Raychem

RAYCHEM
CANADA LTD.

3245 American Drive
Mississauga, Ontario
L4V 1N4
(416) 674-1680

Pay: **GOOD**	Atmosphere: **EXCELLENT**
Benefits: **VERY GOOD**	Job Satisfaction: **VERY GOOD**
Promotion: **GOOD**	Communications: **GOOD**
Job Security: **VERY GOOD**	Personal Development: **EXCELLENT**

★ *Raychem Canada is a wholly owned marketing subsidiary of a U.S.
company that uses radiation chemistry to produce such products as
corrosion-proof insulation. Most of its 75 employees work at the
Mississauga home base. Its 1988 sales were more than $47 million.
Raychem Canada is controlled by Raychem International, which in
turn is owned by Raychem Corp. of Menlo Park, Calif.*

"WORKING AT RAYCHEM isn't a job," says its president,
Robert Gibb. "It's an exciting, dynamic existence."

This is the kind of company where there are no half measures.
As one employee explains, "Once you get to know the company,
you'll either love it or hate it."

The company has grown rapidly, but Raychem is still
characterized by freedom and lack of structure. All employees
build their own careers here. No one shows them an organized
career ladder to climb. It's an informal, unostentatious, yet
professional company. Decison making is done by consensus
within the divisional structure. Administrative decion making is
by consensus among divisional managers. Even when it comes to

hiring, a number of key employees interview prospective workers before the final decision is made.

The company's headquarters reflect the kind of corporate image it's trying to project: modern, beautifully designed and extremely functional. And the employees understand just how functional they are: "Raychem creates an environment that allows people to perform. The idea of performance is in everybody's mind."

After changing the office environment when he took over the top job in 1983, Gibb began converting the corporate culture. He instils a sense of pride and perfectionism into his employees. "People here joke about the fact that I insist everything be done right, whether it be a Christmas party or presentations to customers or the way we treat employees," he says.

The company's corporate objectives clearly state: "We believe that people work best in an atmosphere which is vigorous and stimulating, rather than unnecessarily limiting. To provide this atmosphere, we encourage each employee to become involved with the job, to find better ways of doing it and to make his or her ideas heard."

"We're always trying to do the job better," an employee says. "We're becoming more efficient all the time."

Another employee describes the culture as one of "sophistication and finesse. Everything we do looks good — even the labels on our products are carefully designed."

Raychem also looks for specific character traits in its workers: extraordinary energy and inquisitiveness, a willingness to get involved and the mature self-confidence required to stick one's neck out.

Employees are finding Raychem an increasingly good place to learn. The company has industry-specific internal training courses, and employees are reimbursed and given time off for outside courses, as long as they relate to performance on the job. Says Gibb: "There hasn't been an incidence of us turning down a request. We just do it — it's like the air, no big deal. People know we do this and take advantage of it, and that's what we want."

Raychem pays well, and salaries are certainly competitive with other high-tech companies. The benefits package is superior to most. It includes an unusually high 80% coverage of orthodontic treatment, and the pension plan is non-contributory. The firm encourages employees to buy company stock, and sells it 15% below market price, while allowing employees to contribute as much as 15% of their salaries to the share-purchase scheme.

But the real incentive comes in the form of a cash bonus system, tied to profits and distributed quarterly. In the late 1980s, it averaged about 2%-3% of salary, but it can go as high as 10%.

Promotions are almost always made from within. And given the rate of growth, opportunities look good.

In most cases, employees seem too busy to have any problems, but despite generally good communication and an open-door policy, some say there's room for improvement. And one worker admitted candidly that "freedom brings its own problems, too. We don't always strike the right balance between structure and freedom."

The increased size of the company, whose electronic division alone is bigger than the entire Raychem Canada business was in 1985, has meant a move to a divisional structure for sales and marketing across Canada, but this hasn't changed the way things are done.

Another employee believes more effort could be made to recognize a job well done. "There aren't enough small recognition touches around here."

To succeed at Raychem, you've got to love not only the company, but also a fast-paced, demanding and unstructured environment.

ROYAL TRUSTCO LTD.

Suite 3900
Royal Trust Tower
Toronto, Ontario
M5W 1P9
(416) 981-7000

Pay: **GOOD**	Atmosphere: **VERY GOOD**
Benefits: **EXCELLENT**	Job Satisfaction: **VERY GOOD**
Promotion: **EXCELLENT**	Communications: **VERY GOOD**
Job Security: **VERY GOOD**	Personal Development: **VERY GOOD**

★ *Royal Trustco Ltd. is one of Canada's largest trust companies with more than $100 billion worth of assets under administration. Net income in 1988 was $212 million. The company has 6,000 employees in 130 offices across Canada and another 500 in 22 overseas offices. Royal Trust is 50% owned by Trilon Financial Corp., one of the Brascan group of companies.*

WHAT ARE the characteristics that identify the typical Royal Trust employee? "A person willing to try something new; entrepreneurial, professional, tired and very bright," was the answer given by one keen group of employees.

Under the aggressive leadership of Michael Cornelissen, Royal Trust is now one of the country's most dynamic companies, determined to become the number one trust organization in the world. The price of climbing this pinnacle is a high one for employees.

To succeed in this fast-moving, continually expanding organization takes drive and stamina, coupled with a thirst for challenges. When describing his vision of the future, Cornelissen likens it to running a unique type of marathon race:

"At the 18-mile check, race officials announce that the course has been extended to 52 miles — double the length you planned for. Despite the extra length of the course, suddenly people double and triple their pace. Runners are elbowing you, tripping you, running up your heels. [Then] somebody lets loose a man-eating tiger on the course! That's the environment we can expect in the future [for financial service institutions]."

Marathon runners, in for the long haul, should thrive in this organization, as long as they recognize what they've let themselves in for. Because once the employee has accepted the fact that he or she, along with everyone else in the organization, will be pushed continually to achieve higher and better results, the rewards can be very high.

Ordinary salary levels at Royal Trust are good, but not spectacular. Where you can make gains is in the variety of incentive programs offered. Cornelissen outlines his salary philosophy, which permeates the company: "I don't believe in senior managers getting high salaries and big bonuses. Cash salaries here are well below market salaries. Rewards come through very significant share ownership. This creates a strong feeling of partnership."

Senior managers' incentives include share purchases and share options. Other workers participate through the employee bonus plan and the share plan. Under the latter, the individual worker puts up to 4% of salary into the plan, which converts the funds into company shares. Royal Trust then adds 25% in the form of shares, plus an additional 25% should the company achieve its financial objectives for that year.

Since 1985, the company has been more than matching its objectives, making the share plan a very positive incentive. For example, an employee who joined the plan in 1985 with a salary of $20,000, would have seen his or her own investment of $3,200 become $7,000 by 1989.

Other performance-based incentives also reward initiative, so high achievers can capitalize on their abilities here. As one woman manager says: "The payback is there if you're willing to take the risk."

In the same spirit of partnership, the benefits program requires a higher contribution from the employee than in some other organizations. Vision care, dental and orthodontic plans are all paid for jointly by Royal Trust and the employee. But the range of benefits is certainly extensive, including extras such as mortgage and fitness subsidies. And if an employee buys services from other Trilon companies (insuring a life or car, say, or selling a house through Royal LePage), each transaction earns a set number of Trilon shares.

Benefits for working mothers are also good, and include a six-month maternity leave option and a day care referral plan. Some job-sharing opportunities also exist at Royal Trust. Part-time employment options are also available.

Cornelissen's vision of Royal Trust's future success as a partnership between managers and employees means the company puts a great deal of emphasis on communication. Eleven annual employee meetings are held across Canada and abroad. Cornelissen and his senior managers attend them all. And the focus is on senior management's *accountability* to employees.

"This gives us an opportunity to talk to our employees, and personally evangelize our mission," Cornelissen explains. "It's worth gold to us. We all meet with 75% of our employees each year."

In addition there are bureaucracy-busting breakfasts, lunches with the president and so on. A company ombudsman provides a confidential 24-hour problem resolution service.

Opportunities for growth, advancement and training abound. In 1988, 20% of the employee group were promoted. In that same year Royal Trust spent more than $10 million on training, so that every Royal Trust staffer spent a minimum of four days in courses. A formal career development program takes each employee through a step-by-step assessment to identify potential career paths within the company and plan to get on one of them.

The strength of Royal Trust's commitment to its employees shows in the importance attached to human resources issues. In 1989, all the company's vice-presidents (about 50 in Canada) had at one least one major human resources objective in his or her personal performance plan. The objectives included reducing turnover, say, or increasing training. (Achievement of such personal goals plays a part in determining vice-presidential salaries.)

The disadvantages of working at Royal Trust all seem to stem from the high levels of expectation. As one director said: "The most serious problem I've had has been the sacrifice of family time." When asked what could be improved at Royal Trust, another employee quipped: "Fit 40 hours into 24!"

This is the quintessential high-performance company, demanding initiative, drive, stamina and innovative hard work from its employees. If you're interested in a high basic salary, run a good short-distance race, but you don't have the staying power of the long-distance runner, don't bother to apply. You won't stay the course.

Telesat

TELESAT CANADA

1601 Telesat Court
Gloucester, Ontario
K1B 5P4
(613) 748-0123

Pay: **GOOD**	Atmosphere: **VERY GOOD**
Benefits: **GOOD**	Job Satisfaction: **VERY GOOD**
Promotion: **AVERAGE**	Communications: **VERY GOOD**
Job Security: **VERY GOOD**	Personal Development: **VERY GOOD**

★ *Telesat designs, develops, owns and runs a satellite-based system for nationwide commercial telecommunications. The company sent the world's first geostationary domestic communications satellite (Anik A1) into orbit in 1972, and has put four generations of spacecraft into service without a hitch. It has more than 800 employees, located mainly at headquarters near Ottawa. Operating revenues (from the sale of both communications services and space-related expertise): $128 million in 1988.*

SPACE HAS GLAMOUR, even if you're not a member of the technical priesthood. The excitement of being involved in something truly different gives any job at Telesat an intangible plus.

In fact, while the technology itself has become routine, the launch of a new spacecraft still sends a temporary "high" right through the entire organization. Pride of product and accomplishment accounts for a large part of the company's appeal to employees.

They point out that the techniques and systems developed by Telesat people to control objects in space are the best. And the

95

world is buying them. Revenue from consulting work abroad stood at $8.7 million in 1988, an increase of 60% over 1987.

Prospects for the future excite employees, as well. Telesat has been branching out further into satellite markets. For instance, the company has a unit working on satellite business television. It also has plans for point of purchase radio programs — advertising and music that can be delivered to shopping malls on satellite channels.

Telesat, owned 50% by the federal government and 50% by Canada's nine domestic telecommunications common carriers, is neither a Crown corporation nor a technological experiment. It has proven itself as a viable commercial enterprise (with a net profit of $18.2 million in 1988), and it has no monopoly in the telecom business. Telesat now competes against some of its owners — the telephone companies and their earth-based technologies.

"Telesat has become very market oriented," says Public Affairs Officer Gilles Le Breton. "Telesat used to be a wholesaler of telecommunication services — a telecommunication carriers' carrier. Now we are retailing directly in the marketplace. Our voice and data customers include Hudson's Bay Co., National Bank of Canada, Home Hardware to name a few."

Broadcast clients now account for 57% of Telesat's business, and its 110 industry and government clients provide the remainder. According to Linda Rankin, vice-president of business development, Telesat forecasts that by 1995 it will be a 50-50 split.

The involvement in product marketing since 1985 has had an important effect, says Murray Long, manager of public affairs. "Now we go it alone and take full responsibility for the future, for our whole business base. That means it's a more challenging environment — employees all know our success depends on them. There are greater rewards if we are successful, greater risks if we fail."

In short, the deliberate shift from an engineering-driven to a marketing-oriented corporate culture has made Telesat a livelier place to work. The emphasis has shifted from technology to people. Satellites are a means, not an end. The major product is a bundle of communications services.

"What the company is and what it stands for" played a significant role in attracting one financial man to Telesat. He adds: "It's the kind of company I can cheerfully and voluntarily dedicate a good part of my life to."

A male engineering executive, whose job seems to change every year with the business environment, has taken on an additional marketing venture. "It's whatever you want to do," he says. "That's what this company is all about. If you can identify something, do it."

The difference, according to another man, lies in how the company treats employees who appear to have reached their limits. "Instead of saying, 'Well they're topped off. That's as far as they're going,' Telesat says, 'Well, it's time for a little more fertilizer.' "

Wherever possible, Telesat tries to give individuals with high levels of expertise a free rein. As the president explains: "When they demonstrate they know what they're doing, we try to let them do it."

The man in charge of a key software operation is one of them. He has a broad, general mandate, but no one tells him how to do his work. He comments: "It's not just the work. It's the way I work that appeals to me. I do have freedom and autonomy. I am judged on final results, as opposed to the minute steps I take to get there. And, to do my job, I'm given the facilities I need — not only to get the work done, but to provide a good working environment for the people I'm responsible for."

Employees describe a relatively lean organization with open communications, very few top-level secrets, a warm welcome for new initiatives and a real regard for people. They feel the company has concern for them as individuals. They perceive an organization that prefers to fit the person to a suitable job, rather than force him into a mold.

One woman also discovered what Telesat is all about — "people," she says. The company promoted her into a managerial position with coaching and encouragement. "They gave me a job and said, 'Do it whichever way you want to.' They've measured me on what I've done. They've been very, very supportive. They've helped me grow. It's care and concern about growth — individual growth as well as growth within the corporate ranks — that makes it really different."

The management philosophy at Telesat emphasizes team goals and the part each working unit plays in supporting the whole. The company has taken deliberate steps to bring employees from all disciplines and work areas together. These groups work out plans and programs and have a say in corporate policy. They look at the future and examine their role in terms of the overall corporate future.

The underlying premise is that Telesat has highly motivated, highly intelligent and well-educated employees. Therefore, most of the good ideas for the technical future are probably in-house now. And most of the expertise to convert the ideas into plans is in residence as well.

As a matter of policy, salaries at Telesat are neither the highest nor the lowest in the telecom industry. The average employee income in 1989 was about $41,600. Employees rate the benefits as marginally better on average than those of the federal public service and major private employers.

"We don't go out of our way to have superb salaries or superb benefits," says Eldon D. Thompson, president and chief executive officer. "In fact, our corporate target is to be on the median [in the telecom industry]."

Public Affairs Manager Long adds: "We don't intend to have the highest salaries, but do want to offer an attractive compensation package. We don't want to steal people away from other places, but want to keep our own best here."

And the staff turnover rate is a moderate 6% a year. Many employees say financial gains alone would have to be substantial to lure them away.

The company encourages employees to seek new opportunities and challenges through internal mobility, whenever possible. It has also had some success in moving women out of clerical jobs into technical and general areas.

Telesat has made the advancement of women into management one of the factors the company uses to evaluate its performance and that of its employees (previously only ecomomic and technical factors were considered), but progress isn't rapid. "It has been slow to materialize," Long says. "We have some very visible women, a vice-president, a director, but the senior management ranks still lean very heavily toward men." The reason, he explains, is that there are not many women with engineering degrees, and those who have them are deluged with job offers.

An executive secretary believes the company offers whatever challenges an employee wants to accept. "I don't think there's another company I know of that I'd rather work for," she comments. "I'd rather stay at Telesat and see what I can do here."

The shift to a marketing-related culture at Telesat has made some basic changes in recruiting, though. In the past, the company hired most of its employees on the basis of technical competence. Today, Telesat recognizes its success will be linked with the recruitment of individuals with marketing and management abilities. As the personnel manager put it: "If you've got any good technical marketing people, you send them right here."

TORONTO SUN

333 King Street East
Toronto, Ontario
M5A 3X5
(416) 947-2222

Pay: **AVERAGE**	Atmosphere: **VERY GOOD**
Benefits: **VERY GOOD**	Job Satisfaction: **VERY GOOD**
Promotion: **GOOD**	Communications: **GOOD**
Job Security: **AVERAGE**	Personal Development: **GOOD**

★ *The Toronto Sun is a daily newspaper with a circulation ranging from 300,000 during the week to 475,000 on Sunday. The paper was founded in 1971 by 62 members of the defunct Toronto Telegram. With 870 full-time employees, annual revenues in 1988 of were approximately $150 million. The paper is owned by Toronto Sun Publishing Corp., of which Maclean Hunter Ltd. owns 63% of the shares.*

WORKING FOR The Toronto Sun has many advantages – very good benefits, a relaxed, unstructured environment, and open management. Take, for instance, the controversy over the paper's "Sunshine Girls" and strip club ads. Some employees think they are sexist and should be axed. Others argue that the Sun's very successful formula should not be tampered with.

Whatever the outcome of this internal debate, the openness with which it is discussed is a key part of the Sun's "very good" atmosphere. This openness is an important element of the Sun's management style. General Manager Jim Tighe, for example, walks the building every day. Vice-President Corporate Affairs Trudy Eagan lunches two or three times a week in the cafeteria. And Publisher Paul Godfrey maintains an open-door policy.

There are also newsletters, department meetings, and letters from the president, J. Douglas Creighton, all designed to demonstrate that Sun employees are working together for a common purpose.

Still, some employees feel that the "sixth floor" (executive floor) has become more distant than in earlier years. This is probably inevitable in a company that has been rapidly expanding. In the last half of the 1980s, Toronto Sun Publishing Corp., which owns the paper, has been on a fast track.

It acquired The Financial Post from its parent Maclean Hunter in 1988 when the decision was made for The Post to go daily. Maclean Hunter felt such a move required the daily newspaper expertise of The Sun. That venture has been relatively successful, although it was still operating in the red as the 1990s began.

In 1988, the Sun also started up a daily paper in Ottawa, aquired a majority interest in Bowes Publishers Ltd., which publishes daily and weekly newspapers and also farm publications in Ontario, Manitoba, Alberta and British Columbia, and bought a commercial printing plant in Washington. In 1989, it bought some more weeklies in Alberta and purchased a chain of weeklies and shoppers' guides in Florida.

The cost of growth say some employees has been the loss of "some of that family feeling," for which the Sun has always had an enviable reputation. With 870 employees it is impossible to know everyone's name. In addition, Creighton has to now spend a lot of time on the road visiting his various operations. This limits his accessibility to the Toronto paper's employees.

But there is an upside to the new acquisitions for the Toronto employees. A new building is going up next door to house The Financial Post. This will include a fitness centre and a cafeteria, done cafe style with a wine and beer licence.

Nor has the friendliness that has always characterized the "little paper that grew" disappeared. It remains a friendlier place that most papers, says one staff member. The Sun still strives for the intimate touches that are found in small businesses. The children's Christmas Party in 1989 drew more than 200 kids and their parents. There is an annual golf tournament and a summer picnic.

In addition, the Sun is not a highly structured organization. Indeed, to some new employees the Sun appears to have no structure. "How do we get a product out every day?" wondered a new sales employee after a month. "It's organized confusion. But everybody is easy going and says, 'Don't worry it will get done.' It's a lot of fun." A journalist agrees: "the Sun has always built itself on a wing and a prayer mentality. In editorial it can be pandemonium."

This kind of free and easy environment is only possible in a nonunionized shop, and it certainly has advantages. A sales representative, for example, says how much he enjoys having access to his ads in the composing room. "At other newspapers I have worked at that was impossible to do," he says. "The flexibility of the whole system is outstanding."

All positions are posted internally and with a few notable exceptions, such as publisher Godfrey, the Sun has studiously trained and promoted internal candidates. A female employee of four years says, "I have been promoted three times over people who have been here longer and who are older than I am. It was purely on ability, I can't imagine a company where you can move up faster."

Some editorial staff, however, would like to see expanded opportunities to move up or out of their present domain. And women would like to see the promotion of even more women into senior management.

One of the most attractive features at the Sun is the benefit package which includes the unusual feature of an eight-week salaried sabbatical after 10 and 20 years to help employees recharge their batteries.

And that's just the beginning. The pension plan is fully funded by the company. A deferred profit-sharing plan pays a percentage of salary based on profitability. Besides the statutory holidays, two extra days off are given every year. After one year, there's a Christmas bonus of one-week's salary, three weeks holidays and the opportunity to buy shares with an interest-free loan. After three years, employees get four weeks holiday; after 20 years, they get six weeks. The Sun also has medical, dental and insurance plans. Says one journalist, "Reporters from other newspapers can't believe how good we have it here."

As in many companies, there are a few extra perks for senior people — housing loans for those moving from one city to another, shares for indispensable staff members, and a generous car policy.

The Sun allows employees to take on outside responsibilities

— even high-profile ones such as broadcasting — providing they reflect well on the company.

The company also offers awards for its journalists, the Edward Dunlop awards. The first prize in each category is a $2,500 travel certificate and $1,000 in spending money. "It's a huge incentive for editorial people," says a journalist there.

In terms of comparitive wage levels, the Sun lags "a little behind" Toronto's other major newspapers. But this is somewhat deceptive, as employees note: "when you take account that we are getting 56 weeks pay [after profit sharing and the Christmas bonus] we come out close or on top [of the others]." Even so, the total compensation package is only considered the icing on the cake for most employees because The Sun represents more than a job. It is a way of life.

VANCOUVER CITY SAVINGS CREDIT UNION

515-10th Avenue West
P.O. Box 24807, Station C
Vancouver, British Columbia
V5T 4E9
(604) 877-7000

Pay: **GOOD**	Atmosphere: **VERY GOOD**
Benefits: **VERY GOOD**	Job Satisfaction: **VERY GOOD**
Promotion: **GOOD**	Communications: **VERY GOOD**
Job Security: **VERY GOOD**	Personal Development: **VERY GOOD**

★ *VanCity is the third largest credit union in the world (after those of the U.S. Navy and United Airlines). It has assets of $1.8 billion and functions essentially as a retail bank for about 180,000 owner-members. There are about 783 employees, 165 at head office, the remainder spread among 22 branches throughout Greater Vancouver.*

VANCITY MANAGEMENT recognizes that employees are the key in the financial services industry. They are dealing with a product (money) that is undifferentiated except for the service that employees add to it. And employees at VanCity believe in having fun.

There are not many financial institutions where a branch manager will dress up as Frankenstein at Halloween and sling a cheeky sign across her back saying: "I work for the Bank of Montreal." Rather than frowning on such frivolity, senior management joins in and dons fancy dress for Halloween visits to branches. Some members complained it was too much, though, when one branch brought in rabbits at Easter.

There are other friendly touches. Management sees to it that all employees (male as well as female) get cards on their birthdays and the anniversaries of joining the organization, and handwritten notes from the personnel department or the vice-president of marketing are penned to staff meriting special recognition.

There are awards for people who lose weight, quit smoking or jog 1,000 miles a year. (Somewhat counterproductively, the prize for the latter feat includes dinner at one of Vancouver's finest restaurants.) There are also prizes for branches that write the most business or persuade the most members to switch their registered retirement savings plans to VanCity.

If the organization's management style is light, it has also been sure. VanCity's growth has been remarkable. Founded in 1946 by 22 members, it has grown rapidly, especially in the past decade or so.

Employees rate their job satisfaction as high, and they agree that VanCity actively encourages personal growth and provides the means for this to be achieved. A woman employee comments: "If you want to move ahead, everything is on a silver platter for you if you want to take it. They want you to know as much as you can about everything."

The credit union places great emphasis on training, running its own courses and paying the cost of outside tuition, including university courses.

Many VanCity members bank with the credit union because they feel pride in a thriving home-grown financial institution. They also say it is friendlier than the chartered banks.

New employees, especially, are struck by the pleasant atmosphere. One woman, meeting a senior executive for the first time in a group of about 20 people, was amazed that he later remembered her by her first name.

A woman employee said she feels good about the intensive training she gets at VanCity. "If the competition don't really know about their products and we do, well, that is one up for us." Among VanCity's more unusual products is the popular Ethical Growth Fund, which permits conscientious investors to put their money into companies that don't make military products, are not in the nuclear industry and don't trade with South Africa.

VanCity's roots go deep in its community, and it makes special efforts to support local organizations financially. Each year, it adopts a theme for corporate donations. In 1989, it was multiculturalism, and all requests for donations had to be linked to that theme. Employees also may ask for cash grants (typically $100 to $500) to help support nonprofit community organizations they are involved in.

More than 80% of VanCity employees are women. They occupy 38% of the management jobs, 20% of the executive posts and comprise 35% of the board of directors.

Because it's reluctant to lose the skills and experience of expensively trained employees wanting to take an extended break to care for a young family, VanCity in 1989 introduced a return-to-work program based on European models.

Linda Crompton, vice-president of human resources, explains: "There's a continuing worry about how to get a job when they want to get back into the workforce. We say, 'If you elect you can take two or three years off. We will keep you on the books.' "

Jobs are guaranteed. Employees stay on the staff mailing list and are invited to attend social functions. Twice a year, they are expected to work for a week or two to stay on top of new technology. When the program was announced, 80 women asked to take advantage of it.

Employees sit on a committee that compares VanCity salaries and benefits to those of other financial institutions and makes recommendations to management. Since the committee was started in 1977, its ideas have been accepted without exception.

VanCity does little recruiting outside, except for specialized skills, preferring to promote from within and train staff to handle extra responsibility. In 1989, it was getting about 120 unsolicited applications a month. However, in common with most financial institutions, it was experiencing difficulty in attracting well-qualified people for its more junior positions.

To make the jobs more interesting and justify higher pay rates, VanCity has begun training new entrants for greater immediate responsibility. Rather than simply placing new employees in lowly teller positions where they learn on the job, it began putting newcomers through a month-long training course to acquire the skills for a variety of jobs. This way, it hopes employees will stick around longer in an industry with a notoriously high turnover.

Employees are so enthusiastic about VanCity they admit they occasionally sound "corny." When the credit union asked workers to suggest an advertising slogan, 122 of them replied with repeated references to such concepts as "happiness, pride, friendship and family."

An employee social club, whose directors are elected from among the branches, meets monthly and organizes a Christmas party, a dinner dance, a casino night, a golf tournament, a baseball league, a curling bonspiel and a boat cruise. All are well attended.

As an additional benefit, VanCity also pays the costs (up to $500 a year) for visits to a clinical psychologist. Counseling sessions include advice on problems with alcohol or drugs, marriage breakdown, kids in difficulties. A brochure advertising the confidential employee assistance program says: "You're our most valuable resource. It stands to reason that if we can help you solve outside problems which may be affecting your work, everyone benefits."

Other benefits are low-cost loans for employees. Senior staff, for example, can obtain a mortgage amounting to double their annual salary at half the conventional interest rate.

A woman employee said: "We are not all perfect, obviously, but when there is a bad service given, or we feel it is not up to par, I feel very hurt. At VanCity, a piece of it is mine."

For employees, VanCity has made the usually staid banking business sparkle.

ZITTRER · SIBLIN · STEIN · LEVINE

COMPTABLES AGRÉÉS · CHARTERED ACCOUNTANTS

ZITTRER, SIBLIN STEIN, LEVINE

1 Place Alexis Nihon
Montreal, Quebec
H3Z 3E8
(514) 935-1117

Pay: **AVERAGE**	Atmosphere: **VERY GOOD**
Benefits: **POOR**	Job Satisfaction: **VERY GOOD**
Promotion: **GOOD**	Communications: **VERY GOOD**
Job Security: **GOOD**	Personal Development: **VERY GOOD**

★ *Montreal-based Zittrer, Siblin, Stein, Levine is Canada's 16th largest firm of chartered accountants. A senior personnel consultant describes it as "anything but a traditional accounting firm." There are 377 partners and employees, the majority at the head office, the balance in Toronto. Estimated revenues for 1988 were $25 million.*

ONE OF THE things that makes ZSSL different is that professional employees "learn the meaning of the work they're doing that otherwise would be so boring," managing partner Herbert Siblin says. "If we go to a major meeting with a bank, for example, we will frequently invite staff to come with us just to see the process and see the work they did."

The firm has a strongly people-oriented approach to a profession not widely renowned for high job satisfaction and enrichment among junior employees.

Unlike the more common accounting 'sweatshops,' where low pay, hard work and long hours are the norm for apprentice accountants, even the students seem to like working at ZSSL. In fact, in the past two years, 45 out of 51 summer students opted to return for full-time work.

Once they're on the payroll, ZSSL tries to maintain a sense of individuality and create an intimacy with clients by splitting its operations into 14 distinct audit teams — almost firms within the firm. Each team of 10 to 25, headed by one or more partners, handles a small group of diversified clients on an on-going basis. The client gets continuity and a personal "small-firm touch." He looks on the members of the team as "his accountants."

All of this provides enrichment for employees as well as partners. Even junior staff have the unique opportunity to see all sides of a variety of businesses. Employees can identify with a small group of colleagues, while enjoying the support and benefits of a large firm. Each team develops its own esprit de corps.

ZSSL recently took this philosophy one step further by introducing a mentor program. Recognizing that students often need more than just formal teaching, a mentor, usually a partner in the firm, is assigned to each junior member. The junior member can talk to his mentor about any problems or concerns that may develop, knowing that this person is taking a special interest in his career and personal development. And the mentor is never the person's supervisor.

ZSSL is also making strides to improve its male/female ratio. In a profession formerly dominated by men, the firm recently designated four women to become partners and prinicpals. Four years ago, there weren't any. With a workforce where 46% of the employees are female, 33% of supervisors and managers are now women and 50% of all new recruits are women. The company also adopted a new, more flexible maternity leave policy, allowing women to take up to six-months' leave without jeopardizing their jobs. And in a profession where working overtime is considered part of the territory, another policy rules out the necessity of overtime work for women with young children.

In conjunction with a recent move into newer, more spacious offices, ZSSL built a permanent 280-square-metre training centre, underlining their commitment to continuous training and development. Each member of the firm must attend a minimum of 10days of courses annually. In another new venture, each employee receives a personalized professional-development program to help monitor their own progress. Videos, tapes and other special materials are used.

"Our goal is not to be the biggest accounting firm in Canada," Siblin says, quoting from the firm's mission statement. "We want to become known as Canada's best firm catering to the needs of small and medium-sized businesses."

In order to maintain its position, the firm has turned down several tempting merger offers, preferring to remain reasonably small and trying to retain something of a family atmosphere among staff. "Trying to be the best is far more important than being the biggest," Siblin says.

"From a very early stage, employees are given as much responsibility as they can handle," one partner says. "If they can handle more, we'll give them more. If we see that a person has got potential, ability, commitment, knowledge and expertise, we will push him ahead a lot faster than most CA firms."

Another attraction is that "we admit people to partnership earlier here," Siblin says. "Here, they're eligible five or six years after taking their CA. In more traditional firms, it's usually 10-11 years. It's a tremendous carrot."

While the salaries of ZSSL's administrative employees fall below national averages, professionals and would-be CAs say they're paid on par with counterparts in large accounting firms. The money isn't great at the bottom, but that's an accepted part of what's essentially an apprenticeship. The firm does, however, recognize regional cost-of-living disparities by paying approximately 20% higher salaries at the Toronto office.

"At the partner level, we have one of the highest average earnings per partner in the country," Siblin says.

Sometimes, ZSSL's commitment to personal development goes further than would normally be expected. In 1988, Siblin gave one bright young CA trainee unheard-of time off during tax season to pursue a different kind of training. Heather Stupp went to the International Racquetball championships and returned a winner — 1988 Women's World Racquetball Champion. But that break didn't ruin her concentration. A few weeks later, she wrote her final CA exam and placed ninth in Canada.

The major rewards for professional employees stem from the small-firm environment, the variety and the opportunity to grow. They're proud of the firm's partners — "some really bright people you can learn a lot from," who willingly share their knowledge.

110

THE CHALLENGERS

These are companies coming up fast on the inside, firms to watch out for, the number ones of tomorrow.

ALLEN-BRADLEY CANADA LTD.

135 Dundas Street
Cambridge, Ontario
N1R 5X1
(519) 623-1810

Pay: **AVERAGE**	Atmosphere: **VERY GOOD**
Benefits: **VERY GOOD**	Job Satisfaction: **AVERAGE**
Promotion: **AVERAGE**	Communications: **VERY GOOD**
Job Security: **EXCELLENT**	Personal Development: **GOOD**

★ *Allen-Bradley Canada, whose sales in 1988 exceeded $159 million, manufactures industrial-automation equipment. The company has 1,077 employees and three Ontario plants, two in the Cambridge area and one in Toronto. Allen-Bradley is owned by Rockwell International of Canada Ltd., a subsidiary of Rockwell International of Pittsburgh.*

ALLEN-BRADLEY has a good reputation in Cambridge. Between 1985 and 1990 the company donated $1 million to the local hospital, and was the largest corporate contributor to the United Way campaign in 1988. In 1989, the company set up a community day-care centre in partnership with the Ontario government.

"We encourage our people to be not only good in the company, but in the community," President Bill Hetherington says. "The two go hand in hand." Hetherington is particularly proud of winning an award of excellence from the Waterloo-area Junior Achievement group, recognizing the company for combining product excellence, community involvement and good employee relations. For Hetherington, the award "recognizes that our people here are outstanding citizens."

In fact, the company is so well respected in the community that a new employee just out of school, without a credit rating, went to rent a town house. The landlord, she says, let her have the apartment with no further questions after finding out she worked at Allen-Bradley.

The company has become one of the most computerized in Canada, Hetherington says. "We have tried to be on the leading edge of not only technology, but the way we work with people who apply the technology. Technology frees people, allowing them to have far more self-determination in their careers."

And employees are allowed freedom. "My manager lets me do things my way," a new employee says. "If I have any problems, I can ask for help." Adds another: "If you are a responsible person, management lets you be responsible. If you are not the type of person who can work on your own, they are there to help you along without making you feel like an idiot." Employees say they are encouraged to take chances, with the understanding that they may make mistakes.

Allen-Bradley's ability to cope with change has a lot to do with its management style. "The company has the attitude that you catch more flies with honey than you do with vinegar," a long-time employee says. "Employees are always dealt with in a positive way. Management will say how things can be done better, rather than, 'You didn't do that right.' "

Allen-Bradley emphasizes training. In Cambridge, it has seven full-time and three part-time instructors. Elsewhere in Canada, the company has another four full-time instructors. New marketing employees go through a three-month training and orientation program. And all new employees go through a two-week business course.

All job openings are posted internally and "it is seldom that the company doesn't promote from within," a manager says. The company bases promotion on five criteria: qualifications, experience, work performance and absenteeism. If those criteria are equal for two candidates, seniority decides the issue. Workers with no computer experience are not denied the chance to apply for positions requiring computer skills.

Promotion is limited, however, because the turnover rate is only about 6% a year. The average length of service in the company is 10 years, an impressive figure considering the number of employees grew by 20% between 1985 and 1989.

Allen-Bradley has a policy of hiring ex-employees first, a common-sense way of utilizing their experience. The company also hires family members.

Wages are competitive for the industry and good for the Cambridge area. And benefits are also good. In addition to the usual, Allen-Bradley introduced flexible hours in 1972, making it one of the first companies in Ontario to do so. Through the savings plan, employees can set aside up to 4% of their salary. For every $2 employees contribute, the company adds $1. Allen-Bradley plans to implement a gain-sharing plan in 1991.

For the non-profit day-care centre, the Ontario government provided 80% of the $71,000 start-up cost, and Allen-Bradley put up the balance. About half of the 47 spaces are reserved for children of Allen-Bradley employees. Day-care costs are competitive at $110 a week.

Visitors are impressed by the neatness and smooth organization of the main Cambridge plant. The original hardwood floors from 1954 give the place a certain warmth.

The computer system supplements the company newsletter and notice boards in corporate communication. More than 700 employees have access by terminal to sales and budget figures, product information, and work and purchase orders — in fact, everything except forecasts, payroll and accounts payable. The access has benefited employees. "I now have a better understanding why I can't hire someone or buy a piece of equipment," a manager explains.

The emphasis on communication makes sense. "We don't need the degree of testing we used to, because if people understand what is required of them on their job, they won't produce bad work," Hetherington says.

In the words of one employee: "We are such a progressive company and we have such a great product, so I don't see how we can go wrong. Nothing sits still for more than a couple of years without it being looked at."

B R I T E X LTD. LTÉE

BRITEX LTD.

P.O. Box 460
Bridgetown, Nova Scotia
B0S 1G0
(902) 665-4466

Pay: **AVERAGE**	Atmosphere: **VERY GOOD**
Benefits: **AVERAGE**	Job Satisfaction: **GOOD**
Promotion: **POOR**	Communications: **EXCELLENT**
Job Security: **POOR**	Personal Development: **POOR**

★ *Britex, a small Nova Scotia company that manufactures knitted elastic fabrics, is known across Canada as a venture abandoned by a multinational parent in 1980, but resuscitated by local management. In 1989, sales were heading for the $20-million mark, (three times the 1980 branch-plant volume). with about 20% more employees, bringing the total to 200.*

BRITEX HAS been a unique company right from its 1980 start, when it rose phoenix-like from the ashes of a defunct U.S. company. The firm knew the only way to survive and grow was to build a new management structure.

Success meant involving workers in every aspect of the company, drawing them into decision making at all levels. Sharing both the good and bad meant paying profit-sharing bonuses in good years, and learning to tighten belts in lean years.

A decade later, the company's philosophy hasn't changed. "We still have a damn good team here," President David Graham says. "Anybody can buy the machinery to set up a plant, but it's how you treat your people that makes the difference. And we have a good nucleus here."

115

Britex is still struggling and hasn't made the big gains or rapid growth its managers had hoped for, which might have assured greater job security for its workforce. But it's not for lack of trying.

Free trade has made the company's competitive position even more precarious. Britex, however, is taking things in stride. "Free trade is a challenge but it's also an opportunity for us," Graham says. "It requires us to focus on niches. We can't be all things to all people any longer."

Through committees made up of management and hourly workers, the company has tried to tackle its problems in a collective fashion. The free-trade adjustment committee develops ways of increasing competitive advantage in the U.S. market, while the shipping-effectiveness committee is working on a new "just-in-time" inventory system.

Founder and former president Sandy Archibald is firmly back in control at Britex, after a stint in politics. Today, the company is run by a triumvirate: Archibald, as chairman, looks after manufacturing and runs the plant; Graham handles sales and marketing, working out of the Montreal office; and Secretary-Treasurer Malcolm Inglis is involved in the financial end of the business.

Archibald, Graham and five other managers bought the company with government assistance in 1980. They encouraged employees to join them in becoming owners through a share-ownership program, which sold them the equity at a generous one-third discount. In the early years, close to half the workforce owned shares, an investment whose value rose steadily. The original shares, which sold at $1.35, are now valued at more than five times the original price, excluding past dividends.

But through retirements (when all shareholders must sell back their shares) and some profit taking, the number of employees holding shares has dropped significantly. Today, only 36 Britex workers own equity in the company (the average holding is close to 400). The company, however, is looking at ways of increasing employee share ownership.

Employee committees designed the company's benefit package, opting for life-insurance coverage, but turning down a dental plan. They recently voted for improvements — a contributory sickness-income plan and a vision-care scheme. The company still does not have a pension plan.

116

The annual profit-sharing program, however, pays out 10% of pre-tax profits to employees with more than one-year's service. The plan distributes cash according to a point formula based on pay scale and seniority. In a good year like 1988, the plan paid out the equivalent of about one week's wages, while in poorer years like 1989, something close to one day's extra pay was handed out.

Britex also believes in creating motivation by paying monthly productivity bonuses. Workers are paid an additional 5¢ an hour for every hour they work for each $10,000 of profit achieved by the company that month.

Salaries at Britex are low compared to central-Canadian rates. The base salary for a new worker with no experience is $5.43 an hour. But an experienced worker can pull in $9.23 plus shift premiums, not to mention productivity bonuses and profit sharing. The company is trying to improve the salary structure. "We consistently give raises exceeding the cost of living," Graham says.

A new emphasis on training is another Britex initiative. The firm recently hired an industrial engineer as a full-time training specialist to develop training techniques, with special emphasis on cross-training. The concept involves training individuals to do a variety of jobs, allowing for the gradual development of the team concept. The goal is to have the factory run by teams of skilled workers who rotate through the various job functions.

Britex recently chose eight employees to train as skilled knitting mechanics. The yearlong training course includes sending them to the U.S. for several weeks. Another initiative saw nine employees flown to Montreal to visit the company's largest customer for a demonstration of how Britex products are used.

These initiatives would be unremarkable in a large comglomerate. But in a 200-employee company, the dedication to training and development is a sign of the company's commitment to its employees, and how badly it wants to succeed. Britex remains an excellent place to work in the fragile Maritimes economy for the worker who is prepared to work hard and get involved in the company's activities.

CANADA PUBLISHING CORP.

164 Commander Boulevard
Agincourt, Ontario
M1S 3C7
(416) 293-8141

Pay: **AVERAGE**	Atmosphere: **VERY GOOD**
Benefits: **AVERAGE**	Job Satisfaction: **EXCELLENT**
Promotion: **AVERAGE**	Communications: **VERY GOOD**
Job Security: **AVERAGE**	Personal Development: **EXCELLENT**

★ *Canada Publishing is an umbrella company comprising a number of smaller publishing enterprises: Gage Educational Co., Gage Distribution Co., Macmillan of Canada, Gordon V. Thompson Music, Global Press, Diffulivre, and TMP, The Music Publisher. The privately owned firm, headquartered in Agincourt, Ont., publishes educational and reference books, as well as music and video-training materials, in both English and French. The company employs 200.*

RON BESSE is out to prove that publishing is profitable in Canada. He stands out in publishing circles as a hard-nosed businessman in an industry frequently peopled with dreamers, academics and unfulfilled writers.

Canada Publishing doesn't rank in the big leagues of best companies to work for yet, but it deserves mention because it's trying hard to make the grade. Besse has left his imprint on the firm. He believes in free enterprise and the "entrepreneurial spirit." These notions embody a down-to-earth, business-like management style.

Since taking over in the late 1970s, Besse has streamlined

operations, cut unprofitable divisions and made several acquisitions, turning a fairly small operation into a healthy, diversified publishing empire and making steady profits on sales of totaling $37 million annually.

"We preach the entrepreneurial spirit to our people all the time, even at the lowest levels," Besse says. "Entrepreneurial means trying new things, launching new ideas in publishing. And when they fail, nobody gets upset. We know that in this environment we're going to have failures. But what I do say is that we don't repeat our failures."

Employees are encouraged to be creative — accounting and finance experts as well as those in marketing. The company launched a new marketing thrust, and Besse met with the service people, asking them to suggest ways they could improve their jobs to make themselves part of a marketing team. The response was overwhelming. Many ideas were suggested on how to improve invoicing and speed up shipping.

Publishing in Canada is considered a labor of love because pay is generally inadequate. Canada Publishing is no exception, but Besse is trying to change that through a salary administration program. Entry level salaries have improved and are in line with comparable companies, but in the mid-to-senior levels, compensation is still low.

Even if Canada Publishing does not offer all the rewards of more profitable firms, the atmosphere, communications, and potential for job satisfaction are excellent. If you want to set up a new line of educational textbooks or start publishing a series of children's books, opportunities abound. Employees receive a lot of encouragement from management. Lines of communication are informal and open right to the president's office. It's creative without being bureaucratic, and quality is appreciated.

Employees speak highly of the firm:

• "There's a really good feeling about the place. The people here have a commitment to education as well as to profit."

• "The family atmosphere around the company has really helped it weather the recent organizational change fairly well."

• "The possibilities for personal growth are tremendous, and for professional growth too."

• "It's the small things that count. When you are off sick for five days, the company sends flowers to your home. The same thing happens on each anniversary of your employment."

● "We certainly have the feeling that there's a major effort by management to put the employees on a decent pay footing. Everybody in this company ought to be paid at least 30% more. That impetus comes from working for a good businessman. We feel secure. . . with him guiding us, the company has a future."

Besse is undoubtedly the force behind the changes: employees unanimously stress what a good business-like manager he is, and the fact that he's down-to-earth and approachable. "When he's in the office, he's a boss but when he's in the warehouse, he's like one of us," one employee says.

Communications within the company are managed through informal employee meetings. Memos are discouraged. Company spirit is bolstered through regular social events like the New Year's champagne party held at the end of the fiscal year on March 31. And book sales are held twice a year.

Women have no problem advancing in the company — there is a woman vice-president, and several are co-ordinating editors.

Promotion opportunities are limited because of the firm's small size. Go-getters who work their way through a number of jobs in the firm usually leave to seek other opportunities.

Canada Publishing is a company that's working hard to put itself on a business-like footing and be aggressive in its marketing, while keeping its employees happy. Conditions are not perfect but if Besse succeeds in his plans, it may become one of the best places to work in the book-publishing industry — and a model for others to follow.

DIAGNOSTIC CHEMICALS LTD.

West Royalty Industrial Park
Charlottetown
Prince Edward Island
C1E 1B0
(902) 566-1396

Pay: **AVERAGE**	Atmosphere: **GOOD**
Benefits: **VERY GOOD**	Job Satisfaction: **EXCELLENT**
Promotion: **AVERAGE**	Communications: **GOOD**
Job Security: **AVERAGE**	Personal Development: **EXCELLENT**

★ *Diagnostic Chemicals manufactures specialty chemicals for the clinical diagnostic industry. Based in Charlottetown, P.E.I., the company has 50 full-time employees, and annual sales of $3.5 million; 50% of which are exported. The private firm is owned by its president, Regis Duffy.*

DIAGNOSTIC CHEMICALS IS a great place to work if you're a research chemist, dedicated to living in Prince Edward Island, and don't mind not making a top salary — as long as the job is challenging and offers promise for the future.

Diagnostic Chemicals was established in 1970 by the then dean of science at the University of Prince Edward Island, Regis Duffy. He took over full-time control of the firm in the late 1970s. Since then, he has built the company into a small but thriving chemical specialty manufacturing facility, the only one of its kind in Canada.

Diagnostic's scientists and technicians are mostly young, ambitious and happy with their jobs. They recognize the opportunity that goes along with the risk of working for a small firm, and put a lot of determination, as well as skill, into their efforts.

"People are given a free hand to tackle their jobs, and a chance to experiment," one lab worker says. "This is a progressive company, making new products," says another technician. "You have the leeway to do what you need to do here." "Being small, we get to do a variety of jobs," declares a new employee.

Small also means working conditions and hours are flexible, and management decisions are made by consensus. The recent publication of a booklet outling company policies adds a structure that was previously absent.

The company's mission statement testifies to Diagnostic's belief in training and development: "We encourage our employees to continue their personal growth in knowledge and excellence." Putting money where its words are, the company pays 100% of tuition fees for any educational upgrading undertaken by employees, whether work-related or not.

Salary levels still lag behind those for similar jobs in Central Canada, but this is offset somewhat by the profit-sharing plan, which puts 15%-20% of the total profits in a pool to be divided among employees. Workers realize that it is up to them to improve their earnings by increasing the company's profitability.

Benefits are very good, and contain generous life insurance, very comprehensive extended medical coverage, dental and vision care plans, as well as a pension plan.

And as another worker summed up: "Diagnostic Chemicals allows us to perform in a setting that keeps us in Prince Edward Island and the lifestyle we like."

The company is a fine example of a profitable small business in a non-urban locale.

FEDERAL EXPRESS CANADA LTD.

50 Burnhamthorpe Road West
Suite 1201
Mississauga, Ontario
L5B 3C2
(416) 897-1803

Pay: **GOOD**	Atmosphere: **EXCELLENT**
Benefits: **VERY GOOD**	Job Satisfaction: **VERY GOOD**
Promotion: **GOOD**	Communications: **VERY GOOD**
Job Security: **AVERAGE**	Personal Development: **GOOD**

★ *Federal Express Canada Ltd. is a subsidiary of Federal Express Corp.*
of Memphis, Tenn., a worldwide courier service that delivers more than
a million packages (both parcels and envelopes) daily through 1,300
service centres in 109 countries. In Canada, there are 1,365 full-time
and 299 part-time employees. Canadian revenue in 1988 was $145.7
million.

"PEOPLE, SERVICE, profit," is the Federal Express motto.
And the first emphasis really *is* on people. Even the parent
company's annual report recognizes that it "is employees whose
ongoing efforts account for our continuing prosperity."

FedEx employees are highly motivated, and take a great deal
of pride in what they do. "We do more than just pick up and deliver packages," says a driver. "The company has the insight to realize that it's not the highly paid manager who interacts with the
customer. It's us. And if we're unhappy one day, then the
customer is going to be unhappy." Adds another: "We can make
or break the company." A courier: "We do delivery, pick-up and

sales. To the customer, we are Federal Express."

Federal Express' no-layoffs, Guaranteed Fair Treatment and minority-recruitment policies set it apart from many other employers. According to the 1989 annual report, these practices do more than contribute to good morale. In a service business such as FedEx, the quality of service is a direct result of each employee's efforts.

"The power of this company rests with the employees," explains David Bronczek, vice-president of Canadian operations. "They're the ones who do the job."

"Management works for the couriers," says a driver. "If I have a problem, my manager is there to help me solve it." When something goes wrong, FedEx managers are not interested in finding who is to blame, but in finding out how to correct the problem and prevent it from happening again.

"If an employee is late, you don't say, 'If you come in late once more, you're fired,' " a manager says. "People are responsible for their actions. We ask the employee how he or she is going to solve the problem. They propose the solution, which means they are committed to it. It may be solved by something as simple as changing a shift."

The company will work to find other positions for employees who temporarily or permanently can't perform their current jobs. "It's called light duties," explains a management trainee. "Last week, I had an operation on my foot and couldn't walk. So I was put on desk duty."

Employees take a great deal of pride in their work. "We are class couriers," one of them says. "We wash our trucks every night," Bronczek adds. "We're that obsessive. Our goal is to be the best. It's the image we need to project to companies that hand over a $50,000 contract or a $10.50 letter. And we need our employees to feel that way. It all works hand in hand and generates new business."

Employees are also proud of the technology they use. The Federal Express "super tracker" system lets customer service agents pinpoint the location of any package in less than a minute. Each Federal Express package is bar coded. When a courier handles a package, he or she records the bar code, using a hand-held "super tracker," then plugs the tracker into the digital unit installed in every FedEx van. The unit transmits the information by radio to a central computer.

Under Federal Express' Guaranteed Fair Treatment procedure, an employee unhappy with a manager's decision can appeal it at three levels, including the international head office in Memphis. As one manager explains: "When we take any action, employees have the right to question it. So you have to think carefully about what you do." Adds another: "If you don't solve an employee's problem, he will go to *your* manager. So we work hard to solve employees' problems."

When an employee's performance is poor, for instance, "there are a lot of procedures to discover the reasons why, and devise solutions," says a manager of many years. "It makes it more challenging for managers," adds another, "but it's better to solve a problem than lose the employee." Perhaps this philosophy explains the exceptionally low turnover rate of 1%.

In addition to the open door policy, Federal Express promotes communication through employee meetings, an employee newsletter and daily television broadcasts relayed from Memphis to every FedEx service centre by satellite. The program is usually too U.S.-oriented for Canadian employees, so many don't watch it, but the company plans to launch a daily newscast on Canadian operations.

Federal Express surveys employees annually to identify problems and measure the success of existing policies. More important, says Suzanne Gaal, managing director of personnel for Canada, are feedback sessions where employees discuss problems and come up with workable ways to solve them.

Managers who are not sensitive to employees' concerns and receive low scores in the survey and feedback sessions are evaluated again in three months to measure their improvement. "There shouldn't be any surprises," a manager explains. "Otherwise you aren't communicating well with your employees."

Benefits are good. Employees get three weeks of vacation after three years with the company and four weeks after 10. The tuition refund program encourages continuing education by reimbursing full-time employees up to $1,750 a year and part-time employees $875 per year for successfully completed courses.

After six months with the company, employees and their spouses (dependents, too) get air fare discounts — 50% off on confirmed flights and 75% off on standby flights — from more than 50 airlines, including Air Canada and Canadian Airlines

International. Four airlines offer employees 90% discounts on stand-by tickets.

There are also discounts on cruises, hotels and car rentals — so many that one employee says he never leaves home without his Federal Express card. Employees also may "jumpseat" — fly free anywhere in the world on FedEx aircraft, space permitting.

Under the stock purchase plan, employees may ask for payroll deductions of up to 10% of their gross pay to buy stock of the parent company, purchased quarterly on the New York Stock Exchange. Employees get it at 85% of the price of stock on the first or last day of the quarter, whichever is lower. Only 15% of the employees in Canada participate in the plan, but one courier who does participate thinks those who don't are missing out: "Last quarter, the stock started at US$43 and three months later was $US51, so I paid 85% of US$43. What a deal."

Wages across Canada are standard. A courier in Fredericton earns the same as one in Toronto. It makes for very happy employees in Fredericton, but employees in Toronto feel they need a premium to compensate for the much higher cost of living. (At the time of writing, the company was addressing the issue and going through pay equity review.)

Federal Express recognizes exceptional efforts of employees through the company newsletter and "bravo zulu" awards — a pin and occasionally cash.

Road safety is crucial for a courier company. Every Federal Express driver who goes a year without a preventable accident receives a pin and is eligible to compete in the safe driving championships, where drivers negotiate obstacle courses. The top driver from each of the three Canadian regions competes in a lavish all-expenses-paid international competition in Memphis. Each international competitor wins US$500 just for qualifying. The top prize in 1990: US$10,000.

Drivers who remain accident-free for five years receive a watch; for 10 years, a gold ring; for 15 years, a diamond.

Federal Express benefits from the full potential of employees — their talent, creativity and loyalty — because of its strong commitment to equality and fairness.

HONGKONG BANK OF CANADA

300 - 885 West Georgia Street
Vancouver, British Columbia
V6C 3G1
(604) 685-1000

Pay: **GOOD**	Atmosphere: **GOOD**
Benefits: **GOOD**	Job Satisfaction: **GOOD**
Promotion: **AVERAGE**	Communications: **GOOD**
Job Security: **GOOD**	Personal Development: **GOOD**

★ *Hongkong Bank of Canada provides a wide range of financial services to personal and business customers through 61 branches across the country. It is a subsidiary of Hongkong & Shanghai Banking Corp., which has consolidated assets in excess of $138 billion and a staff of more than 50,000 worldwide. In Canada, Hongkong Bank employs 1,739 people. Its size mushroomed in 1986 when the Hongkong Bank (150 employees) swallowed the Bank of British Columbia (1,550 employees).*

FOR MANY of those who lived through the severe financial troubles of the Bank of British Columbia, their new careers with the Hongkong Bank are secure and exciting. Pay and benefits are good, training and communications are getting better and the impressive Asian connection has given them an entrance to international banking and trade finance they didn't get while opening Bonanza accounts for customers in Smalltown, B.C.

More than 50 managers at all levels have been to Hong Kong for training, and more go each month. There are also regular two- to three-year international secondments for fast trackers.

The Hongkong Bank is favored by many new Canadian residents of Chinese origin who are well acquainted with its famous parent. About a quarter of the bank's business comes from this growing market.

One manager explains how the bank tries to help Asian immigrants. "A lot of people who come over want to know about how to buy a house and choose schools and how to get around. When we were the Bank of B.C. we shied away from specifically recommending a real estate agent or an accountant or a lawyer. Part of being in the Asian market, serving these new people is, in fact, to find a driving instructor and driving them around the city personally to find homes and introducing them to real estate agents. They want to know about schools and universities and restaurants and the transit system."

Another manager says she would give her right arm for a switchboard operator who spoke English, Mandarin and Cantonese, preferably without an accent. The Asian connection produces interesting challenges.

The old Bank of British Columbia, rescued from bankruptcy in 1986, had a great deal of regional pride. It had a strong retail presence in Alberta and British Columbia, and showed a lot of innovation in new banking products: special deals for senior citizens; one of the first package accounts; and the calculation of daily interest when the big chartered banks still said it couldn't be done. Current management at Hongkong Bank is pursuing new business more aggressively than the Bank of British Columbia, a regional financial institution with more limited goals.

Managers say their challenge is to encourage the merging of distinct cultures: the retail banking atmosphere of the Bank of British Columbia and the international finance skills of the Hongkong Bank. The "them and us" attitudes that arise in all mergers have largely been put to rest.

Prior to the Hongkong Bank takeover, the Bank of British Columbia laid off 550 people, and following the merger a further 90 people were let go. The management style changed radically. Three levels of the hierarchy between the CEO and the customer have been eliminated. Grant Spitz, vice-president of human resources says, " The best way to describe the difference is we went from a paternal approach to a team approach." Given this recent history, one would expect unease. However, employees say they feel secure in their jobs and, responding to an attitude survey in September, 1988, more than 94% said they thought the future of the bank was good.

Bank President Jim Cleave says: "Our staff has been able to come out of the foxholes and stop ducking the bullets that have been coming at them."

Employees have been told that it is now "business as usual" and there is much evidence that this is true. The bank has been recruiting new staff in response to increased business and has been spending money redecorating and providing branches with new furniture and office equipment. Hongkong Bank's aggressive desire for growth has created a high level of optimism and morale.

Generally the bank gets good marks from its employees for atmosphere. The employee survey showed that more than 91% felt management was open to suggestions for improving work flow and procedures. At the same time, almost 94% said they had sufficient information to do their job and almost 75% said they felt the bank's communications overall were straight and open. The survey also showed that 93% felt the bank's customer relations were satisfactory compared with the competition's, and 85% felt their work was satisfying. Significantly, 81% said they would encourage a friend to work at the bank.

Employees enjoy a couple of unusual benefits. They can arrange the lease-purchase of a home computer from the bank at very favorable rates, and they can purchase optional bank uniforms (smart dresses and business suits) at very attractive subsidized prices. Managers can also get mortgages at 5% less than the rate charged customers.

Says an employee working in a bank branch in Vancouver's Chinatown: "It's like working in another country. It's wonderful. There's a lot of energy. It's a very busy place."

With this changing culture, Hongkong Bank is an exciting company to be part of.

LABATT BREWERIES OF CANADA

150 Simcoe Street
London, Ontario
N6A 4M3
(519) 673-5050

Pay: **VERY GOOD**	Atmosphere: **VERY GOOD**
Benefits: **EXCELLENT**	Job Satisfaction: **VERY GOOD**
Promotion: **GOOD**	Communications: **VERY GOOD**
Job Security: **GOOD**	Personal Development: **VERY GOOD**

★ *Labatt Breweries of Canada brews and markets a broad range of beer, ale, malt liquor and stout from 17 plants and offices across Canada. The company has 4,870 workers, 60% of whom are unionized. Headquarters are in London, Ont., with executive offices in Toronto. Annual sales are more than $1.6 billion. It is a subsidiary of John Labatt Ltd.*

LABATT has made the transition from a very paternalistic place of work, to one that places more emphasis on training to encourage employees to attain their fullest potential. Currently the company is developing inhouse training to prepare workers for the complexities of the '90s.

From its family-run origins in the mid-1800s, Labatt has become big business while retaining a caring attitude towards its employees. With growth has come change, and many of the old traditions have lapsed. Gone are the days of the 24-hour pub, open for workers to have free beer. Now the pub is open for limited hours, and workers must wait until the end of their shifts to quaff their daily quota of two free suds. In addition, each employee is entitled to a free case of beer a month.

Treating employees well remains a cornerstone of doing things "the Labatt way," Labatt's Brewing Group President Sidney Oland says. "Beer is a friendly business, and creates an atmosphere of general liking for people." The company credo spells this out: "We know our strength comes from our employees. We provide clean, modern, efficient work facilities. We insist on fairness, respect, and the opportunity to improve, and we reward excellence. We promote regular, open, two-way dialogue between managers and employees — we try to benefit from the ideas of all employees."

In practice, two-way dialogue means that President Pierre Desjardins meets with employees within each region twice a year to review business goals and achievements with workers, and to reply to any questions they might have.

Relations between management and workers are not always rosy. But the confrontational style of past management has given way to one that is more oriented towards employee involvement – a work-team concept. "We have now got ourselves into a situation where the labor climate is not perfect, but I think we try and treat people more as individuals," a manager explains. "We got through the last two collective agreements without a work stoppage, and that was basically the first time in 25 years."

Labatt's does provide a number of unusual programs for employees. Take *Smile Across Canada*, for example. In a typical summer, 130 children between the ages of 12 and 14 from different parts of the country spend a week with Labatt's families in other parts of Canada or the U.S. Later in the summer, the children of the host families make return visits. Travel costs are paid by the company.

Labatt is also involved in sponsoring the arts. Recent projects have included *The Phantom of the Opera* and The Rolling Stones' *Steel Wheels* tour.The firm also encourages employee participation in the arts by planning discount theatre trips. The atmosphere in the company is very positive, exuding vitality and enthusiasm. Individual workers are given plenty of scope to be inventive and expand their job descriptions to fit their talents. There are many examples of ambitious workers getting ahead, with Labatt's encouragement. Susan Laberee began as a secretary in the personnel department 12 years ago. She went to university part-time, with Labatt's paying for her courses. After getting her degree, she became personnel manager of the Kitchener-Waterloo plant. She is now manager of training at head office in Toronto, where she co-ordinates the company's national training program.

Inge Russell, manager of research in microbiology/genetics, started as a junior lab technician 19 years ago. She now has her doctorate in microbiology — tuition fees and books having been paid by the company — and is engaged in advanced research and genetic engineering, making better and faster-acting yeasts.

"If you have the energy, I don't think anything is going to stop you at Labatt's," she says. "But you have to be willing to work hard, and long hours too. We're enthusiastic and succeed because the company encourages us."

Job security is the one nagging fear in employees' minds. The highly competitive nature of the beer industry, together with the evolving technology in the field means some jobs are at risk. Labatt's combats this not only with training, but relocation when necessary.

Pay levels are high and the benefits package is comprehensive, including such extras as eyeglasses and orthodontistry. A share-purchase plan is also available to all full-time employees through payroll deduction. Education costs are reimbursed upon successful completion of courses or degrees. And a scholarship program pays tuition fees to send 14 children of Labatt's employees to university each year.

Labatt offers very good pay, excellent benefits and the opportunity for employees to maximize their potential.

L. E. SHAW LTD.

P.O. Box 2130
Lantz, Nova Scotia
B0N 1RO
(902) 883-2201

Pay: **GOOD**	Atmosphere: **EXCELLENT**
Benefits: **GOOD**	Job Satisfaction: **VERY GOOD**
Promotion: **AVERAGE**	Communications: **EXCELLENT**
Job Security: **VERY GOOD**	Personal Development: **EXCELLENT**

★ *L.E. Shaw is a diversified manufacturer of construction products, specializing in clay brick and concrete block. The company also owns a trucking division and a land developer, Clayton Developments Ltd. It has manufacturing plants in Nova Scotia and New Brunswick and about 400 employees, half of whom are unionized. The company, owned by 11 of its senior managers, records annual sales of approximately $40 million.*

ALLAN SHAW is the president of a company started in 1861, when ancestor Robert Shaw began firing brick at a small plant in rural Nova Scotia. On the surface, this looks like just another family firm.

In this case, though, appearances are deceiving, because Allan Shaw didn't inherit his presidency — he earned it. When his father retired from the firm in 1979, nine senior managers, including Allan Shaw, bought the company. Only after he worked his way through various positions did the owners elect Allan to the top job.

The change in ownership brought a fresh atmosphere and a variety of changes, all positive, employees say. One worker:

"Allan Shaw said to us, 'People are our main asset,' and to prove his point we've seen increases in pay, a sickness protection plan, a quality of working life program and a profit-sharing program. Everything has reinforced that statement."

Today there are 11 owner-managers, and they are considering broadening the ownership base to include more employees. With this long-term aim in mind, they sent five employees to a Halifax college for an employee management participation course, two days a month for two years. Success in that venture has led the company to send 40 employees to a course at the Advanced Management Centre at Dalhousie University.

L.E. Shaw's continuing commitment to excellence has been demonstrated by the initiation of quality circles. After one year, 18 quality circles were operating in manufacturing, retailing, engineering and administration.

Although the company maintains a small office in downtown Halifax, the largest group of employees works at Lantz, N.S., about 60 kilometres east of the city. The site of one of the company's old clay quarries has been transformed into a superlative and unusual work environment.

The central office building has been built in a pleasing colonial style, constructed around the employees' lounge, a room with a cathedral ceiling, large fireplace, easy chairs and a lunchroom. A hot lunch is served daily at a nominal cost.

Outside, the old clay pits have been partially filled in and flooded to create ponds that have become a bird sanctuary, home to a flock of wild Canada geese. The company also cleared a jogging trail through the woods for fitness enthusiasts.

L.E. Shaw's sensitivity to environmental issues, demonstrated by its continuing efforts to restore former quarries to their natural beauty, won the company a Nova Scotia Provincial Environmental Award in the industrial business category.

Many corporate decisions are made only after consultation with employees. For example, there is the annual employee benefit meeting to decide on what new benefits, if any, the company should bring in. Up to 1989, for example, employees have resisted bringing in a dental plan, feeling that other benefits (such as vision care) mattered more to them. Not all employees agree, but the majority rules.

Salaries are good, taking into account regional disparities. And the incentive pay program, which can increase salary by between

5% and 10%, is certainly an effective motivator.

The company puts 10% of pre-tax profits into the profit-sharing plan, and workers share the proceeds equally. In 1989, each employee received $1,800, half in cash, half deferred and invested on the employee's behalf. In addition, the company has a separate pension plan.

Employees take the profit plan seriously. One secretary says: "You really think twice about taking a sick day, because you know it might mean a loss in the profit share." Another worker: "Profit sharing has communicated to everyone that 'you're all in this together and pulling in the same direction.' "

Staff turnover is very low. In fact, there is a tradition of several generations of the same family working at L.E. Shaw, and the company's reputation ensures a pile of applications for the occasional job opening.

Workers are generally very positive about the company, which allows them great freedom and creativity to do their jobs. As one woman says, "I left my previous two jobs because I couldn't stand the pressure. Here you have incredible freedom to do your job the way you want. The pressure is still there, but you want to perform. It's not imposed from above."

The only potential problem stems from the company's popularity. Low turnover means fewer chances for promotion. While workers see possibilities for lateral moves, there aren't many chances for management positions. Still, it doesn't seem to be a major issue at L.E. Shaw.

"I don't think we wave the flag enough and tell people how great we are," one enthusiastic worker says. "We're proud of this beautiful building, and of the excellent people the company has been able to attract."

LIPTONS
INTERNATIONAL LTD.

29-2 Connell Court
Etobicoke, Ontario
M8Z 5T7
(416) 251-3121

Pay: **AVERAGE**	Atmosphere: **GOOD**
Benefits: **VERY GOOD**	Job Satisfaction: **GOOD**
Promotion: **GOOD**	Communications: **VERY GOOD**
Job Security: **GOOD**	Personal Development: **VERY GOOD**

★ *Liptons designs, manufactures and retails women's fashion. The company has 67 stores under the names of Liptons, Goodman Manteau, Heritage House, Easy Pieces, Xanthé, Finds and Stefano in Ontario, Quebec, Alberta and Manitoba. In 1989, the company had 410 full-time and 126 part-time employees. Sales in 1988 were $54 million. The company is privately owned by Evelyn and Marvin Goodman.*

THE SECRET OF Liptons' success is that Evelyn and Marvin Goodman don't expect employees (called associates) to do anything they wouldn't do themselves. Marvin can often be found fixing the photocopier at head office. "Evelyn is a full-time salesgirl and buyer," a manager says. Adds another: "Every Saturday, she is on her knees pinning dresses. She still wants to serve customers she has known for 30 years."

A seamstress relates how Evelyn found her sweeping up dirt and said, "What are you doing? Your time is too valuable. I can do this, but I can't do what you do. I'll clean up the mess." Whereupon she did. "Everyone is treated like a human being here," the seamstress says.

"Evelyn wears many hats, and expects everyone else to," an associate says. As a result, employees are able to develop because they "do not have strict roles. If you need help and support from the rest of the company, it's there. You're allowed to move within a great area and test yourself." Employees say they are given relatively free rein to develop new ideas.

Liptons also listens to its employees:

● "The company is progressive and willing to change."

● "Nothing is carved in stone, except working on Saturday."

● "At other companies, you could be old and gray before management listened to you. Here you can act on ideas faster than anywhere else."

● "Marvin says, 'Don't come to me with a problem unless you have a solution.' "

● Marvin believes in bringing others into the decision-making process, because "the odds are in favor of a good team succeeding more readily than an individual hero."

But with so many creative people contributing to the decision-making process, chaos is sometimes the result. Instructions are not always effectively communicated.

The Goodmans take their business very personally. "Every time a new store opens, Evelyn and Marvin say they have a new baby," a saleswoman says. One assistant manager says when Evelyn leaves her in charge of a store, it's like a mother entrusting her child to someone else's care.

Many employees have the same attitude. "Those of us who have been here for some time feel we own this company," an employee of 11 years says. "I go into one of our stores and if I see something wrong, I tell the manager."

The company was among the first of its size in Canada to introduce a flexible benefits plan and an employee-assistance plan. Liptons' benefits are tailor-made for four groups: young and older single employees, and employees with young and older families. All four packages have a core of insurance coverage, but each module differs in the amount of long-term disability and the type of extended health and dental coverage. Associates choose the package best suited to their needs, and can change annually. If an employee's marital status changes before yearend, she can switch immediately.

Liptons has a profit-sharing plan that pays employees $300-$400 in April and December, because companies should "share with the people who made it possible in the first place," Marvin says. In addition, employees receive $500 for referring job candidates, provided the new employees remain with the company at least three months.

Marvin's philosophy on benefits is simple: "The more we can do for our associates, the more our associates will likely do for our clientele."

Employees feel the company is very considerate of their needs, and that Evelyn and Marvin Goodman care about them. One manager tells of the excitement of an employee who received a birthday card at home with a cheque in it.

"It's a company with a heart," an employee of two years says. And a mother says:"The company will work to accommodate you. They are very considerate of the trials that go on in your personal life."

But employees complain the sick leave at six days a year is insufficient. While the number of days can be extended, employees don't feel it should be left to managers to decide.

Turnover is high, but Marvin points out that "retail has never been considered an end profession in itself." When he started the business, he "was determined to improve the level of professionalism in retail merchandising."

At Liptons, professionalism means "we respond to clients immediately," a manager says. The company invites comments from customers through postage pre-paid forms available at all store counters. Managers must respond to complaints within four days. Feedback — both positive and negative — is circulated to all stores every three weeks. "Yes, we make errors," one employee says, "but we try our hardest to correct them." A manager explains that any employee praised by a customer is sent a letter saying, "We love you because you loved the client who now loves Liptons."

Sales staff work together. "If someone is busy with a customer and doesn't have time to put away the clothes, someone else is there to help," a seamstress says. And an employee in a new store says: "You would never have thought we opened only two weeks ago. It looks as though we have been working here together for years. We're like glue. This shows what kind of company it is."

Most of the staff are women, a fact most associates enjoy. "I really feel women are a lot better to work with," an associate of three years says. "We bring our other life persona in here — our sensitivity, caring and nurturing."

To Marvin, it seems obvious that women would be running the business, given its nature. Women make up 96% of the work force, 98% of management and 80% of the executive ranks. "They are in the best position to determine what's right for other women. The company has benefited greatly by being able to call on the under-used brain power that women possess, both from the business and aesthetic side."

The company's expansion plans mean more opportunities for promotion. A training program encourages associates to develop skills necessary to manage a store. For a company its size, Liptons is very progressive, and offers women with drive the opportunity to create their own positions.

MACDONALD DETTWILER & ASSOCIATES LTD.

13800 Commerce Parkway
Richmond, British Columbia
V6V 2J3
(604) 278-3411

Pay: **GOOD**	Atmosphere: **GOOD**
Benefits: **GOOD**	Job Satisfaction: **VERY GOOD**
Promotion: **GOOD**	Communications: **AVERAGE**
Job Security: **GOOD**	Personal Development: **VERY GOOD**

★ *MacDonald Dettwiler is a world leader in the development of computer-based systems for aerospace, resource management and electronics manufacturing. Its clients include NASA, the European Space Agency, the Australian Department of Transportation, the U.S. Jet Propulsion Laboratory, the U.S. Air Force and the Canadian government. Almost all of its 666 employees work at its headquarters in Richmond, B.C., although it also has offices in Europe, Asia and the U.S.*

MDA IS BURSTING with youth and brainpower. The employees' average age is 32, and about 60% of the them have university degrees, mainly in electrical engineering, computer science and physics.

As one of them says, "The youthfulness and energy of the company breeds ideas and innovation galore."

Not surprisingly, the company is hot on continuing education and encourages employees to stay technically current. MDA runs a score of in-house courses on subjects ranging from assertiveness to effective decision making and stress management, and the company pays 100% of the tuition for career-related programs.

MDA assists employees to add to their academic credentials. Each year, it selects an employee to return to university at company expense ($12,000 a year for two years) to complete a master's degree. In 1989, a woman computer scientist was taking a master's in meteorology at the University of British Columbia.

The company receives about 500 applications from university graduates annually. It interviews approximately 100 and hires from five to 10. In addition, MDA recruits on-campus at major Canadian universities. There is also a year-round co-op program, with six $1,000 awards given annually to co-op students.

Walking through MDA's spanking new office complex in a Vancouver suburb, a visitor is easily misled by the relaxed atmosphere. The working environment is fairly unstructured and largely cerebral, with lots of opportunity for creativity and innovation. Most people wrestle with problems by tapping at computer terminals in pleasant private offices or huddling in groups of two or three in small conference rooms.

Employees laugh when asked if the atmosphere is relaxed. It is anything but, they say. In their own words, it is "volatile," "intense" or "hectic." In a primarily contract-driven atmosphere, MDA must work hard to maintain a competitive edge.

MDA attracts high achievers, who thrive on the stress of deadlines and overtime, pumped up by the satisfying knowledge they are at the leading edge of technology. The company exports 80% of its product, and has sales and service offices worldwide.

Employees also know they can make an impact. The company has an "I Told You So" Award given to workers for persistence and ultimately proving their idea to management.

Pay is competitive, and increases are merit-based. Management and staff jointly set quarterly objectives. The company pays a $1,500 recruiting bonus to any employee who helps to bring a needed professional into the fold.

Benefits are good. One popular plan is the registered retirement savings program. MDA does not have a conventional pension plan, but makes an RRSP contribution equal to 5% of regular salary up to a maximum of $3,750 a year. This way, the company's contribution is immediately vested in the employee, and he or she can take it with him if he leaves.

Women make up 43% of the workforce, and over the past few years they have begun to move up the ladder. Although MDA does not supplement UIC maternity benefits, it will grant a one-to-six-month leave of absence on a merit basis.

Flextime has proven popular, allowing many employees to choose when to start and quit, provided they put in their hours. The company insists only that they be around in the middle of the work day. Some prefer to work nights, when they can get the computer's full capacity. Others, pressured to complete projects, stay late and work weekends, but no one complains if they take a few days off when the pressure eases.

MDA is privately owned, and about 80% of its employees are shareholders. The company splits the cost of share purchases with the employees.

Several employees said they like MDA because it is Canadian owned, or at least run by local management. Many technical employees who had offers from other firms, picked MDA partly because of location, preferring British Columbia to the frigid high-tech colonies in Saskatoon and Ottawa.

MDA was started in 1969 by John MacDonald, a former University of British Columbia electrical engineering professor, and Vern Dettwiler, an engineer who once headed the new products group at the UBC computing centre. Both are still around: MacDonald as MDA's chairman; Dettwiler as chief engineer.

The company they founded is now the world's leading supplier of earth resource satellite ground stations. These units capture data transmitted in digital form by orbiting space satellites and convert it into pictures used for mapping, weather forecasting or spotting potential mineral deposits.

There are spin-offs, too, such as film image recorders that convert digital data from computer sources into film transparencies at high speed and with great resolution. The company has also branched out into flight operations management, air traffic control systems and high-resolution, high-speed photoplotting systems for printed circuit board design.

In the words of one employee, "What sets MDA apart are its high standards, its people orientation, abundant vertical and lateral opportunities and the fact that it is a world leader in some technology areas."

Manufacturers

MANUFACTURERS LIFE INSURANCE CO.

200 Bloor Street East
Toronto, Ontario
M4W 1E5
(416) 926-0100

Pay: **GOOD**	Atmosphere: **VERY GOOD**
Benefits: **GOOD**	Job Satisfaction: **VERY GOOD**
Promotion: **GOOD**	Communications: **GOOD**
Job Security: **AVERAGE**	Personal Development: **VERY GOOD**

★ *Manufacturers Life is Canada's largest insurance company, with assets of more than $23.8 billion and 3,339 full-time employees. It ranks among the 12 largest life insurers in North America and sells financial planning products through 175 offices worldwide, 44 of them in Canada. International headquarters are in Toronto, while the Canadian division's head office is in Waterloo, Ont.*

MANUFACTURERS LIFE HAS a long tradition of being a company people want to work for. During its history of more than a century, it has become known as a progressive and caring employer.

Manufacturers Life built the reputation on a foundation of respect for its employees, providing superior pay and benefits, strong job security and above average promotional opportunities, all offered in a superlative office environment.

But that reputation became slightly tarnished when the company undertook major organizational and administrative changes. What had been seen as a secure and stable work environment altered drastically. In 1982, Manufacturers began to decentralize its Canadian operations. Then in early 1985 it acquired and absorbed Dominion Life Assurance Co. Ltd. of Waterloo, Ont.

Dominion's location in Waterloo provided an excellent opportunity to speed up the decentralization by moving the Canadian operation's head office to Waterloo. Suddenly, Manufacturers Life employees were either being asked to move to Waterloo or to change jobs in Toronto. Some positions were made redundant and workers were asked to leave. Insecurity replaced stability, and morale took a nosedive.

By 1988, however, the merger and decentralization processes were virtually complete, and a renewed sense of stability began to re-emerge. But the new atmosphere was tougher, less country-club and much more business-oriented. Under new CEO Tom Di Giacomo, who came up through the investment side of the business, a clear message came across that although people would not be forgotten, profits came first.

In a 1988 organization assessment, the company stated: "Our priority, as with any other business, is to realize optimum profit. Acceptable profit levels will enable the company and employees to be successful. At the same time, we recognize that what will set us apart from, and ahead of, our competitors is the quality and commitment of our people and the service we provide."

Di Giacomo confirms this philosophy: "There are three areas of value to us: customers, employees and shareholders. And you have to keep the three in balance. However, we are definitely demanding more from our employees today."

In spite of this more hard-nosed approach, Manufacturers recognized that the events between 1985 and 1988 had affected employee morale. As a result, in late 1988, a comprehensive organizational reassessment was undertaken at the Toronto head office to identify weak areas and attempt to improve them.

The results of that sounding confirmed that employees view Manufacturers Life as a good place to work that provides them with interesting jobs in good physical working conditions. Employees also gave top marks to the company's performance appraisal program and to management credibility.

But the uncertainties precipitated by recent changes were reflected in the weaknesses identified by employees. A lack of understanding of the company's overall direction, together with concern about compensation, job security and inadequate career development indicated that management was not communicating its new thrust effectively to its workforce.

After several large employee meetings to discuss the results of the survey, followed by more than 50 smaller group sessions, a new human resources initiative was launched. The three-pronged thrust includes: development and education through an in-house continuous learning centre; better communications and employee involvement; improved reward and recognition programs.

Improved career development opportunities are now available to employees through the more than two dozen courses offered by the company's new training centre. Courses range from time management, executive development to a work and family group course. In addition employees can also participate in eldercare seminars, or take advantage of the dependent care computer referral system.

Compensation is viewed as competitive at Manufacturers Life headquarters in Toronto, but not always flexible enough to reward employees appropriately for their contributions to the company. Consequently, in 1989 the whole salary area was under review to try to improve links between performance and appropriate rewards.

Within the Canadian division at Waterloo, some 105 kilometres from Toronto, salary levels are viewed as superior, compared locally, although by Toronto standards they would be seen as average. Dominion Life employees were the real beneficiaries of the merger with Manufacturers, because the first thing the new owners did was to give all clerical staff $1,000 raises to bring salaries more into line with community levels.

The benefits program is comprehensive (including vision-care and orthodontic coverage), although some areas need adjustment, and most of the benefits apart from the pension plan are company-paid. The package also contains a number of extra perks of real value to employees.

Under a subsidized mortgage program, Manufacturers Life will underwrite a mortgage of two and a half times an employee's annual salary, up to a maximum of $150,000, at a 20% discount off the company's current mortgage rate.

Toronto employees can have the use of a state-of-the-art in-house fitness centre for a low monthly fee. In Waterloo, there are plans to create a more modest exercise room in the new headquarters building. Both locations offer workers subsidized cafeterias, and both major head offices provide subsidized parking, an increasingly important perk in high-priced downtown Toronto.

This company shines in the advancement of women. Manufacturers set up a task force in 1976 to deal with this issue, and the results are satisfyingly obvious.

In an organization where 67% of the employees are women, they also make up 40% of management. But where the real gains are visible, compared to similar large organizations, are in the executive ranks. Until the departure of highly visible Jalynn Bennett, vice-president of corporate development, Manufacturers Life had four women vice-presidents, including one (Rose Patten, senior vice-president of corporate human resources) as a member of the inner circle, the corporate executive committee.

In 1985, Manufacturers Life received the Ontario Women's Directorate Award in recognition of their promotion of women.

The company goes out of its way to provide support to its women, in the form of alternative working arrangements, including flex-time and job-sharing. It also offers courses in topics such as assertiveness training and career planning. The company supplements UIC maternity benefits to ensure that each woman receives 60% of earnings while on maternity leave.

Manufacturers Life attracts high performers, drawn by its pre-eminent position in the financial services industry, the variety of the job opportunities and the participative team environment. As one ex-Dominion Lifer (now proudly a Manufacturers employee) summed it up: "Manufacturers offers a high-paced, competitive, aggressive and innovative environment, where decision-making is pushed right down into the organization."

Micronav
A Leigh Company

MICRONAV LTD.

P.O. Box 1523,
Sydney, Nova Scotia
B1P 6R7
(902) 564-8833

Pay: **AVERAGE**	Atmosphere: **EXCELLENT**
Benefits: **AVERAGE**	Job Satisfaction: **EXCELLENT**
Promotion: **GOOD**	Communications: **VERY GOOD**
Job Security: **AVERAGE**	Personal Development: **VERY GOOD**

★ *Micronav designs, develops, manufactures and installs microwave landing systems. Based in Sydney, N.S., the firm employs 82 people. Sales run at about $3 million a year. Micronav is a subsidiary of Leigh Instruments of Kanata, Ont., which produces a wide range of aerospace products.*

OFFERING HIGH-TECH opportunities in a place more usually associated with fishing and mining, Micronav is viewed as an oasis for young engineers who want to live and work in the Cape Breton area.

The young workforce is enthusiastic and committed to the company and its future. Because the average employee age is only 32, and most of the workforce has been working in the microwave landing systems field for more than five years, it looks as though they're in it for the long haul.

Micronav also offers its workers tremendous learning opportunities and challenges. "I've been doing things at Micronav that I wouldn't do in most companies for years," says one employee. "I've gained a lot of experience here very quickly. The potential for growth is tremendous."

The spirit in the company is positive and entrepreneurial — because that's the only way small firm can compete with bigger, fatter competitors. Non-stop training also gives Micronav an extra competitive edge. The company pays in full for off-site courses, and conducts in-plant training sessions regularly. On average, each worker attends a skills-upgrading course once a year.

Employer and employee share the cost of benefits equally, and (apart from the absence of a pension plan) the package is as good as any larger corporation's. There is a form of gain-sharing that allows workers to share in profits generated by a reduction in a project's costs, as long as quality standards are maintained.

"The payout to the employee can be as high as 10% of salary," says Micronav President Nick Coyle. "In one case, a team managed to get a 10% gain share twice in one year." Unfortunately, this program generally excludes office and secretarial staff, being limited to engineers and technicians.

Pay brackets don't approach levels in central Canada, especially for the clerical staff. "However, engineer's salaries are at the low end of competitive levels," Coyle says.

Most of the workers are in the company for long-term gain, banking on future growth and profits. As one explained it, "Salaries are a wee bit low, but the combination of benefits and experience here, along with the potential for growth, more than makes up the difference." Or, as another employee put it, "The pay is lower, but job satisfaction is much higher."

Another advantage in a small firm is very good communication. All employees meet at least once a month to discuss current programs and upcoming events, and a social gathering follows to encourage informal dialogue.

Chances for promotion are as good as your ideas and initiative make them. As one employee said, "this place is so small that you're near the top no matter where you are."

Micronav is a great place for young engineers, keen for diverse job and learning opportunities, unconcerned about current pay levels, but prepared to work hard in exchange for the potential to achieve greater rewards in the future.

The future has looked even brighter since Leigh Instruments acquired Micronav in January, 1988, giving the Cape Breton company more secure financial backing. Leigh's support already shows in the form of a new plant and state-of-the-art equipment.

NOVATEL
COMMUNICATIONS LTD.

1020 - 64th Avenue N.E.
Calgary, Alberta
T2E 7V8
(403) 295-4500

Pay: **GOOD**	Atmosphere: **EXCELLENT**
Benefits: **GOOD**	Job Satisfaction: **EXCELLENT**
Promotion: **AVERAGE**	Communications: **GOOD**
Job Security: **AVERAGE**	Personal Development: **EXCELLENT**

★ *NovAtel employs more than 1,300 people in the research, development, manufacture and sale of cellular telephones and cellular systems worldwide. It is a wholly owned subsidiary of Alberta Government Telephones, though it is managed separately from the telephone utility. Head office is in Calgary, with ultra-modern production facilities in both that city and in Lethbridge, Alberta. It also has sales and distribution centres in Atlanta, Georgia; Fort Worth, Texas; Montreal; Mississauga, Ont., and in Britain. It is not unionized.*

NOVATEL CHAIRMAN John Burrows says: "Our company is a brain power company. Our natural resource is the brain power of our people. We don't have natural resources such as timber or coal. Every dollar which comes in next year will come out of the brains of our people."

With that emphasis, it is easy to understand some of the unusual lengths that NovAtel goes to in recruiting employees. Before candidates are even interviewed for a production job at its plant in Lethbridge, they are required to attend a three-day workshop — without pay — where their problem-solving and team-building skills are assessed. If they surmount this hurdle, and subsequent interviews, they are then put on a six-week training course before they have a hand in actually producing the company's cellular telephone equipment.

Says Chris Groves, the company's vice-president of computer integrated design and manufacturing: "We decided to build quality in at the front. We are really looking for two things: team play and the ability of employees to think for themselves."

When a young engineer was recruited from Ontario, he had an initial interview in Toronto, numerous phone interviews and then eight interviews in Calgary before he was offered the job. In another instance, NovAtel insisted on paying for the visit from Toronto to Calgary of not only a potential employee but also his fiancee.

NovAtel, which competes against some of the best international electronics firms for its share of the rapidly expanding cellular telephone market, scours the world for the talent it needs to help it stay ahead. Recruiting trips to the Orient brought in 30 people, all of whom but one were engineers. Those hired included several robotics experts from Singapore to work on the design of an automated production line.

Says a recruiter: "We are so high-tech, and the robotics that we are putting into our manufacturing plants is so leading-edge there isn't anyone in this country that does it. There is a technology problem. NovAtel's kind of manufacturing is both capital and knowledge intensive. We are going to robotics and our schools are just not producing enough good engineers or software people specialized in this kind of machinery. So we have to go offshore to find it."

Some employees work in super-clean rooms and look like medical personnel in an operating theatre. The company is seeking "six-sigma" quality — a level of 3.4 defects per million parts or process steps.

NovAtel was founded in 1983 and got in on the ground floor of the cellular telephone revolution. In 1989, the average age of employees was 33.

Executive Vice-President Sandy Moore says 1989 sales were more than $309 million, compared with $153 million in 1988. "Not bad for a bunch of rookies," he comments. As he looks ahead, he says: "We are talking about 30%- to 40%-a-year growth."

NovAtel expects to achieve 15% of the world market share of transportable cellular phones by 1992. But it could reach that lofty target in 1991, Moore says. "We are in the fastest-growing industry in the world. If all I do is retain market share, there is probably a 20% growth built in" each year. In 1989, 2% of the U.S. population owned cellular telephones. This is expected to increase to 8% by 1994, which means that more than 16 million Americans will be dialing each other by cellular phone. "There will be another eight million units going into the U.S. marketplace over the next five years, and basically we expect to make two million of them."

In 1989, NovAtel committed $37 million to expand production in Calgary and Lethbridge.

Burrows says: "Our smallest competitor is Northern Telecom with $6 billion in sales. We are just a little flea on the giant's back. If he catches us, we're dead. I don't feel any sense of lack of security. It is the exhilaration of competing and winning. This kind of ambience and atmosphere is very exhilarating for a young person."

As NovAtel was expanding furiously to keep pace with the exploding demand for its product, this meant lots of overtime, not a little stress but also the thrill that comes with working at the leading edge of technology. NovAtel, while a stimulating company, is not yet a mature firm and is still making the transition from a research and development organization to a modern manufacturer.

Some employees who joined from larger, more structured organizations say they found the atmosphere unsettling at first. Often, they discovered, there were no established procedures and they had to make up their own rules. But after a while, this freedom of action became enjoyable. For one thing, they were given far more responsibility than they would be offered in a more mature firm.

Says an engineer: "It's the first company I have worked with that the lower-level people's voice could be heard so easily. In some bigger companies where I worked, if you wanted your voice to be heard, you had to go up through several divisional managers, writing up proposals which had to be endorsed by so many signatures you forgot where you started off. In this organization, one memo will probably get you a hearing with a vice-president."

The opportunity for professional development — and the types of experience that enrich a resumé — are big attractions for many employees.

President Del Lippert says: "We are in an industry that is constantly changing. For example, the half-life of an engineering education is five years. We need people who thrive on change, who are willing to try new things, learn new ideas, make mistakes and learn from those mistakes. As a company, we must encourage people to learn and explore new ideas. NovAtel must be a place where people can continue to learn for the rest of their lives. We need to create an environment where people can adapt to change and progress with changing technology."

A young technologist, who says he can easily find a better-paying job elsewhere, says he prefers to stay with NovAtel because of the opportunity to learn from a company doing pioneering electronics work. Before he was only 26, he had already been sent to install cellular systems in China, Mauritius, Costa Rica and the U.S.

So far, much of NovAtel's manufacturing has been done in Japan, Korea and Hong Kong, but this activity is being repatriated to Canada with the big investment in automation.

Burrows says: "We can get the labor component to 15% or lower with robotic manufacturing processes and so we can absorb the labor rates in the Orient here." (In 1989, NovAtel was paying $2 to $2.50 an hour in Korea versus $8 in Lethbridge). "We have done that with our peripheral products. These are all produced in Lethbridge. They used to be produced in Korea."

Investment in automation doesn't necessarily mean fewer staff. As its business grows, NovAtel is building up its work force.

For those who like a high-tech environment, NovAtel offers an exciting future.

PROCTER & GAMBLE INC.

4711 Yonge Street
North York, Ontario
M5W 1C5
(416) 730-4711

Pay: **VERY GOOD**	Atmosphere: **VERY GOOD**
Benefits: **EXCELLENT**	Job Satisfaction: **EXCELLENT**
Promotion: **VERY GOOD**	Communications: **GOOD**
Job Security: **VERY GOOD**	Personal Development: **VERY GOOD**

★ *Procter & Gamble's 2,500 Canadian employees produce and market a variety of widely known consumer brands — such as Tide, Pampers, Crest, Duncan Hines, Head and Shoulders. The Toronto-based company has plants in Hamilton, Belleville, and Brockville, Ont., as well as in Pointe Claire, Que., and Grande Prairie, Alta. This subsidiary of Procter & Gamble Co. of Cincinnati, Ohio, has annual Canadian sales of about $1.1 billion.*

PROCTER & GAMBLE is one of the few companies with a known, widely accepted reputation in the job market. It is seen as a very successful, middle-of-the road company, with high ethical standards; a company that takes a great deal of time and care in developing its products, and more recently, as a company that is beginning to react more quickly to consumer concerns about environmental protection issues.

P&G started a 12-member waste management leadership team at the beginning of 1989 to address public concerns and work with government to help solve disposable waste problems. Its aim is "to minimize the impact of products and packages and their manufacture on the environment and on solid waste disposal." One change was to reduce the size of Crisco containers by 30% to take up less space at landfill sites. Another was the development of lightweight reusable plastic bottles.

P&G is also renowned for the development of its employees, a factor that contributes to the remarkable number of expatriate P&Gers found in key executive positions with other companies. Procter & Gamble workers take a perverse pride in being able to say they've done a superb job of training their competitors. As one manager explained it: "People who leave P&G can go to Kimberly-Clark, for example, and say, 'Here are the three things P&G does best. Let's copy them. And here, on the other hand, are the three things they do worst. Let's avoid them.' And then they can do it — and do a better job than we can."

The company's dedication to its employees is stated prominently in all its literature. Around its famous man-in-the-moon logo is the motto "caring people committed to excellence." The Canadian company's statement of purpose begins with:

"We will provide products of superior quality and value that best fill the needs of consumers. We will achieve that purpose through an organization and a working environment which attracts the finest people; fully develops and challenges our individual talents; encourages our free and spirited collaboration to drive the business ahead; and maintains the company's historic principles of integrity and doing the right thing."

Employees bear out the genuineness of this philosophy and point out a variety of ways in which these qualities are maintained. A professional woman explains: "I used to work for a temporary help agency, and I saw about 30 different companies over three years. Every time I came to P&G I was impressed by the attitudes here. The environment was always so friendly, and yet people worked hard to get the job done, because they had really good goals both for themselves as well as for the company. So, when I was ready to apply for a permanent job, I came to P&G because I had been so impressed."

People within the company have a very clear idea of the qualities an ideal P&Ger should possess: "They should be dynamic, intelligent, get along well with others, be team players, self-starters, organized, fast-paced, with a clear set of goals to achieve, yet they should always be polite and respectful," says one manager.

Employees believe that the general public reputation enjoyed by P&G is essentially correct, and express a great deal of pride in their association with such an elite company. They also believe the organization is steadily improving and changing for the better: "The pace has changed here over the past few years," explains one product manager. "There is now a pitch of excitement that didn't exist before. And we have proved that we can move faster." New products include Tide with bleach, Clearasil medicated pads, Luvs boy/girl diapers and the refillable Enviro-Pak line.

Another employee adds: "In the last five years we've become a lot more flexible. Although we do seem to spend more time developing our products than anybody else, usually we come out on top because we've done our homework better than anybody else."

Communications in the company are also easier than they have been in the past. As one long-time staffer commented: "We used to operate on a 'need to know' basis. Now we're moving to a more open attitude. Once a year the company now gives us an honest assessment of both good and bad news about the organization. It's called the 'State of the Business' talk."

Opportunities for promotion abound in a company that has increased both sales and profits, while cutting down on staff levels. And opportunities for women seem remarkably good. With women making up 35% of the total workforce, a satisfactory 29% of managers are female, while the number of women executives has tripled in the past four years to 15%.

"I was promoted after I had been here for only three months," one woman said. "Wow! I didn't even think anyone knew who I was."

The company's policy of recruiting only at the entry level and then aiming to keep employees for a lifetime means that promotion from within is almost always the case.

Pay levels at P&G are above average, but not outstanding. Says one worker: "I could always make more money working in a bank. But money's not the important thing here — it's the people orientation that counts."

Employees do agree that their benefits package is outstanding. It is certainly one of the most comprehensive. Some of the extras P&G offers as part of its regular benefits are: a maternity benefit of 95% of full salary, adoption leave, vision-care, generous orthodontistry coverage, tuition aid, a scholarship program for children of employees, an employee counseling service, a stock-option plan and early retirement supplements.

P&G's newer plants operate in a team mode. Democracy and participation are the twin cornerstones of the team management system works. The Belleville disposable diaper plant makes a good example. Right from opening day in 1975, technicians (the name given to all workers) were assigned to teams of six. Each team runs one section of plant operations, whether a section of the production line or the storeroom. All jobs within each team are interchangeable, and no one does the same job for long, because the workers rotate through the functions. Eventually everyone has to do a stint on the production line. Team members, regardless of sex, handed a tool box when joining the company, and made responsible for routine maintenance of the machinery they work on.

This team style gives employees a sense of responsibility. Teams set monthly work quotas, and try to exceed them. They compete with each other for efficiency and productivity, and are proud of their results. "We're flexible," explains one employee. "People do a number of different jobs — therefore they can do things that really interest them."

The whole philosophy of the plant is based on the idea that people are capable and want to do more. "People should understand why they're doing things, and have a say in how it affects them personally. We're always on the lookout for ways to improve the work environment," says another employee.

One of the most impressive qualities shared by many P&G workers, both in the plant and head office environment, is their thoughtful evaluation of the company, summing up both positive and negative characteristics. They seem genuinely eager to discover ways of improving it and making it an even better place to work. Some of their constructive criticisms include concerns about:

● Bureaucracy: On one hand, workers view it as an necessary protection within a large organization. They say, "It's one way of developing good organizational skills." On the other hand, they see attitudes toward red tape changing: "One of the mottos we've heard a lot in the last few years is *Sacred cows make good steaks.*"

Another worker says: "You don't have to be a workaholic to succeed, but there's always been a current around here that

says, 'My God, it's four o'clock. You're leaving on time today —
what's wrong with you?' "

● Promotion: "The expectation of all our people is to become
senior managers some day. We're all upwardly mobile. But what
happens when growth slows and we all hit senior levels at the
same time? We need to give people more lateral moves to
broaden work experience."

Personnel Development Manager Edward Payne says some
concerns expressed by employees, such as understaffing and
overwork, have been rectified. And he is optimistic that other
problems will be dealt with too. "We want to have a very caring
corporate culture," he says.

Another senior manager adds: "This company's not perfect.
It's very, very good, close to perfect, but not quite."

SUN MICROSYSTEMS OF CANADA INC.

100 Renfrew Drive
Markham, Ontario
L3R 9R6
(416) 477-6745

Pay: **VERY GOOD**	Atmosphere: **VERY GOOD**
Benefits: **GOOD**	Job Satisfaction: **GOOD**
Promotion: **VERY GOOD**	Communications: **GOOD**
Job Security: **GOOD**	Personal Development: **GOOD**

★ *Sun Microsystems of Canada Inc. is a supplier of computing systems for professionals. The company has 188 employees in seven locations across Canada. This subsidiary of California-based Sun Microsystems Inc. posted 1988 sales of more than $60 million.*

SUN MICROSYSTEMS is another aggressive, dynamic and determinedly ambitious high-tech company to emerge from California. The attitudes and values that drive this brash upstart have a familiar ring: flexibility, autonomy, quality, excellence, teamwork, absence of bureaucracy and (above all) sales, sales, sales.

Sun has a record of doubling its sales every year, and President Everett Anstey predicts Sun's astounding growth will continue — with the Canadian company reaching 1,000 employees and $500 million in sales by 1995.

Sun's technology is the hottest in the market, according to employees proud to be working for an industry pace setter. "If you want to be in marketing, I'd rather be selling a Cadillac," one employee says. The California-style hype — "we try for the impossible and settle for the absurd" — is a by-product of the energetic environment.

Employees thrive on the autonomy and responsibility they are given, and are challenged to use their creative abilities to the fullest. "You are listened to," one employee says of management's responsiveness. "You don't have to sell an idea through 17 layers of bureaucracy to get an idea implemented."

Change is central to the environment. The company is so adept that it is able to change its entire product line in response to market demands within 90 days. Being in on the ground floor of this ever-expanding operation gives young employees a charge. The average age in the company rose to 32 in 1988 from the previous year's 28.

Sun pays its staff very well — "at the 75th percentile" in fact. And the quarterly bonuses are equally generous — 2% of salary if sales objectives are met. The company puts up another 2% at yearend if annual sales exceed target, and it is quick to reward outstanding work with still other bonuses.

The benefits are quite good and include vision, dental and even an orthodontic plan. The only thing missing is a pension plan. Not surprisingly in such a young company, this doesn't concern workers too much. Other benefits include a fitness subsidy, an employee-assistance program and a generous stock-purchase plan. Employees can deduct 1%-10% of their salary for semi-annual stock purchases. The price is 85% of market value at the start or end of the six-month period, whichever is lower.

The company is constantly hiring new people to keep pace with expansion. Most are internal referrals, rewarded by recruiting bonuses of $1,350 ($4,000 for a sales representative) if they remain at least a month. The referrals foster a sense of camaraderie. But turnover is high — at 20%, it is double that of other companies in the industry.

Employees describe themselves as people who can take dynamic change in stride, have a type-A personality, and are flexible and outgoing. They must also have stamina and be "task and job oriented."

The company's drawbacks relate to its rapid growth, and include very heavy workloads and long hours. Anstey admits enabling "people to keep up with the growth is a big problem. That's where career development is so important. That's our biggest challenge today." In response, he is committing more money to training to help ease the workload.

"It's like running a marathon race," says Andy Kroen, director of corporate resources, describing the process by which new employees adapt to the Sun culture. "At the 15th or 16th mile, when you think you have nothing left to give, that's when the culture shock really hits. But when you complete the 26 miles, you survive and begin to enjoy it."

Why do people remain in this demanding environment? "It's fun!" Anstey says of what motivates his employees, some of whom work between 50 and 60 hours a week. "It's not hard to put in the extra effort when the work is fun."

For people who like loose, unstructured, fast-paced, ever-changing work environments and thrive on challenge and variety, Sun Microsystems is an excellent place to work. Its "small-company" approach with a minimum of rules works. Can Sun maintain the entrepreneurial atmosphere while growing rapidly? One thing is certain: Sun's dynamic environment provides an excitement not found in many other companies.

SYNCRUDE CANADA LTD.

200, 9911 MacDonald Avenue
P.O. Bag 4023
Fort McMurray, Alberta
T9H 1S7
(403) 790-6111

Pay: **EXCELLENT**	Atmosphere: **GOOD**
Benefits: **VERY GOOD**	Job Satisfaction: **GOOD**
Promotion: **VERY GOOD**	Communications: **GOOD**
Job Security: **VERY GOOD**	Personal Development: **GOOD**

★ *Syncrude, owned by a consortium of oil companies and the Alberta government, produces synthetic crude oil by mining and processing oil sands at Mildred Lake near Fort McMurray in Northern Alberta. It is the biggest operation of its kind in the world and has 4,700 non-unionized employees, almost all of whom work at the plant site.*

AT FORT McMURRAY it is 40 degrees below Celsius early on a January morning and the sun will not make a hesitant mid-winter appearance for several hours. In the frigid darkness, a fleet of 100 buses chartered by Syncrude cruises from door to door to carry a small army of employees to work from the neat residential sub-divisions built by Syncrude.

The work site is 40 kilometres distant at Mildred Lake, where the earth is being stripped of bitumen-impregnated sand by machinery so gigantic it defies adequate description. Syncrude, a $3.7-billion frontier megaproject, produces about 10% of Canada's crude oil needs, or 55 million barrels annually.

Most of the workers will put in 12-hour shifts, or longer if needed, before being conveyed back to their homes. Syncrude does its best to make their lives comfortable. All lunchrooms have fridges and microwave ovens, and people working overtime can order in meals and call for a free taxi ride home, if necessary.

Syncrude, which began production in July, 1978, is not yet a mature company, as its own executives are quick to point out. It has suffered many teething troubles as it sought to perfect the difficult techniques of mining the sticky Athabasca oil sands and extracting the crude oil.

While unable to boast of an especially long track record as an employer, it has made a number of impressive moves to draw workers to remote Fort McMurray and treat them handsomely. Employees feel they are well paid, well trained and work for an expanding company that offers much potential for promotion and long-term stability.

As testimony to its popularity as an employer, Syncrude receives about 12,000 job applications a year in its recruiting office in Fort McMurray, although it only needs 450. For a frontier operation, Syncrude has an impressively low turnover of 6.8% a year.

Significantly, numerous attempts to unionize the largely blue-collar work force have failed. One employee explains it this way: "I think people look at what they see on television and in the papers about strikes and contract disputes. Then they look at Syncrude and say, 'Hey, we don't have that here and we have no need of it.' The company looks after us, and we really don't have to fight for every inch of ground as a union might have to."

Another worker comments: "A few years ago, the employee relations people used to send all employees a form, and you would fill in what you would like to see for improvement in benefits. In the past few years, they have got away from that, because I don't think there is very much more you could ask for."

Syncrude aims to pay better than comparable industry averages, although it doesn't want to lead the pack. To ensure it remains competitive, it regularly surveys 15 top companies in the mining, oil and utility industries, aiming to be among the top five.

Since Syncrude wanted to create a stable workforce, it decided it had to get into the housing business, and so it set up its own building subsidiary, which constructed about 3,400 housing units — apartments, condominiums and family homes.

Because housing is more expensive in Northern Alberta than in many other areas of Canada from which it recruited people, Syncrude offered employees interest-free loans of up to $32,500 (subsequently reduced to $25,000) to help with home purchases. These loans were once necessary to entice people to settle in small communities, but now that's no longer the case and the company has stopped offering them.

Later, as an active private market developed, Syncrude offered significant incentives to employees selling their homes to do so privately and thus relieve the company of earlier buy-back guarantees it had given. The incentives were generous, amounting to $7,000 on a $100,000 home, plus up to $1,000 in legal fees. Occasionally, when it feels there is a need, it also assists with five-year second mortgages to help newcomers buy their first homes.

The 12-hour work shift was introduced at the insistence of employees. Says one worker: "I love it; it is the only way to go as far as I am concerned." Employees work a total of 14 days in a 28-day cycle and shifts often fall so they can take a seven-day vacation once a month, if they choose. Some workers, typically office staff, work a more conventional, shorter work day.

The company offers significant financial support to the Syncrude Social Society, which organizes a variety of events. For example, the company paid for a series of super barbecues — steak and entertainment for almost 9,000 people (all employees plus one guest each). To feed so many, the festivities continued for five nights.

Syncrude also encourages the hiring of family members. One satisfied worker said: "I have myself and my wife and two sons working here, a daughter and a daughter-in-law are summer students [with summer jobs at Syncrude], and two of my sons are going to university on Syncrude scholarships."

Another employee summed up a feeling of optimism about Syncrude this way: "You could come up here and get hired on, raise a family and see your children grow up and take their education here. There is a future for several generations. If you took a big business envelope and imagined that as the resources that are available in the tar sands and you put a postage stamp in one corner — that would represent what has been developed so far. There is just a fantastic future here."

Syncrude, with 260 natives on its payroll, is the largest

private-sector employer of natives in Canada. Not only does it makes special efforts to train native workers, it also encourages native groups to provide contracting services. One Indian band, for example, earns more than $1 million a year running a bus service for the Syncrude operation.

If you don't mind the cold and isolation, you'll probably catch the enthusiasm.

TELEMEDIA

TELEMEDIA INC.

1010 Sherbrooke Street West
Montreal, Quebec,
H3A 2R7
(514) 845-6291

Pay: **AVERAGE**	Atmosphere: **VERY GOOD**
Benefits: **AVERAGE**	Job Satisfaction: **VERY GOOD**
Promotion: **GOOD**	Communications: **EXCELLENT**
Job Security: **GOOD**	Personal Development: **GOOD**

★ *Montreal-based Telemedia Inc., a publicly traded company, has diversified communications interests including 23 radio stations, 16 magazines, (such as TV Guide, Canadian Living, Equinox and Harrowsmith), as well as 27 community newspapers and a book publishing house. The company also runs six broadcast networks, and is involved in promotional marketing, consumer couponing, advertising sales and contract publishing. Telemedia is a partner in a Quebec sports specialty television network, Le Reseau des Sports. Most of its 1,429 employees work in Toronto and Montreal, but about 100 are based in Vancouver.*

TELEMEDIA IS A is a company in transition. Started in 1971 by Philippe de Gaspé Beaubien, renowned for his success at running Montreal's fabulous Expo 67 world's fair, it began as a small group of radio stations in Quebec. The company took its personality from that of its dynamic, entrepreneurial and fun-loving founder. Telemedia quickly attained a reputation as a people-oriented company that valued its employees highly.

Even in the mid-1980s, people were still drawn to it by its unique culture. A manager tells about being offered a job in the company. He asked what the company was in business for. As the manager recalls it, the reply from the president and chief executive officer, John Van de Kamer, went like this: "We're in business basically to make money and have fun. And if making money gets in the way of having fun, then we'll make a little less money." The answer appealed to the manager, who accepted the offer.

De Gaspé Beaubien, Telemedia's chairman, described the company's guiding values and principles in these words: "Doing things right and doing the right thing (competence and ethics). Having some fun along the way. Building on the potential of our people." But today the atmosphere at Telemedia is more business-like and the emphasis on fun has definitely diminished.

A magazine editor explained it this way: "As the growth is stopping, they're getting serious. We're getting to be a big company now, so we'd better grow up and act like it." A broadcasting sales manager adds: "When I started here, the company was like 'Philippe's little toy.' But now the company is getting serious, and growth is slowing. It's no longer fun, the way it used to be."

Other workers say the fun still pops up every now and again, even if the atmosphere isn't as zany as it was when the company was small. Telemedia's light-hearted and freewheeling philosophy has of necessity been reined in.

But Telemedia maintains its distinct personality. One of the things that sets it apart is the method used to hire managers. The company uses a current job description and another for five years in the future (looking for the individual's capacity to grow). The next step is a "candidate profile" — an outline of the key qualities sought for the specific job.

Managers then apply a scale to the candidate profile, assigning weights to each of five key qualities within a total of 100%. The company rarely hires anyone scoring under 75%, but even topping 80% won't necessarily open the door.

There are other key questions to be answered. Do you really want to do the job? Is it something you truly like to do? "[For example], some people write very well, but they don't really enjoy it," says Nan-b de Gaspé Beaubien, the chairman's wife and the organization's vice-president, human resources. "We don't want that, because there's no point. You're not going to be happy."

The crucial last question is whether the candidate likes the culture of teamwork and interdependence. If you prefer to work on your own, look elsewhere. A employee explains: "It's always a matter of putting the right person in the right place at the right time."

And Telemedia line managers who get careless in their people skills feel it where it hurts, because "20% of their bonus is what we call qualitative — based on people-development. That's how important we think that part of their job is," Nan-b (as she is called by everyone) says.

However, this bonus scheme, although universally applied throughout the managerial ranks on the broadcasting side of Telemedia, is far less visible on the publishing side of the company. Below the editor rank, no one has even heard of the bonus scheme.

There's a decentralized management system (called "loose-tight" internally) which gives the manager full responsibility. Once a month, however, he and his boss sit down in an "ops meeting" — an uninterrrupted, as-long-as-it-takes, one-to-one discusssion of the manager's performance and those of the people who work for him. Employees are almost unanimous in their praise for these ops meetings. "They're great," explains one new employee. "Employees are really made to feel part of the process here — and are given feedback on a regular basis."

The company calls the annual employee review a performance "appreciation" rather than an appraisal, because of its interactive nature. Telemedia employs a full-time trainer for communications skills, who even teaches employees how to give "negative feedback" (criticize the boss).

In this participative environment, planning originates with middle management and goes upward, not the other way round. As a matter of policy, senior management responds and reacts to ideas from below. The ideas may be rejected, reworked or accepted, but the process works upward, not downward.

"The planning process and management style placed over it does give middle-to-senior management a unique quality that I have never seen before in any communications company," says a middle manager who spent 19 years elsewhere in the industry.

The pay in Telemedia seems to depend a lot on where you stand in the organization. Although employees agree that pay levels have improved over the past few years, entry level salaries, particularly in publishing, are low. And in general, five-year journalists also could do better elsewhere.

Managerial salaries, on the other hand, seem to top national averages by substantial amounts. And most managers also have the handsome bonus scheme.

The benefit program has been upgraded recently, most notably by the addition of a money purchase pension plan. And the wellness program, which includes quit-smoking weight watching and stress management courses, as well as fitness club fees, goes a long way toward eliminating the sense of a "no frills" approach to benefits that used to pervade the organization.

The company's recent growth has reduced career opportunities in some areas. As one broadcasting employee says: "At the senior management levels, many new hirees are coming from outside the company. They're not training us inside for these senior positions." Many employees feel the need for more guidance and direction about internal career development.

The company seems to be aware of this need, and has started a five-day in-house management development program, but employees don't believe this one program is enough, and want to see more done at the middle managerial level.

Another concern is the perception that it's difficult for women to rise into senior levels. And statistical evidence backs this up. Although half of the workforce is composed of women, only 21% of the managers are female, and only 12% of executives. One woman middle manager adds: "There's a finite limit here I can rise fairly quickly up to a certain point, and then if I'm not part of the old boy club, that's as far as I'll go." Other women back up the perception that Telemedia's senior management group has the reputation of being an "exclusive old boy's club."

Employees also give management black marks at handling communications where firings are concerned. A number of highly visible terminations are signs of "poor communications," says a radio sales manager. Another employee adds, "The company doesn't seem to have enough respect for employees' intelligence to explain the situations properly. For a communications company, they're very naive about the press."

Richard Dubuc, vice-president, human resources, publishing, says communication has become an issue because of Telemedia's growth. "We have doubled in size since 1986, and that brings with it such problems as come up in a large organization," he says. Instead of relying on word of mouth, he says specific, formalized communication programs are being developed.

Despite some criticisms, Telemedia employees feel valued. Each year, on the employee's anniversary of joining (in most divisions, except for broadcasting), the company presents a gift, always tasteful and expensive (such as a coffee-table book). Though it may sound a mite corny, this type of personal touch delights the staff.

TEMBEC INC.

Temiscaming, Quebec
J0Z 3R0
(819) 627-3321

Pay: **GOOD**	Atmosphere: **EXCELLENT**
Benefits: **GOOD**	Job Satisfaction: **VERY GOOD**
Promotion: **VERY GOOD**	Communications: **EXCELLENT**
Job Security: **VERY GOOD**	Personal Development: **VERY GOOD**

★ *Tembec, a producer of wood-cellulose products, specialty plywood and forest-based chemicals, is probably Canada's best known example of local ownership taking over after multinational management failed. The Montreal-based company, serving worldwide markets from northwestern Quebec, in 1988 had net sales of $226 million, up by 39% on previous year. In January, 1990, the company announced plans for a new pulp mill at Temiscaming. There are 1,250 employees, three quarters of them unionized, mainly in the Canadian Paperworkers Union.*

TEMBEC IS PROOF that employees can make a difference. In 1972, a large multinational corporation shut down its "unprofitable" pulp mill at Temiscaming, Que. — sudden death for a town of 3,500.

But ex-employees and other residents (spearheaded by a group of former mill managers) rallied, with financial aid from the Quebec government, to form Tembec Inc. They bought the mill for a bargain-basement price of $2.5 million.

By December, 1973, after toiling long hours, employees watched the first roll of Tembec pulp come off the machines. There was no looking back.

The first full year of operation in 1974 produced an after tax net income of $9.3 million, and employees shared in more than $1 million of profits. In 1988, a record $3.2 million was shared out among workers.

Charles Gagnon, director of corporate relations, recalls that while the new company then enjoyed a thriving market, it also had something more important – the motivation and drive of its people.

"They felt it would work," Gagnon explains. "They took lower wages and benefits than the rest of the industry. The compensating value was a job for life."

The employees not only had a large measure of job security, but also a whole new way of working life. As a group, they owned a substantial portion of the company and the right to two places on a 14-seat board of directors. Whether they held equity or not, they also shared in 4% of the gross profits from their own productivity.

Through a dozen labor-management committees whose decisions are binding on both sides, the employees have a direct say in job-related decisions. In fact, there are no "management rights" at Tembec.

"We have a *responsibility* to manage, but we have no rights. Our whole concept is based on consultation," Gagnon explains.

A hiring committee (two union members and two managers) makes the final decisions about new employees. A job-posting committee selects jobs to be filled from within, while a job-classification committee puts dollars-and-cents numbers next to job descriptions.

There's a four-member committee to decide whether employees are entitled to special leaves of absence. An automation committee weighs the potential effects of technological change on individual workers.

Since 1973, Tembec has spent more than $100 million on a drive to modernize its facilities. Its newest project was the erection of a $310-million coated paperboard mill, expected to create 170 new jobs in Temiscaming.

Another initiative has been a $78-million environmental protection drive. It was one of the first pulp and paper companies to reduce water pollution by using a recovery boiler and evaporator in producing sulphite pulp. Its new process doesn't use chlorine bleach, and doesn't release dioxins into the air.

A program to reduce sulphur dioxide emissions has been completed, enabling Tembec to recover 90% of the waste. It plans an additional $25-million investment to treat secondary effluent.

Possibly the most important group in the Tembec mill, the disciplinary committee (one union man and one manager), serves as an impartial tribunal in cases of on-the-job misbehavior. It's a point of pride that about 98% of the decisions are unanimous.

The interaction also goes beyond the formal processes. A mill worker explains: "Usually we settle our differences right here [on the shop floor]. You can talk to different bosses. If things don't pan out, you can phone the manager for an interview. The door is open. You're welcome."

The pay, while regionally high, is still slightly below the forest industry average, although the gap has narrowed. An entry level mill worker at Tembec starts at $32,000 a year. And the benefits package is at least as good as the industrial average. A share purchase plan, allows employees to buy shares up to a maximum of 10% of earnings at 10% off the market price.

Job security and profit sharing make up for the slightly lower wage scales. In 1988, most Tembec workers received an average $4,200 profit share. And not only has Tembec not had any layoffs, but present expansion plans make the future look bright.

For its workers, Tembec stands for many things — including a way of life. One man puts it this way: "We started with low wages, but I felt a lot more comfortable with Tembec than I did with [the multinational]. There's no comparison whatsoever. I feel that I'm contributing something. I wouldn't trade it for the world."

XEROX

XEROX
CANADA INC.

5650 Yonge St.
North York, Ontario
M2M 4G7
(416) 229-3769

Pay: **VERY GOOD**	Atmosphere: **GOOD**
Benefits: **GOOD**	Job Satisfaction: **VERY GOOD**
Promotion: **GOOD**	Communications: **GOOD**
Job Security: **GOOD**	Personal Development: **GOOD**

★ *Xerox Canada is a major supplier of office technology, equipment and services, and a manufacturer of photocopier components. Sales in 1988 were $1.1 billion. The company's 5,113 full-time and 111 part-time employees, 6% of whom are unionized, work in all major centres in Canada. Xerox Canada is a subsidiary of Xerox Corp., Stamford, Conn., but 21% of the company's shares are publicly held.*

"WE'VE STILL got a lot to do, but I'm not sure there's a lot of people out there doing it much better than we are," says Xerox Canada's vice-president, senior staff officer, Thomas Watson, in discussing management's efforts to make Xerox "an employer of choice."

But there was a time when many companies were doing it better than Xerox. The company weathered a turbulent period in the mid-1970s, when competition from similarly priced, more innovative Japanese products knocked Xerox off its customary perch atop the Canadian photocopier market. Employees who had been enjoying excellent working conditions, high pay and a comprehensive benefits package found themselves working for a company lagging behind industry leaders.

Since then, Xerox has fought back hard and regained much of the market it lost. An elegant and impressive head office building in Metro Toronto's North York heralded the company's return to a competitive market position. And Xerox has taken the time to study the quality of the employment it offers.

In 1983, Xerox implemented its "leadership through quality" program, insisting on quality and customer satisfaction. It has helped keep Xerox employees on side by instilling in them a sense of pride in their work. And the effort has paid off. In 1989, Xerox Canada won the first-ever gold Canadian Business Excellence Award presented by the federal government.

During the difficult times of its battle back to the forefront, Xerox has consistently remained a demanding environment. And there are two ways to get to the top — through plain hard work or by exhibiting ability. "If you have your own initiative, you can really work the system here to your advantage," says one employee.

"You see a lot of people here really challenged by their jobs," says another long-standing employee. "In a positive sense, there's always more to do than you'll ever have time to do it in."

Many of the best and brightest are attracted to Xerox. The company hires 40 to 50 co-op-program students throughout the year. Experience at Xerox looks good on a resumé, and the company has a reputation for offering one of the top-notch marketing training programs in Canada. Sheer numbers make it difficult to move to head office from outside, but a formal career program has been designed to give sales employees a sense of direction.

Employees are also encouraged to work in different areas of the company to keep their work environment challenging. And succession planning means high-potential people are flagged and put on fast-track career development programs.

Xerox has made an effort to promote women. Women currently make up 45% of the professional ranks, up from 31% in 1986. But only 9% of managerial/executives are women, and one woman sits on the 12-member board of directors.

Employees see more benefits than drawbacks in working for Xerox. The company has gone a long way toward regaining its former reputation as a well-paying employer. For instance, about 7% of employees received a 10% salary increase for good performance in 1989. Employees whose performance needed improvement received up to 3% increases, depending where they were in the pay scale, and all other employees got merit increases of between 1% and 8% depending on salary range, performance and their position.

The suggestion plan also gives formal recognition to useful ideas. There are three levels: the Appreciation Award, with a maximum value of $100; the Award of Merit, worth up to $500, and the Award of Excellence, maximum $2,000.

The "leadership through quality" program was started to increase employee satisfaction at Xerox by giving workers an acheivable goal: to make customers happy. Now that Xerox has clearly succeeded in that goal, a similar program for the 1990s will focus on employee satisfaction. Through programs like these, Xerox management aims to please.

THE
MAINSTREAM

Cautious companies with a definite focus on the future and change, but with one foot firmly planted in the past.

Bell

BELL CANADA

1050 Beaver Hall Hill
Montreal, Quebec
H2Z 1S4
(514) 870-1511

Pay: **GOOD**	Atmosphere: **GOOD**
Benefits: **VERY GOOD**	Job Satisfaction: **GOOD**
Promotion: **GOOD**	Communication: **SATISFACTORY**
Job Security: **VERY GOOD**	Personal Development: **EXCELLENT**

★ *Bell Canada, a subsidiary of Montreal-based BCE Inc., is the country's largest telecommunications company, with 1988 operating revenues of $6.6 billion. Bell has about 55,000 employees (traditionally 50% female), most of them unionized (in the Canadian Telephone Employees' Association and the Communications & Electrical Workers of Canada).*

THESE ARE challenging days for Bell Canada, which is fighting to maintain its monopoly on long-distance calls. The challenger is CNCP Telecommunications. Bell, which had to swallow the 1980 loss of its monopoly on renting and installing all equipment hooked up to its lines, argues CNCP doesn't want competition, just a modified monopoly where it gets a piece of the action. Bell is worried CNCP will confine its service to the most lucrative markets, leaving Bell the burden of servicing other markets. It also believes CNCP's entry into this market will mean higher charges for local service, since long-distance charges currently subsidize local service costs.

Meanwhile, Bell is eyeing the cable market. "The technology

has advanced and we're converging toward the point where one network would be appropriate," Bell President Jean Monty says. Naturally, Rogers Communications Inc., which owns 40% of CNCP (with Canadian Pacific Ltd. owning the other 60%), doesn't want to see Bell invade its market, particularly if CNCP doesn't get a piece of the long-distance market.

"The telecos would like telephone subscribers to pay for the wiring of their homes with fibre optics so they can distribute videos," Rogers President Ted Rogers argues. "This entry into the cable-television field would be financed on the backs of residential telephone customers."

It's going to be quite a fight and one that should make Bell an interesting employer.

There will, of course, be changes but Bell prides itself on adaptability. The company is convinced there are no jobs its employees cannot handle.

A new environment is indeed being created. "Although the security associated with the 'Ma Bell' image of the company has definitely lessened, a new culture based on competitiveness, respect for and commitment to employees seems to be unfolding," Jean Bernard, vice-president of personnel, says.

Bell introduced several programs in the late 1980s to help with transition. A team award, based on financial performance and customer service, provides an incentive to managers and professionals of 5%-10% of their salary. Many departments now have non-monetary awards for entrepreneurship and excellent service.

Individual productivity measures have been reduced in favor of group-performance measures and quality-of-service indicators, and there are now employee-involvement programs in many areas. A reference book, containing information on major jobs for clerical and wage employees to aid in career counseling, has also been published. For managers, Bell has developed a job-information system and a self-assessment skill process to enhance management career planning.

In addition, Bell has an employee-suggestion award system, a cash award for ideas that help cut costs or enhance revenue. Awards range from $50 to $20,000. In 1989, 5,700 employees submitted suggestions and about $650,000 was paid out for ideas that were adopted. The company saved about $12 million.

One thing not changing is the company's belief in generous

treatment to active and retired employees — a philosophy born in the 1920s and 1930s when the telephone monopolies were among the first corporations to introduce pensions, benefits and the concept of lifetime careers. Bell is, and probably will remain for some time, a fine place to work.

Bell has generally had good labor relations, with only three strikes in more than 100 years. The last one was the longest, lasting four months in 1988.

Bell rarely fires employees except as a last resort. The company prefers to put a lot of effort into what it calls "salvaging or redirecting."

A job at Bell can offer variety, personal development, good pay and benefits, including a non-contributory pension plan. For a woman who started working for Bell as a mail girl at age 16, and is now an assistant department head, Bell represents opportunity, mobility and enormous scope.

"You could work for 10 different companies in the one company," she says. "You can definitely set your career goals working through the organization. You also get lots of re-enforcement. The more departments you've worked in, the more points you get."

Another career woman says management training emphasizes "teaching your employees what you know, so they can perform to their fullest, and offering them the opportunity to do things beyond what their own jobs have allowed." A man who has worked in advertising and marketing systems, and for Bell's project in Saudi Arabia says: "You don't get bored. You're not doing what you've done for the last 20 years."

For those who do not possess great ambition, Bell's other attractions include excellent training programs and flexible shifts. They can also take vacations at different times of the year — a luxury to many hourly rated factory workers. (The essential nature of Bell's service means no annual vacation shutdown.) In May, 1989, a trial four-day, 36-hour work week, involving clerical and associated members of the Canadian Telephone Employees' Association, began. The move appeared successful after the first eight months of what is to be a one-year trial.

Bell's policy of opening all jobs to anyone makes it a good place for women. Those in management say the company offers more opportunities for them than many other organizations.

Yet, only 2.4% of operators are male. Only 7.3% of men hold

clerical jobs and account for 3.9% of service representatives in business offices. In 1975, women represented 0.4% of installers and repair people. By 1988, after a deliberate effort to draw more women into those trades, the number of women in skilled craft and trade positions rose to 1.8%.

In 1990, Bell will set up another project in hopes of drawing more women into non-traditional jobs. The Qualifications Development Program is a joint project with the union. Qualified female applicants receive six-months' training in craft and service jobs. Those who are successful will be eligible for permanent positions.

Employees seem to lack a corporate-family spirit, but they do experience something perhaps more important — a sincere belief that the firm will always treat them fairly.

BRITISH COLUMBIA BUILDINGS CORP.

3350 Douglas Street
Box 1112
Victoria, British Columbia
V8W 2T4
(604) 387-7211

Pay: **VERY GOOD**	Atmosphere: **VERY GOOD**
Benefits: **VERY GOOD**	Job Satisfaction: **VERY GOOD**
Promotion: **VERY GOOD**	Communications: **GOOD**
Job Security: **VERY GOOD**	Personal Development: **GOOD**

★ *Government-owned B.C. Buildings Corp. manages 20.5 million square feet of space throughout the province. Its 800 employees help run more than 3,000 properties, ranging from 19th century heritage buildings to ultramodern office complexes. In fiscal 1988-89, the Crown corporation earned $28 million on revenues of $260 million. About 75% of its employees are members of the B.C. Government Employees' Union.*

EMPLOYEES OF B.C. Buildings Corp. bristled when asked to differentiate their organization from the provincial civil service. They were emphatic. They are not civil servants — and don't let anyone forget it.

While owned by the provincial government, their corporation (of which they seem especially proud) marches to a different drummer. The employees are driven by client satisfaction and market pricing for their company's services. They argue they are innovative, cost conscious, respond to deadline pressures and aspire to excellence.

B.C. Buildings Corp. was created in 1976 to bring accountability to the provision and allocation of government accommodation. The company functions much as departments of public works do in other jurisdictions, but with one important difference: it uses a market-based pricing system (to the best extent it can) to establish rents charged to government ministries for the space they occupy. It also services buildings for a number of noncaptive clients.

The corporation has real estate assets worth more than $600 million. Its employees help manage office blocks, isolated highway maintenance yards, residential institutions, courthouses, correctional centres, fish hatcheries, and the three-city-block Law Courts and Robson Square complex in downtown Vancouver. About 800 workers now do what a staff of more than 2,000 used to. One measure of the corporation's efficiency is the square metres of space managed per employee. This increased from 1,802 in 1985 to 2,358 in 1989. At the same time, gross revenues grew from $234 million to $260 million.

The corporation has cut the fat from its payroll by a combination of 240 voluntary early retirements and attrition over a five-year period. Not one person has been laid off for economic reasons and employees say they feel secure in their jobs. The corporation re-trained workers when it found it had more people than it needed in certain classifications. For example, cleaners were trained to become clerks, stationary engineers and trout hatchery operators.

Pay and benefits for the unionized workers are negotiated as part of a collective agreement involving 28,600 government employees working for a variety of ministries and agencies. While the pay is good and some benefits are excellent (an indexed pension, for example), it's not possible for the corporation to offer bonuses or profit sharing schemes, but it doesn't seem to bother employees. One reason for this is the abundance of opportunities for promotion. In the 1988-89 fiscal year 177 employees were either promoted into new positions or received an upward reclassification because they were handling more responsibility.

Says Property Manager Michael Marasco: "I'm a bean counter by trade. In the eight years I have been here, I started as a systems analyst and got promoted to a buildings superintendent, which was totally another area of expertise, but they provided me with training and guidance. I got promoted back into an accountant's job and now I'm a property manager. All this was in a relatively short period of time, and I'm not unique. There are people here who have had five or six promotions over a 10-year period."

Employees enjoy the opportunity to work with little or no supervision, the readiness of management to listen to ideas, and the corporation's encouragement for those who want to educate themselves for better jobs. Employees participate in quality circles and meetings with clients where the corporation's performance is discussed, promoting openness and good communications.

In September, 1989, a large group of employees — from management to the most junior — who worked at the Riverview Hospital in the Vancouver suburb of Coquitlam, went on a weekend motivation course at the Harrison Hot Springs resort in the Fraser Valley. Response was strong and participants encouraged coworkers "to grow." Another new direction in the corporate attitude is that employees at all levels who feel they can contribute are being encouraged to volunteer for environmental committees.

Current in-house training programs include such diverse subjects as cleaning management, effective meetings, time management, supervisory skills, coping with stress, management process skills and so on. These courses aren't mandatory, but they are popular and well-attended.

Grant Hastings, an electrician at the Riverview Hospital and chief shop steward of B.C. Government Employees Union, Local 1503, says the difference between working for the government and working for the corporation was "like night and day." For example:

• "The corporation has goals; we have a five-year plan on projects. The government ministry was day to day.

• "With the government service you just didn't have the direction you have with the corporation. B.C. Buildings really strives to make you team players.

• "In 10 years I have had three grievances which had to go beyond the local level. That's excellent. I used to have one a month with the government. I spent more time in union headquarters probably than on the job."

• "We have very good union, employee-management

relationship."

Hastings also says the "paranoia" of working for a government ministry has disappeared. "Now, if the employer thinks the union ought to be involved, they tell me I ought to come to a meeting. It's the reverse."

There are meetings and surveys in which employees are asked: "How do you think we can run this place better?"

Says Hastings: "Ideas count and it makes you feel like a human being. You are not just a tractor runner."

B.C. Buildings Corp. tries to be a cut above.

BRITISH COLUMBIA
TELEPHONE CO.

3777 Kingsway
Burnaby, British Columbia
V5H 3Z7
(604) 432-2151

Pay: **VERY GOOD**	Atmosphere: **VERY GOOD**
Benefits: **VERY GOOD**	Job Satisfaction: **GOOD**
Promotion: **AVERAGE**	Communications: **EXCELLENT**
Job Security: **AVERAGE**	Personal Development: **VERY GOOD**

★ *British Columbia Telephone, Canada's second largest telecommuni-cations company, provides regional and worldwide telephone and telecommunications services. B.C. Tel and its subsidiaries employ 15,000 employees who design, manufacture and market a wide range of voice, data, text and image products and services. About 80% of the workforce are unionized, mainly in the Telecommunication Workers' Union. B.C. Tel is 50.1% owned by Anglo-Canadian Telephone Co. of Montreal (a wholly owned subsidiary of GTE Corp. of Stamford, Conn.).*

A DECADE ago it would have been laughable to suggest that B.C. Tel was one of Canada's best employers. In 1979, and again in 1981, labor-management relations sank to an all-time low as the company and its workers fought battles characterized by lawsuits, intimidation and allegations of violence.

Clearly, a very determined effort had to be made to steer the company into the future. To its great credit, B.C. Tel has succeeded magnificently. A new atmosphere is apparent to the most casual customers; in the friendliness of staff at its

PhoneMart stores and the courtesy that has replaced the once-familiar snarls from B.C. Teloperators.

In 1981, the company took a close look at its own health and didn't like what it saw. It recognized it had failed to communicate with its employees and their union. There were no recognition programs, no vehicles for employee participation. And there was much frustration with a highly centralized management structure that ensured almost all decisions affecting the province-wide business were made in Vancouver.

Since then, management has been decentralized and become more responsive. Now the company's communications rank as excellent. (The company conveys its messages by employee magazines, electronic mail, videotapes and numerous departmental meetings. Some workers even complain goodnaturedly they now have too much company information to absorb.)

B.C. Tel encourages employee participation in many ways, including quality circles — Japanese-style groups in which employees brainstorm to solve common problems — for which about 2,000 leaders have been trained. Some results have been striking.

For example, a female employee's suggestion on how to repair faulty telephone handsets saved the company about $153,000. Her reward: $10,725. Another woman earned $12,000 merely by suggesting that a final notice be sent to customers with overdue accounts before they were turned over to a collection agency. No one had thought of it before. B.C. Tel saved $120,000 in four months.

The company has its own training centre, where employees learn everything from technical to management skills. It is heavily used. In 1988, for instance, there were 27,232 employee training visits. The centre is so successful, in fact, that B.C. Tel makes its services available to other companies. The phone company, which produces in-house about 60-70 training videos each year, recently has been hiring people from TV and radio news to give the videos extra topicality and polish.

B.C. Tel's benefits are exceptional, and now amount to 36.4% of payroll. Apart from the sort of pension, medical and dental benefits one expects from a major employer, the company offers generous vacations and numerous perks. For example, at head office in Vancouver, there is a subsidized cafeteria, a splendidly equipped fitness centre and a room set aside as a social club for long-time employees and retirees.

There is much more. The company offered a $300 subsidy to anyone who wanted to buy a computer for home use. The social club can negotiate 15% discounts on vacation cruises. There are courses in good nutrition, stress management and so on. An employee can even get a preferential deal on a car lease and pay for the vehicle (and the insurance) by payroll deduction. B.C. Tel also encourages employees to become shareholders (by putting up 25¢ for every $1 an employee invests), and almost half the workforce has done so.

As a federally regulated company, B.C. Tel must have an employment equity program. Its efforts to promote qualified women have been successful, and the results exceed the Canadian labor force average. Women represent 44% of the total payroll, 29.7% of management and 18.7% of the executive ranks.

Donald Champion, vice-president of administration, says the company has reduced its workforce by about 2,000 since 1981 (about half through early retirements, the rest by attrition), increased its efficiency and improved sales. "It has been a very satisfactory period for us in those terms," he explains.

"We have tried to keep employees aware of competition and to help them to understand the impact," Champion adds. "When you come from 100 years of being a regulated monopoly, it is very difficult for employees to make that transition. Many of them joined the company because of the high degree of security that is involved, and it is very difficult for them to change, to adapt to that."

In recent surveys, more than 90% of employees said they would recommend B.C. Tel to their friends as a good place to work. Three quarters of management employees and two thirds of nonmanagement employees said they would stay with B.C. Tel if offered similar jobs with another company at similar pay.

While B.C. Tel has lost some market share in the terminal and data business, it had not lost business in the one area it is most concerned about — long distance service.

B.C. Tel is a fine case study of how competition's stiff breezes have reinvigorated a once-complacent monopoly. Management, acutely aware of the possibilities of losing market share, preaches the doctrine of quality and excellence, and employees now respond with enthusiasm.

These days everyone hired by B.C. Tel, including blue collar workers, undergoes psychological testing. Test procedures have been modified to try to select people who are entrepreneurial-minded — risk-takers rather than those seeking a high degree of security.

B.C. Tel is making the right connection to accommodate changing times.

CANADA TRUST

275 Dundas Street
London, Ontario
N6AZ 4S4
(519) 663-1400

Pay: **AVERAGE**	Atmosphere: **VERY GOOD**
Benefits: **VERY GOOD**	Job Satisfaction: **VERY GOOD**
Promotion: **GOOD**	Communications: **VERY GOOD**
Job Security: **VERY GOOD**	Personal Development: **VERY GOOD**

★ *Canada Trust is the commonly used name for Canada Trustco Mortgage Co. and its wholly owned subsidiary, Canada Trust Co. They are in turn owned by holding company CT Financial Services Inc. The group is owned by holding company Imasco Ltd. of Montreal. Canada Trust is the country's largest and oldest trust company, with assets of $29 billion and net earnings of $232 million in 1988. It has about 11,500 full-time employees and 4,200 real estate representatives in more than 532 locations. The company has an executive office in Toronto.*

CANADA TRUST has gone through turbulent changes since 1985 — first having been swallowed by Genstar Corp., then merged with Canada Permanent Mortgage Corp. Genstar was then taken over by Imasco. Yet, throughout this process, Canada Trust has remained a fine place to work.

Much of the credit must go to Merv Lahn, chairman and CEO, who has maintained a large measure of autonomy and management continuity throughout a potentially troubling period.

In 1985, enthusiastic employees who enjoyed working for the company said very positive things:

- "I think the three words that stand out most in my mind are opportunity, challenge and, most of all, recognition."

- "There's no limit to where you can go. I feel Canada Trust really supports you to the hilt."
- "It's a very people-managed company. Everybody cares about one another. We help each other."

In 1989, employees were still saying positive things:

- "If you want to move ahead here, your options are open."
- "The best thing about working at Canada Trust is the open style of management."

This is a company that recognizes initiative and encourages independent action. And as the company moves into the 1990s, the new emphasis is on career development."Our competitive edge is people," says Duncan Tilly, vice-president of human resources.

A five-step job evaluation emphasizes career development. At the start of the year, employees discuss their personal objectives with their managers. There are at least two reviews a year in addition to a yearend in September. "Managers are committed to never surprising anyone with the final review," a manager says. Part of the final review covers career development, and employees identify talents they would like to develop further in the coming year.

Training is a big part of the company's commitment to career development. "I have never been told that we can't afford training," one supervisor says. "It is worth its weight in gold."

"There is a growing recognition that continual attention to training is the key to stability and fulfilling our strategies," Tilly says. "We surveyed our employees and the No. 1 factor that motivated them was training. Training gives you a competitive edge."

Canada Trust has set up a facility, Canada Trust Management Institute, to give supervisory personnel regular management training. Many of the employees are finding the lessons invaluable. "I'm new to management," a former student explains. "I learned how to deal with staff as 'people.' " Many courses are open to all levels, from the most junior teller up, broadening opportunities for improvement and advancement.

"Your future is yours," one employee says. "If you do a good job, they reward you for it." A supervisor adds: "I am allowed to make decisions without going through eight layers of approval. They trust us to make decisions. Even if it turns out to be a wrong one, they don't thump you."

"You have got to tolerate mistakes," Tilly says. "Otherwise, how do people learn?"

Canada Trust has a toll-free hot line for employees with grievances, and a neutral arbitrator who will help to resolve problems between employees and managers.

Another big plus is the generous benefits package. In addition to pension, health, dental and vision care, the company offers some extras. There's a stock-purchase plan, to which Canada Trust contributes 25¢ for every $1 contributed by the employee. And if the company's return on equity exceeds 17%, the company's contribution may rise to a 50¢-a-dollar ceiling.

Other extras include a 20% mortgage discount (up to a maximum of $75,000) as well as comparable discounts on loans and other financial services.

The company would not divulge pay data, but employees rate their pay as average for the financial-services industry. "We're not going to get rich working at Canada Trust," a branch manager explains, "but we're going to live very comfortably."

However, pay for entry level positions, particularly tellers, is considered too low. Several managers admit they are well paid, but wish they had larger budgets for their tellers' salaries. "After all, they're in the front lines, dealing with customers. They're really our customer-service representatives," a manager says.

Salary administration is another area of contention. The system by which performance pay is allocated, together with Canada Trust's complex salary structure, sometimes means that accepting a promotion reduces an employee's salary. Most employees say this area tops the list of problems in the company.

There are also complaints about the low number of women in senior management. In a group of some 50 top managers, there are only five or six women. Some employees feel Canada Trust is not as accomodating as it could be with women. They cite the lack of extended maternity leave and flexible hours for working mothers.

Canada Trust is an exciting, friendly place to work for the ambitious employee who wants training and development opportunities. "As far as the industry goes, Canada Trust is No. 1," an employee says. "The best company is going to be here tomorrow and deliver the best products. I think the challenge is to be with Canada Trust."

 CARGILL

CARGILL LTD.

Box 5900
300 - 240 Graham Avenue
Winnipeg, Manitoba
R3C 4C5
(204) 947-6251

Pay: **AVERAGE**	Atmosphere: **GOOD**
Benefits: **GOOD**	Job Satisfaction: **GOOD**
Promotion: **VERY GOOD**	Communications: **AVERAGE**
Job Security: **AVERAGE**	Personal Development: **GOOD**

★ *Cargill is a wholly owned subsidiary of Minneapolis-based Cargill Inc., which has operations in 40 countries. The Canadian operation (annual sales: more than $1 billion) employs about 1,700 people from Quebec to British Columbia in the livestock, feed, seed and agricultural chemical industries, as well as in grain merchandising, its lifeblood. The company operates more than 110 country grain elevators*

CARGILL HAS the reputation of being one of the most aggressively managed companies in Canadian agribusiness. So it's not too surprising to learn that its president, Kerry Hawkins, was promoted to the job while still in his mid-40s and that many of the regional and division managers are still in their 30s.

The company has a strong belief in promoting from within, and it's anxious to attract bright talent. To do so, it has worked hard to dispel the belief that the grain business is dull.

The director of human resources, Bob Johnson, with Cargill since 1974, says when he first ventured onto university campuses, he practically had to stand in the halls and say to students: "Hey, do you want to come in for an interview." He comments: "Cargill Grain did not seem very sexy to someone who had just finished four years in commerce and his buddies were going to Procter & Gamble."

While it is of limited value to junior employees, being part of a multinational organization offers very definite opportunities for advancement to the ambitious. Canadian managers have moved to Cargill operations in Australia, Switzerland, the U.S., Britain and Brazil.

Cargill views itself very much as a growth company in Canada. In 1985, Hawkins was spending about 20% of his time looking at opportunities for expansion. This work has borne fruit. Since the first edition of this book was published in 1986, Cargill has moved strongly into Eastern Canada by buying the grain division of Maple Leaf Mills (300-350 employees) in Chatham, Ont., and the fertilizer division of Cyanamid (120-130 employees) in Markham, Ont. Almost a third of its workforce is now in Ontario and Quebec.

Cargill has also built a $50-million beef slaughtering and processing plant at High River, Alta., which went into operation in 1989.

An example of rapid promotion is Rick Hill who, at 29, was made the controller of the High River project, which has a payroll of about 470. He was recruited directly from the commerce program at Concordia University in Montreal. At Cargill, he worked his way through several internal auditing jobs at a fast clip, getting promoted at times before he felt he was completely ready. "I've been very fortunate in my career. I've been at the right place at the right time." He says Cargill has lived up to every promise it made in its campus recruiting. The company is exciting to work for, he explains, and its rapid growth offers great chances for promotion.

Other employees concur. One woman manager said she had had four different types of jobs in five years. "When I look back, it has been very good. Sometimes you are thrown into a position that you are not quite prepared for. If they are short of people, or they feel you can do that, they will [let you] do it and challenge you."

A secretary said when she went to work for Cargill, her friends said: "Why do you want to work for a big place like that? There are so many employees there, you will get lost in the shuffle. But I don't find that; if you talk to people, they respond. I think it is a great place to work."

Cargill has a system of employee involvement teams, roughly patterned on the Japanese working circles. Small groups of employees meet regularly to suggest improvements in working conditions or procedures. Three subjects are taboo: personalities, company policy and pay (which is about average for the industry).

Cargill, like an increasing number of companies, offers employees counseling on drug and alcohol abuse. While the problem is not big, the counseling is certainly useful. One manager says: "I am very grateful because it saved my life. I was called in by my boss, but they had searched out a practical answer [referral to the Alcoholism Foundation of Manitoba] before confronting me."

Joy Gardiner, an accounting clerk, who moves on crutches, calls Cargill a caring company. She says most interviewers have a negative response to a disabled person. "I would send out my resumé in the mail, and I would get letters indicating that they were interested in me, but when I went to the interviews I was given the brush-off. But with Cargill and the people who interviewed me, I felt totally different. I felt they were willing to hire me on my ability. They are willing to compromise if the filing cabinet is too far away or my desk needs to be in a certain area, they are willing to do anything. Here I feel totally comfortable."

The company is decentralized. "You just can't manage a business as large as Cargill with a half dozen managers in Winnipeg removed from the operations." says Jim Prokopanko, general manager of the Ontario based fertilizer division. Responsibilities that used to be carried out by the divisional head office are being pushed down to the local level.

Accounting is an example. Previously the Ontario head office took care of accounts payable for the division. "When it's your name that goes on the bottom of the cheque you feel more responsible," says Prokopanko, referring to local managers. "Now local offices deal directly with suppliers to solve billing problems."

"You are given the responsibility to do the job, and management doesn't tell you what to do," says an employee who has been through four different responsibilities in three years. Adds another: "it's as close as you can come to running your own business."

The company policy of hiring from within, as a manager points out, means one promotion can have a domino effect, resulting in four or five different employees changing jobs. Job changes are also fostered by annual reviews, in which employees identify job related objectives with their immediate managers. "It allows you to shape your own destiny," as one employee puy it.

Another adds: "The agriculture economy may not be the best at this time, but we are with the best company. We are head and shoulders above our competition."

Management makes a point of talking to all workers. "Cargill makes everyone at the plant level feel important. If the little guys feel important, they will work for the company," says a female employee. A worker in the industry for 20 years and unused to such treatment agrees: "When [head office] managers come around, they don't only go into the manager's office. They come around and talk to employees on the plant floor." For Proko-panko, this direct contact is essential to stay in touch with what is really going on in the company.

But in an organization as large and diverse as Cargill, the atmosphere naturally varies from location to location. At the Nutrena Feeds division in St. Boniface, Man., for example, there was some unease in 1989 following a corporate restructuring that passed control of the division from Canada to Minneapolis. The transition hasn't always been smooth.

There were also some concerns about job security, and it was not always clear to employees what was expected of them by head office in the U.S.

Taken overall, though, Cargill is a great place to grow in agribusiness.

FINNING

FINNING LTD.

Great Northern Way
Vancouver, British Columbia
V5T 1E2
(604) 872-4444

Pay: **GOOD**	Atmosphere: **VERY GOOD**
Benefits: **POOR**	Job Satisfaction: **GOOD**
Promotion: **POOR**	Communications: **AVERAGE**
Job Security: **AVERAGE**	Personal Development: **AVERAGE**

★ *Finning sells, leases and services Caterpillar earth-moving equipment throughout British Columbia, Alberta, Yukon and the Northwest Territories. About 63% of the 1,510 employees are unionized by the International Association of Machinists & Aerospace Workers. Vancouver-based Finning has 24 sales, parts and service facilities in British Columbia, Alberta, Saskatchewan and Washington state. It also has service depots in eight locations and resident representatives in 11 others. It has a wholly owned subsidiary in Britain, Finning Ltd.*

WORKER MORALE at Finning has remained consistently high in good times and bad. This is testimony to astute management, because Finning, long regarded as one of Vancouver's better employers, rides the same economic roller-coaster as its customers in the construction, forest and mining industries.

During the recession of the early 1980s, the company suffered, but remained in the black throughout. Late in the decade, it was enjoying the heady experience of a full-throttle economy. In 1988, Finning's North American earnings of $21 million exceeded the previous high set in 1979.

Fully 70% of Finning employees are shareholders under an

easy-purchase scheme. Employees feel they not only are better paid than workers in comparable firms, but also enjoy an enviable harmony in their workplace. The company has never had a strike or lockout, and union shop stewards are proud that most grievances are settled without costly formal arbitration.

Bob Garrity, who in 1989 had been chief shop steward at Finning for 13 years, said he discouraged his members from filing formal grievances when problems arose, finding it more effective to take a low key approach. "I talk to Charlie Loyst [the human resources vice-president] about a problem, and he doesn't have to take an official stand on it. Once the company takes an official position, it is hard to move."

Finning has an informality that employees appreciate. There are few titles, no one stands on ceremony and senior executives line up with hourly paid workers for lunch in the cafeteria — sitting wherever there happens to be a vacant chair.

Small gestures by management also make them more popular on the shop floor. One incident is typical. Finning regularly bought Vancouver Canucks hockey tickets to entertain customers. Those not used were given to the office staff. When a shop steward suggested a more egalitarian distribution, a big supply of tickets soon arrived at the plant. And they continue to arrive.

Hourly rated workers say management's responsiveness is good. There are monthly meetings at which shop stewards can invite anyone from senior management to discuss problems. But a number of employees say communications between branches, spread across Western Canada, could still be improved.

Toward the end of the 1980s, Finning was experiencing difficulty in recruiting skilled tradesmen. It offered its employees a $500 recruiting fee for every heavy duty mechanic they introduced into the firm.

Despite the shortage of experienced workers, Finning introduced a scheme in 1989 that enables workers to retire on a generous pension at age 61, rather than 65. Garrity praises Finning for this, because it was a company initiative and not a result of collective bargaining.

Human Resources Vice-President Loyst says the early retirement scheme became possible because of the strong success of pension investments, managed by outside consultants. Finning has for years enabled workers to take early retirement on an ad hoc basis, recognizing the strenuous physical demands made on a heavy duty mechanic.

Employees praise management for going ahead with long-range projects even while the company was struggling through the early-1980s recession. For example, it invested then in a successful remanufacturing centre, where used equipment is refurbished and given an extended life.

During difficult times at the bottom of the economic cycle in the early 1980s, Finning also bought two Caterpillar dealerships in Britain. This turned out to be a smart investment, and the British operations now account for 43% of Finning's bottom line.

In September, 1989, Finning made another significant move when it took over R. Angus Alberta Ltd., an Edmonton-based Caterpillar dealer with 900 employees in nine locations throughout Alberta and the Northwest Territiories. This $220-million purchase made Finning the largest Caterpillar dealer in North America — and possibly the world.

Angus itself was a large operation, with 1988 revenues of $270 million and total assets of $175 million. Finning decided to take an arm's length approach to Angus' personnel policies, and indicated it was in no hurry to change Angus pay scales, pensions and other benefits.

Finning's exhibits a social conscience by the way it encourages employees to support the annual United Way campaign. It offers prizes ranging up to two weeks' extra vacation for employees who donate a day's wages to the charity drive. Employee participation has been as high as 90%.

In good times and bad, in a tough business, *Finning does care.*

HALLMARK CARDS CANADA

2 Hallcrown Place
Willowdale, Ontario
M2J 1P6
(416) 492-1300

Pay: **GOOD**	Atmosphere: **VERY GOOD**
Benefits: **GOOD**	Job Satisfaction: **VERY GOOD**
Promotion: **VERY GOOD**	Communications: **GOOD**
Job Security: **EXCELLENT**	Personal Development: **VERY GOOD**

★ *Hallmark manufactures and distributes greeting cards and other social-expression products. The company has 1,467 full-time and 1,412 part-time employees in 112 retail stores across Canada, a distribution centre in Aurora, Ont., a sales office in Montreal, and a Toronto head office and manufacturing site. Sales in 1988 exceeded $150 million. The company is a wholly owned subsidiary of Hallmark Cards Inc. of Kansas City, Mo.*

HALLMARK'S SLOGAN, "When you care enough, send the very best," has been adopted and modified by employees: "When you care enough, you do your very best."

John Kempster, president of Hallmark Canada, believes "99.9% of employees want to do a good job. You just have to give them an opportunity to do it." The company gives employees that chance through a program of continuous improvement.

One employee in the order department believes Hallmark has been successful because it recognizes that employees provide the competitive edge. "If the order filler doesn't do the job well, Hallmark makes a mistake," one manager says.

Employees feel the emphasis on improvement is good for the company. Just-in-time delivery is becoming a widespread practice. "Companies not doing it are falling behind," another manager says. "It's good to know Hallmark doesn't have its head in the sand."

"Management aren't harping at you to get this or get that done," one worker says. "Employees know what to do and the work gets done."

Hallmark realizes that improved customer service is crucial, and the focus is not only on the traditional customer. "We are also becoming more focused on departments being customers to each other," one manager says.

The philosophy has fostered teamwork. "They make people feel that they are needed and that everybody is an important part of this company and we are all working as a team," one clerk says.

"We have weekly meetings to work on problems," another clerk adds. "Employees get involved and are recognized. Supervisors tell you they appreciate what you do."

"With the employee involvement, communication is getting better," one employee says. "People can go to their manager and express their opinion and get some feedback. Before, if you had a problem, you left it with your supervisor." Another adds:"Instead of bitching, people are more apt to work together and reach the same goals." So the program has fostered a sense of togetherness.

Emphasis on training and development helps reinforce positive attitudes toward the company. Analytic Trouble Shooting (ATS) is a week-long course open to employees. "Truth is perception. Perceptions are the product of our combined past experiences," Kempster says. "Everyone has had different experiences, so they will have a different perception on the same subject."

ATS gives employees a common language and method of problem solving. As a result, decision making at Hallmark is more focused. "ATS can be applied to anything — to your home life or your job," one employee says. "It is a questioning process. It emphasizes teamwork — if you have a problem, it is not just your problem."

Hallmark Canada pays 100% of all successfully completed external courses, and employees are encouraged to take first-aid

200

and CPR courses. Education is also emphasized through cross training. An employee of 37 years points out that employees benefit by learning new skills, which increase opportunities for promotion and lateral transfers, while the company benefits from having a more skilled and interchangeable work force.

"Literally hundreds of employees a year are moved through the skills-exchange network to help departments with a heavy workload," one supervisor says. "It improves the atmosphere and employees appreciate the new experiences, meeting new employees and seeing how different departments work." The exchange has helped break down barriers and improve communication among departments.

All jobs below that of manager are posted internally. Management would rather promote a good worker who has been with the company for five years, but may be lacking skills, and train her than hire somebody from outside who may quit after six months. Employees appreciate Hallmark's loyalty to them, and they in turn do a better job.

Despite the emphasis on continuous improvement, one supervisor feels the company is still "too conservative and unwilling to take chances and move ahead as fast as we can." An employee of seven years agrees: "We are a subsidiary of a large U.S. parent and, as a result, we are not as creative, innovative or dynamic as we would be if on our own. We do not have the R & D that takes place in the U.S. — we simply look at their innovations and cherry pick. We are too dependent on the U.S. parent, which impedes change." These employees feel Hallmark Canada should become more aggressive in assuming a lead in some areas.

The company's emphasis on personal development has created some problems. Employees who have taken ATS expect "things are going to change overnight," one manager says. "When they see things aren't happening right away, they get down about it. It will take time." Moreover, as some have yet to take the course, employees are operating at different speeds. It is Kempster's hope that everyone will have taken ATS by 1991.

"Because we haven't always had the authority to do things on our own, we have to learn to walk before we run," one salesman says. "As we get better at it, maybe we will have the opportunity to do things on our own."

In addition to all the traditional benefits, there is a subsidized cafeteria in the Markham headquarters. Employees can also have a free card every day and 100 free cards at Christmas. And they pay only a nominal rate for wedding invitations — the money goes to charity. The company takes care of its employees in times of difficulty. "If you need time off for a problem, you can take it," one says. And Hallmark has a strong social and family orientation. Activities centre on a different sport each season, such as bowling, curling, hockey and baseball. There is a Christmas party for children, aged 10 and under, where each receives a generous gift. The company also holds an annual summer picnic.

The seasonal nature of the card business means that work is not spread evenly throughout the year. "We hire a lot of people during peak periods on a temporary basis," the manager of personnel administration says. "They know when they start that is the case. We have never laid off a permanent employee."

"Hallmark is very well known as being a secure place to work," an employee of five years says. "You have to go out of your way to cause trouble to get fired."

Employees are proud of the company. "It is a fun product. Everybody gets pleasure out of greeting cards," one engineer says. And employees are proud of Hallmark's ethics. "The company tries to do the right thing for the customers, the suppliers and retailers," a new employee says. "That makes it easy for me to say its a good company to work for."

Hallmark is a company that shows traditional care and concern for employees, while offering interesting and varied work experience and a strong sense of security.

HAYES-DANA INC.

1 St. Paul Street
P.O. Box 3029
St. Catharines, Ontario
L2R 7K9
(416) 687-4200

Pay: **GOOD**	Atmosphere: **VERY GOOD**
Benefits: **GOOD**	Job Satisfaction: **VERY GOOD**
Promotion: **VERY GOOD**	Communications: **VERY GOOD**
Job Security: **AVERAGE**	Personal Development: **VERY GOOD**

★ *Hayes-Dana, with seven divisions and 10 plants, manufactures and distributes automotive components. In 1988, the company (52% owned by the Dana Corp. of Toledo, Ohio) reported net income of almost $22 million on record sales of $570 million. There are about 2,400 employees across Canada, 53% of whom are unionized, many by the Canadian Autoworkers.*

THE WORD "excellence" is used a lot at Hayes-Dana. The company doesn't hesitate to study the best in other countries' manufacturing facilities and adopt what it finds.

In particular, it is willing to learn a great deal from the Japanese. Take, for example, the ideal of "excellence in manufacturing." EIM companies strive for zero defects, zero inventory, zero through time and zero set-up time. Hayes-Dana admits these goals may be hard to reach but it's prepared to make the effort.

Rank and file employees play a big part in the pursuit of excellence. As part of its EIM program, selected employees undergo intensive six-week training sessions, including classroom work and two-week plant tours in Japan. Those selected are known as "facilitators." Most are in management, although hourly workers have also been picked. Candidates are chosen for their ability to absorb what they see and pass it on to fellow workers.

Facilitators return to their plants "full of piss and vinegar," as one executive puts it. They lead the management team through the improvement process and co-ordinate individual teams of plant people to work on specific problems. Getting plant-level workers involved in productivity improvement pays off. In many facilities, cost reductions of 50% or more have occurred through cuts in through time, inventory levels and direct labor hours.

Hayes-Dana runs a much leaner operation than in the past. Its total workforce has been cut by about 600 people since 1986. The reduction was achieved mostly through attrition. The company has periodically laid off people as orders have dried up. It has chipped away at payroll by recalling fewer workers when production started up again. And about 200 workers moved with the sale of one of its divisions.

For those who remain, Hayes-Dana is a stimulating place to work.

Part of the company philosophy is to push responsibility downward or, in current jargon, to "empower" lower-level employees to think and act for themselves. "Involve everyone; make every employee a manager; communicate fully; [and] let the people decide, where possible." These statements are part of the corporate guidelines. Outsiders are sometimes astonished that the system works.

The philosophy (known simply as the Hayes-Dana style) also states: "Control only what's important; decentralize; provide automony; simplify; minimize paper use; discourage conformity; break organizational barriers; [and] keep facilities under 500 people." Accordingly, Hayes-Dana doesn't have "top management." There are no corporate procedure manuals, and the term "paperwork" has an almost derisive connotation.

The organization chart shows only four levels, and the fourth consists of "PEOPLE" whose function is "participation."

The organization functions on a statement of "goals and policies." Within the framework of those basic rules, division managers run their operations as they see fit.

The Hayes-Dana style, for example, calls for promotion from

within, while other mandates state: "Share the rewards; provide stability of income and employment; [and] make all Hayes-Dana people shareholders." Each operation must honor the principles, but there's no uniform way of doing it.

As a result, there are no corporate pay scales or benefit packages. Even in unionized plants, these factors depend on each facility's financial situation.

In general, however, Hayes-Dana figures its people come out near the top in the automotive league.

And there are other differences. In some operations, employees are salaried regardless of their work. All divisions share productivity gains, but some do so through individual incentive programs and others through group bonuses.

There's only one company-wide benefit — the stock-purchase plan. For every $1 an employee invests in the purchase of Hayes-Dana shares, the company adds 25¢.

There's an interesting example of Hayes-Dana's attitude toward its employees involving the plant at Barrie, Ont., which produces heavy-duty axles. As far as the company is concerned, the people who make axles are uniquely equipped to talk about them.

Potential customers are encouraged to ask them. Visitors won't get a skilled marketing pitch on the plant floor, "but they'll get the truth," says Paul Redfearn, general manager, regional assembly division. "We're very open with anybody who wants to come in here and talk to our people."

They still talk about the time when Volvo put its axle business up for bids in Canada. A team of Swedish experts arrived at the Hayes-Dana drive-train facility, where the division manager stunned his visitors by ushering them out of the offices and into the plant.

"It blew their minds," McLaughlin recalls. "He went out on the floor and took those men with him. He stopped the operation, called the axle people around and said, 'Here are the guys from Volvo. Here's what they want. Can you do it?' "

The workers delivered an emphatic "yes," McLaughlin says. "Our guys committed themselves to it. Management didn't commit them to it. As a result, Volvo came back and said, 'Okay, you'll be the sole supplier.' "

Hayes-Dana has proven to be a great place to work for the person who doesn't want to sit back and take orders.

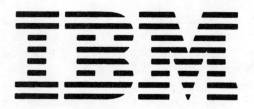

IBM CANADA LTD.

3500 Steeles Avenue East
Markham, Ontario
L3R 2Z1
(416) 474-2111

Pay: **VERY GOOD**	Atmosphere: **VERY GOOD**
Benefits: **EXCELLENT**	Job Satisfaction: **GOOD**
Promotion: **GOOD**	Communications: **VERY GOOD**
Job Security: **EXCELLENT**	Personal Development: **GOOD**

★ *IBM is by far the largest Canadian computer company, generating about one third of all computer industry revenue, with products ranging from mainframes to PCs. The company has more than 12,605 employees, offices across the country and two manufacturing plants, in Metro Toronto and Bromont, Que. Annual revenues are $3.7 billion. The firm is a wholly owned subsidiary of IBM World Trade Corp., Armonk, N.Y.*

PEOPLE WHO work for IBM just love the sense of identity with "Big Blue," as the company is sometimes called. It's a sense of security, of belonging to one of the biggest and best. If you make the grade, and it's not easy, because IBM has exacting standards, you'll have a stimulating job.

More than 70 years ago, IBM founder Thomas J. Watson instilled these beliefs in the organization:

● Respect for the individual: We care about the dignity and rights of each person in the organization.

● Customer Service: We work to give the best customer service of any company in the world.

• Excellence: We believe that all jobs should be done in a superior way.

"We recognize that people are our most important asset," says Pat McCue, director of personnel relations. "Our full employment tradition means that our employees can be confident of job security. The result is a high level of commitment on the part of our employees."

It would be hard to remain uncommitted to a company that does many things so well for its people. The benefits are extremely comprehensive and include all the usual programs, as well as some extraordinary perks, such as a program of financial assistance for the special care of mentally or physically disabled children. IBM pays 80% of the expenses involved in adopting a child. The company doubles any gift to a university, college or hospital up to a maximum of $5,000. IBM pays for fitness courses and successfully completed stop-smoking courses. Women on maternity leave receive 95% of their salary for six weeks. There is an assisted stock-purchase plan and part-time employees who work half the average week receive pro-rated benefits.

IBM will reimburse 100% of tuition fees, and registration fees, and course the cost of textbooks after successful completion of a recognized course. In addition, children of all regular, retired or deceased employees are eligible for 12 university scholarships of $2,000 annually, and six community-college scholarships of $1,000 per year. Employees who take an education leave of up to one year are guaranteed a job at the same salary — and, while they are away, receive extended health-care coverage.

Communication is another area where the company tries to excel. IBM has instituted a number of programs to eliminate that "getting-lost-in-the-shuffle" feeling, which can happen all too easily in a company of more than 12,000 employees. An open-door policy enshrines the principle of a worker's right to discuss any problem with his manager. Employees meet annually with their immediate supervisor, and can confidentially submit complaints, questions or comments. The letter is forwarded by a co-ordinator to the appropriate senior executive, who respond via the co-ordinator.

Performance evaluations are an integral part of the company's incentive system. All employees are evaluated annually, and pay increases are determined on this basis. Standards are high. Employees must rate three rungs above the satisfactory level to be considered outstanding.

IBM's job-security net (in *Canada* in *1989,* we emphasize) was so firm that employees did not appear worried about the rigorous evaluation scheme. As one worker said: "Even if you're not performing, you get a chance to improve."

Merit pay is only one of several incentives used to make people at IBM strive for greater productivity and excellence. One of the smallest but most satisfying rewards is descriptively called "Dinner for Two." This $90 award is one any manager can offer in recognition of individual effort.

IBM's suggestion program recognizes money-saving or revenue-generating ideas, and pays workers 25% of the company's savings in the first two years. In 1985, Brenda Boyd received $118,994 for a suggestion concerning warranty extensions. And in 1989, she received $200,000 — the maximum allowed — making her the largest winner in the company's history. "A computer may be installed in January but actually purchased in June," Boyd says. "Though the customers do not begin paying for the machine until June, they are obliged to pay for maintenance from the January date." Because of Boyd's clarification, IBM is collecting $1 million of revenue a year that had previously been overlooked.

Because IBM refuses to divulge pay information, verification depends on what IBM personnel tell outsiders. Former employees say pay is high at Big Blue, but one programmer says, "When you take into account how hard they expect you to work, it's not really that high." IBM will also not release figures on the number of women in its work force.

IBM supports a range of community health and welfare, civic, cultural and educational activities. Their 1988 contributions, in the form of cash grants, equipment and other resources, totalled more than $3 million.

Each summer, IBM hires about 1,600 students, in addition to hiring 900 co-op students during the year.

Not everyone loves working at IBM. Comments from those who have left the fold indicate some of the problems:

● "The sheer size of the organization and resultant bureaucracy are negative qualities."

● "The corporate spirit is too stifling and doesn't leave enough room for individual effort and recognition."

● "Being successful in so large a company means playing

company politics."

- "Sales predominate over other areas in the company — so it's tough to get ahead if you're in another department."
- "It's not a good place to work if you're an average performer."

But some former employees extol the virtues of having worked for IBM:

- "It's a good place to come from, and there's great technical training."
- "They have a fast-trackers program for women."
- And last, but certainly not least, "IBM is a winner, and it's great to work for a winner."

Imperial Oil

IMPERIAL OIL LTD.

111 St. Clair Avenue West
Toronto, Ontario
M5W 1K3
(416) 968-4111

Pay: **VERY GOOD**	Atmosphere: **GOOD**
Benefits: **VERY GOOD**	Job Satisfaction: **GOOD**
Promotion: **GOOD**	Communications: **VERY GOOD**
Job Security: **VERY GOOD**	Personal Development: **GOOD**

★ *Imperial Oil is Canada's largest energy company, with 1988 revenues of $7.2 billion. It has 10,697 employees, based in virtually every major urban centre. U.S.-based Exxon Corp. owns 69.6% of Imperial's equity. Most of the other shareholders are registered in Canada.*

COMPENSATION HAS TO be one of the main factors that make Imperial a good place to work. Imperial pays *extremely* well. "When I was approached to come to Imperial, it took me 10 minutes to decide," says a librarian. "Not only were the benefits good, but the money was unbelievable."

"We like the benefits," says a controller. "People outside Imperial can't believe them." The benefits package has such extras as refunds for physical fitness, hearing aids and eyeglasses. All benefits (including the pension plan) are company-paid, with the exception of 50% orthodontic coverage.

Under the savings plan, employees can contribute up to 5% of their salary, which the company matches dollar for dollar. There's a share-ownership plan, too. The company provides

$1,800 scholarships to children of present employees and retirees, provided the students leave high school with averages of 70% or higher. Thereafter, students only have to stay enrolled in university to renew the scholarship. For employees, Imperial refunds 100% of all tuition and book fees upon successful completion of work-related courses.

"We are tagged as a very conservative company, but we are changing," says an employee of 18 years. Imperial introduced a leadership challenge program in 1989 to improve managers' "people skills" and focus on company core values. "It's too early to tell how well it will work, but a lot of money is being spent on it. Two thousand managers will go through it in the next 18 months," one gas station manager commented.

Imperial is changing from a paternalistic company to one that encourages employee creativity and initiative. Management feels this leads to more committed and productive workers. Employees seem extremely loyal, hard-working and dedicated to accepting challenges.

Employees are proud of Imperial's highly ethical stance. "I've never had to question the ethics of anything we're doing," says one employee of more than 20 years. "I've never been asked to compromise myself."

"We could save a lot of money by cutting corners," adds another, "but we just don't do it. We sometimes spend millions of dollars on one cleanup, and no one ever asks, 'Is it necessary?' "

In 1989, a proposed merger of Imperial Oil with Texaco Canada was a major challenge for Imperial's employees. Newsletters kept employees constantly updated. Those not working directly on the merger took on extra workloads to keep the base businesses running smoothly.

A manager comments: "At times like the merger, 12-to-14-hour days become a way of life." And long hours were common for several months after the merger was first proposed.

"People work long hours at this company," says an employee of eight years, "but not all the time. If I am working longer hours on a project, once the project finishes I don't hesitate to leave early if there is nothing to do. It's up to you to manage your time."

In normal times, employees can take every third Friday off, in return for an extra half-hour's work daily.

Career development is an employee's responsibility. "It used

211

to be that your manager worked out your career path for you. Now it is up to you to manage it yourself," says an employee in retail sales. "And there are so many opportunities in this company."

Imperial was one of the first companies in Canada to index pensions for inflation voluntarily. The first $16,000 of pensions are indexed, and "while it is only about half the rate of inflation, the point is the company doesn't have to do it at all." says an employee of 27 years.

Out of concern for employee health, the company has health centres with staff physicians and industrial hygienists. If asked for, their services are available to all workers. All employees under 40 are entitled to a company medical examination every five years; those between 41 and 50, every two years; beyond 50, annually.

In employees' eyes, some areas require improvement. "Women are having a tough time breaking into management," says a female employee of 18 years. In 1989, women made up 23% of the total workforce, but only 6% of managers.

"Women get to a certain level and quit. Once they start getting higher, they perceive they have to be like a man to get ahead. Forget ever having children, forget ever being married and having a home life. In order to get into upper management, they either have to have a husband who stays at home or they give up their family. Women are saying times have to change."

Apart from complaints like that, Imperial Oil stands out as a generous, stimulating, challenging, people-oriented and responsible company to work for.

JACOBS SUCHARD CANADA INC.

P.O. Box 2170
Vancouver, British Columbia
V6B 3V6
(604) 420-2511

Pay: **VERY GOOD**	Atmosphere: **VERY GOOD**
Benefits: **GOOD**	Job Satisfaction: **GOOD**
Promotion: **AVERAGE**	Communications: **GOOD**
Job Security: **VERY GOOD**	Personal Development: **AVERAGE**

★ *Jacobs Suchard, through its Nabob Foods Division, roasts coffee at its plant in Burnaby, B.C., and markets it across Canada. It also produces packaged tea. The Coffex Division produces decaffeinated coffee for the North American "gourmet" trade. The company also markets Suchard and Tobler confectionery products imported from Europe. It has about 180 employees, 45% of whom are in manufacturing, the rest in sales and administration. About 40% of its employees are members of the United Food & Commercial Workers Union. The company, a wholly owned subsidiary of Jacobs Suchard AG of Zurich, Switzerland, has annual sales of more than $100 million.*

GETTING HIRED by Jacobs Suchard is a bit like taking holy orders. The recruiting process is rigorous, because the company searches both for technical skills and congeniality. One blue-collar production worker says he was called in for five interviews and asked to take a psychological test before being offered a job. His conclusion: Jacobs is a fine company that cares for its employees and makes them feel like important team players.

Certainly the company works hard at making employees feel

at home. The president invites new workers to his office for coffee and a brief chat. He often walks through the plant, not to check up on operations, but to see if the workers are happy.

About 13% of Jacobs employees belong to the Quarter Century Club (and in 1989 a 96-year-old retired worker was still turning up for company sponsored social events). Obviously, a mature workforce and a low 6.7% annual turnover rate don't make for plentiful promotional opportunities.

The company does encourage excellence, however. It keeps a sharp eye on the competition, and expects its employees to hustle to stay out in front. Several workers point with approval to a credo that states: "Our company is built on exceptional teamwork and high growth orientation. Our people are dedicated to building their company through an entrepreneurial spirit which encourages innovation. We strive to be 'Number 1' in everything we do."

Jacobs Suchard Canada's predecessor was launched in 1894 as a tea and spice company by Kelly Douglas. It was a subsidiary of the Weston grocery empire until 1976, when it was acquired by Jacobs, the leading coffee roaster in Switzerland, Germany and Austria.

At the time of the Jacobs acquisition, the company was handling too many products and losing money, says President John Bell. "We made a decision that we could do well in one or two areas," he recalls.

The reorganization was difficult. From a payroll of 550, the company cut back to 140 by 1983. Since then, it has obviously grown again.

In 1980-81 the company suffered a five-and-a-half-month strike/lockout, Bell recalls. "It was really the survival of the company. All of our employees were on a four-day work week. We had to become a low-cost producer to survive."

He adds: "Today, we have a wonderful relationship with the unions." If there is any lingering bitterness from that lengthy labor dispute, it is not in any way apparent.

In 1976, the Nabob division introduced vacuum bag and "quick roast" technology. Those innovations, the company says, have been important in helping it gain a significant market share of the coffee business in Canada.

Jacobs tries in many ways to show employees they are important to its future. It even commissioned an original song,

The Difference is You, which was recorded by Vancouver singer Susan Jones. Everyone got a copy. In addition to the usual Christmas dinner-dance, summer picnic and so forth, the company every year takes its entire workforce to a hotel for a day to discuss progress and present recognition awards.

It tackles social events with style. One summer evening in 1989, for instance, it rented the entire Vancouver Aquarium and had a barbecue on the deck, while employees and their families watched a performing whale show. Each year, the company also presents original Christmas gifts that have included a limited-edition watercolor, season passes for Expo 86, an Expo souvenir book, a coffee maker, brandy glasses and a product hamper.

The company took issue with the questionnaire for this book, which it said was highly weighted to benefits and personnel policies. Human Resources Director Richard Ames argues it is the corporate culture that makes Jacobs Suchard a great place to work. The company encourages teamwork and recognizes achievements.

The company pays well above the food industry average. And, measured by sales per employee, it is the most productive food company in Canada. In a survey of employee attitudes, its workers ranked Jacobs Suchard at 8.1 on a scale of one (poor) to 10 (excellent).

Employees said the company is receptive to ideas, and will act on them if possible. More important, though, they value highly the pleasant "family" atmosphere.

LONDON LIFE INSURANCE CO.

255 Dufferin Avenue
London, Ontario
N6A 4K1
(519) 432-5281

Pay: **GOOD**	Atmosphere: **VERY GOOD**
Benefits: **EXCELLENT**	Job Satisfaction: **GOOD**
Promotion: **AVERAGE**	Communications: **GOOD**
Job Security: **EXCELLENT**	Personal Development: **EXCELLENT**

★ *London Life sells insurance and financial services throughout Canada. With assets of $9.3 billion and an annual return on equity averaging 16.9% from 1980 to 1989, it is a major force among Canadian life insurers. The company has 5,239 employees, of whom about half are in sales. Headquaters are in London, Ont., with close to 200 regional offices coast to coast. Through holding company Lonvest Corp., it is part of Trilon Financial Corp., a division of Brascan Ltd.*

LIFE INSURANCE companies have become exciting, career-challenging places to work in the past decade. Intense competition for qualified business employees and sales agents has sharpened workplace practices, stimulated the use of modern technology and forced companies to adopt the latest in management/staff relations techniques.

London Life has for the past 10 years been recognized as a leading proponent of change, due largely to the unconventional leadership of Earl Orser, who was appointed by Brascan in 1978. He was a rarity in the industry: an outsider and an accountant rather than an actuary.

Orser made changes to what had been a sleepy, family owned insurance company. He introduced an award-winning productivity improvement program (and later coupled it with one of the first employee gain-sharing systems in a financial institution), incentive contracts for senior executives, a new mix of senior people from outside London Life (sometimes from outside the insurance business) and detailed strategic planning.

In 1989, the gain-sharing program was reorganized to increase incentives and make payouts easier to attain. Under the new scheme, gains in productivity of between 2% and 4% are shared 100% among employees, while gains between 4% and 10% are split equally between workers and the company. In 1990, for example, an employee with an annual salary of $25,000 would receive a $750 gain share if the company had a 6% increase in productivity.

Under Orser's direction, women were promoted to management and the "women in management" results earned London Life an Employment Equity Award from the Ontario Women's Directorate in 1986. Over the past four years, the percentage of women in management has risen to 13.9% from 8.3%, and each vice-president has been given a target to achieve. Considering 70% of its workforce is female, London Life still has some catching up to do.

Flexible work hours and job-sharing opportunities took on new meaning in the 1980s because of the necessity for two-family incomes. They also fit the needs of single-parent employees. Flexible hours give employees many options, such as working a 36-hour work week over 4½ days or nine eight-hour days and having the 10th day off. Fifty people are currently part of a job-sharing program, employing a variety of work-hour options to share jobs.

The highly successful "count on me" customer-service recognition program recognizes teamwork and special efforts in serving the company's more than two million customers. Employees have their achievements published in the company newsletter, in addition to being presented with an award.

Pay levels are above average, with increases based on performance. The benefits are outstanding, offering many perks above the norm. Mortgage subsidies, for example, are offered at two times annual salary up to a limit of $100,000. A maternity benefit ensures eligible employees receive 60% of their normal salary for 15 weeks. A special Toronto allowance increases salaries by 5%, in recognition of the city's high cost of living.

A wellness subsidy pays an annual $150 toward an employee's choice of either fitness, stop-smoking or weight-control programs. Other perks include free parking; subsidized cafeteria; private park with tennis courts, baseball diamond and picnic grounds; employee assistance program; and 100% tuition-refund program.

Early in 1989, Orser was promoted to chairman, while Gordon Cunningham was named president. Cunningham, a lawyer, came to London Life from Trilon, where he had been president. He brought with him a fresh, less-structured approach to interpersonal relationships.

One of his first decisions was to remove security devices from the executive-suite doors, declaring that everyone was welcome to come and see him if they wished. "I believe if we break down some of the longstanding barriers between people and departments, we can strengthen our abilities and stimulate the total energies of all our people to be a more successful organization," Cunningham says.

He decided the name "operating committee" was a little intimidating for the executive management group, so he had it renamed the "senior-management partnership." To kick off the 1990s, he declared the first working Monday a day to celebrate both the new decade and the values of working together. No meetings or traveling were allowed and staff wore casual clothes. Nerfball golf was played through the halls and everyone was encouraged to call or visit new people and find out what they did for the company.

"I've worked in this building for 20 years and I had a good talk with someone I hadn't really seen for 10 years," one staff member says.

The new president plans to follow up the casual start of 1990 with annual employee meetings at eight locations across Canada, so everyone has a clear, personally delivered message on how well the company is doing and what is needed for continued success.

Cunningham's basic management philosophy stresses the need for everyone to commit to the same vision, purpose and values, so that success can be achieved in a world that is becoming more complex and challenging.

"We need to empower all our people and recognize that our people often know more than we do," Cunningham told a management conference. "I'm absolutely convinced that in order to be among the successful companies of the future, we will have to share a winning attitude and recognize the contribution of all. I believe in building on our legacy."

Cunningham and a management group — a team he expanded through internal appointments — like to use the acronym "TASTE," reflecting new directions in effective management. TASTE refers to trust, accountability, support, truth and effort — all necessary ingredients for winning in the 1990s.

"There's certainly a fresh, new spirit of openness around here," one long-time employee says. "Earl Orser broke us of old habits when he arrived in 1978 and helped us to appreciate our position as Canada's leading insurance company. Gordon Cunningham is now telling us that everyone's view is important and that every partner in London Life brings some special skill to the table. That's kind of exciting."

Part of London Life's challenge is having to deal with a changing market. While life insurance remains the company's core product, London Life has broadened its portfolio to provide for the needs of an aging population and customers who want sophisticated investment-, savings- and retirement-planning products.

And the company is looking far beyond its traditional markets in Canada, having opened offices in Michigan, New Jersey and Barbados. While Canada remains the primary market, potential business in Taiwan, Hong Kong and Europe is being explored. Cunningham is also anxious to broaden the potential for sales of London Life products through associated companies like Royal Trustco, Trilon, and The Optimum in Quebec, and, at the same time, strengthen the companies so they can compete with the large Canadian chartered banks.

To help London Life people think globally and deal with the complexities of the future, new emphasis is being placed on training and upgrading skills. Management has completed Phase I of an in-house training program called Management Development Institute. MDI, Phase II, focuses on leadership style and improving communication skills.

On any given day, 140 training staff provide full-time instruction at all employee levels. And in 1988, more than 980

London Life employees took post-secondary courses. Successful students were reimbursed the cost of both tuition and books.

Promotion is one of the few problems at London Life. Low turnover and the introduction of new technology have created the all-too-familiar bulge around the middle — too many talented people in middle management with nowhere to go. The situation has eased somewhat because of business growth, expansion of subsidiaries and increased work with associated Trilon companies, leading to a demand for knowledgeable workers. More people are being rotated through a variety of jobs and special projects in order to provide training and a broader experience. In 1989, more than 100 employees took advantage of the company's job-posting system to advance their careers.

"I thought we'd bitten off quite a chunk 10 years ago when we said we wanted to be the leader of our industry in the 80s," says Norton Campbell, senior vice-president of human resources. "I don't think many of us thought today we'd be confident we had reached that goal and that we'd now be planning quantum leaps onto the world stage for financial insitutions. One thing I've always believed is that our people have the skills to help that happen and, encouraged in the right way, they'll do some pretty terrific things."

MERCK FROSST CANADA INC.

MERCK FROSST CANADA INC.

16711 TransCanada Highway West
Kirkland, Quebec
H9H 3L1
(514) 630-2616

Pay: **VERY GOOD**	Atmosphere: **VERY GOOD**
Benefits: **GOOD**	Job Satisfaction: **VERY GOOD**
Promotion: **VERY GOOD**	Communications: **VERY GOOD**
Job Security: **VERY GOOD**	Personal Development: **EXCELLENT**

★ *Merck Frosst is a diversified pharmaceutical company producing prescription drugs and over-the-counter products such as 222s. The company also has a strong research and development division. Sales range from $200 million to $300 million annually. Most of the 915 employees are based at the suburban-Montreal headquarters. The firm is a wholly owned subsidiary of Merck & Co. Inc. of Rahway, N.J.*

MERCK FROSST is a company that takes pride in its achievements. "We get it done," is how employees describe their approach to business.

As a leading pharmaceutical firm, it is very conscious of its professional image within the scientific community: "We pride ourselves on the high quality of our products, and on our ethics and integrity," a sales manager explains. "As a result of this attitude, people here really believe in the place."

The atmosphere is fast paced and demanding. "The company expects a lot from you but rewards you well," one researcher says.

Employees agree Merck pays very well. It's necessary in

order to attract the kind of high flyers Merck needs to be "the pre-eminent Canadian company engaged in discovering, developing, producing and marketing high-quality, innovative, cost-effective agents for improved health care," its mission states.

The benefits are good, but there are few of the extras offered by other top-ranking firms. There's no vision care, and the stock-option plan is only open to senior people. Some improvements include increasing the fitness-club reimbursement to 100% from 50% and making early retirement possible from age 55.

Merck Frosst's management approach has changed from a traditional, hierarchical style to a more participative, consultative one. "We are less concerned about traditional structures, and work in a team," says Don Miller, vice-president, human resources and corporate affairs. "Who we report to is of less importance than what we can accomplish. We aren't hesitant now to stick our toes into other people's waters."

The one area that has shown dramatic improvement is the company's affirmative-action program. Much has changed at the manager, professional and technical-entry levels. Since 1985, the number of women in these groups has almost doubled to 27% from 14%. Overall figures for the company are also encouraging: women make up 38% of the workforce and half have reached executive ranks. In 1989, two out of three people hired in sales were women, and of 100 new employees designated management, professional or technical staff, 47 were women.

Research workers and scientists don't have to keep their noses pressed to the grindstone and concentrate solely on producing marketable pharmaceuticals. They are given the freedom and funding to work on independent research projects, and are encouraged to publish papers in scientific journals. They have developed five commercially successful pharmaceutical products since 1986, including cholesterol-reducing therapy. They also have "state-of-the-art" research equipment and are constructing a $60-million research facility in Kirkland, just outside Montreal, to be completed next year. "We are actively recruiting scientists to join the research team; this is a very exciting place to be," Miller says.

On the sales and marketing side, trainees are treated just as generously: "We have one of the most extensive training programs in Canada for sales reps," one sales manager says. Several sales people who left the company for another firm came back to Merck within two years because they missed the firm's drive, stimulus and get-ahead attitude.

Brian McLeod, vice-president of marketing, says they go beyond traditional programs and try to see things from their customers' perspective. The mentor program, for example, allows sales staff to meet four times a year with specialists and physicians to learn about medicine, diseases and customer concerns.

Job security is excellent, especially since the company announced plans to commit $200 million to Canadian research over the next four years. Spending includes construction of new research facilities. Opportunities for promotion are very good in Canada, as well as in Merck's international divisions.

Communications are thorough and professional. A quarterly management meeting allows workers to pose questions to the president. In addition, the Employees' Advisory Council, made up of employees and two vice-presidents, reviews concerns on a monthly basis. The council handles everything from the children's Christmas party to job postings.

The Merck Frosst work environment is both stimulating and demanding, and is particularly good for self-starters who prefer less structure. It's also a great place for a research scientist to develop a career.

NORANDA FOREST SALES INC.

4 King Street West
Suite 700
Toronto, Ontario
M5H 3X1
(416) 365-0710

Pay: **AVERAGE/GOOD**	Atmosphere: **VERY GOOD**
Benefits: **VERY GOOD**	Job Satisfaction: **VERY GOOD**
Promotion: **AVERAGE**	Communications: **VERY GOOD**
Job Security: **GOOD**	Personal Development: **GOOD**

★ *Noranda Forest Sales markets and distributes forest products and building materials for its parent company, Noranda Forest Inc. The subsidiary employs 225 people in Canada, the U.S., Britain and Japan. Approximately 90 employees work at the Toronto head office. Annual sales are in the region of $800 million.*

THE RECESSION of the early 1980s was particulary bad for the forest industry, and the situation at Noranda Forest Sales was no exception. In 1982, the company was just struggling to survive. In 1983-84 the company lost millions. And yet in 1989 Noranda was immensely successful and profitable, and a good place to work.

Noranda's improvement on the business side has been recognized by two awards: the 1988 Canada Award for Business Excellence in Marketing and a 1987 Canada Export Award.

The change is primarily due to the drive and determination of one man, Arkadi Bykhovsky, and the way he injected his employees with the spirit and enthusiasm to turn the organization around.

"A few years ago, all we had was a bunch of lounge puppies here, who took three-martini lunches," recalls a finance manager in disgust.

"When I first came here," adds a vice-president, "we couldn't get people to come and work for us, our reputation was so bad."

Bykhovsky joined Noranda in late 1983, after being lured away from a competitor. It soon became apparent to him that company had to embark on a "strategic thinking process," which had to begin by adopting a "clear vision and a well defined business philosophy." When he became president in 1986, that's precisely the path he followed.

"There weren't any goals or clear directions for the company until Arkadi came along. Now we know exactly what we're trying to achieve," explains a senior lumber trader.

Bykhovsky decided on a two pronged approach: an effective marketing thrust (including a hands-on familiarity with production operations) combined with a recognition that "people must be our principal strength and asset."

The results of this strategy are reflected in what is described by employees as a lean, dynamic, entrepreneurial organization with a friendly atmosphere and an abundance of fairness. The employees value their autonomy above all — "the chance to run our own show."

Workers attribute the change in atmosphere directly to the president, who is described as "a strong, visionary," "an intriguing character," someone who is "open-minded and down-to-earth." Bykhovsky sums up his approach to management very simply: "I don't tolerate mediocrity, and I believe in emphasizing team spirit. To my mind, communications are the single most important aspect of managing people well."

Bykhovsky demands a lot from his people, but rewards them when they do well. Under a bonus pay program, employees in profitable divisions get generous bonuses at Christmas. In 1988, for example, clerical workers received $750; salesmen and traders, $1,500; middle managers, $2,000.

The bonus augments a salary structure that most employees view as fair and competitive, although it may be slightly low for clerical workers. Mindful of the high cost of living in Toronto, the organization pays a special Toronto allowance for managers. For instance, an executive being moved from Quebec to Toronto saw his salary rise from $90,000 to $130,000 to compensate for the difference in costs.

The benefits are generous, and include such extras as fitness subsidies, weight-loss classes, day care seminars, and a home computer purchase plan. In addition, Noranda has recently hired a full-time French instructor to enhance communications between English- and French-speaking branches. At the end of one recent French course, the company sent the whole class to one of its Quebec mills for a weekend as a reward for their increased fluency.

The work is challenging, and employees believe they get a chance to grow and develop on the job. However, promotion opportunities are limited by the company's small size and the youth of the senior management group. One young sales coordinator admits: "I'm at a standstill with the company right now. I've been with the company for a few years and have enjoyed myself very much, but now it's either my managers's job — or that's it. You get more responsibility as you go along, but not so many promotions."

A young woman also feels held back by the number of men in the company. "It's a bit harder for women in certain areas to get ahead." Most women work in clerical, administrative or accounting jobs, but the organization has begun to recognize the necessity to advance women. Of all 190 Canadian employees, 86 are female. And of 59 management and supervisory personnel, 15 are female. Noranda now has three female lumber traders, one of them handling the company's biggest account.

Communications in such a small organization are relaxed, informal and regular. Many departments hold monthly meetings, while others hold quarterly sessions to discuss problems and concerns.

A manager sums up what really sets this company apart: "We're basically left to run our own show here, and the same applies to our boss too. We really call our own shots. And the results are visible. In the last couple of years, we've really begun to make some money."

PCL CONSTRUCTION GROUP INC.

5410 99th Street
P.O. Box 8
Edmonton, Alberta
T5J 2H2
(403) 435-9711

Pay: **AVERAGE**	Atmosphere: **VERY GOOD**
Benefits: **AVERAGE**	Job Satisfaction: **GOOD**
Promotion: **AVERAGE**	Communications: **ADEQUATE**
Job Security: **AVERAGE**	Personal Development: **AVERAGE**

★ *PCL is one of Canada's largest general contractors, and about a third of its business is in the U.S. About 575 employees own 85% of the equity; Great-West Life Assurance Co. holds the remaining 15%. The PCL group of companies has a core salaried staff of about 950. Its hourly paid work force (about 65% unionized) usually varies from 2,000 to 3,000, according to business demands, but at mid-summer 1989 it stood at about 1,820. Its total billings in 1988 reached about $1.2 billion.*

PCL IS NOW a large organization spread across North America, but it tries to maintain the sensitive relations with its employees that distinguish small, family-run companies. For instance, when the recession of the early 1980s forced layoffs, PCL took the unusual step of calling up competing firms to see if they could offer employment to some PCL had to let go.

Because the firm (originally called Poole Construction) has been around since 1906, it has a well-established reputation, particularly in its home province of Alberta. One employee says having a PCL decal on your hard hat is almost like having cash in your pocket if, as has happened, you are stuck on a remote road with a flat tire and no money to pay for a repair.

Having industry contacts also means that PCL staff can purchase building materials, such as lumber and cement, at trade discounts of 20%-40%. It's even possible to buy a side of beef cheaply if you work for PCL in Edmonton (the meat company has supplied company barbecues for years). If you want, you can pick up a couple of dozen eggs at the office on a Friday afternoon.

A junior employee says: "The first day I started work I was really impressed, because my boss took me from office to office introducing me to project managers, engineers and accountants. And the people would say, 'Welcome aboard; it's nice to have you.' You sincerely felt as if they were meaning that. You get that feeling, right from the start, of a close-knit family."

Maintaining a family-like atmosphere is difficult, though, because of the company's widespread operations. For instance, pride in the company expressed by employees at its Edmonton base is not nearly so evident at its regional office in Vancouver, where the identity is less well established. One employee said the firm was occasionaly confused with a bus company (Pacific Coach Lines).

PCL Chairman Robert Stollery says because the company's operations are so diverse he looks for people who are self-reliant. There is, he says, significant branch autonomy. "We have a whole bunch of racehorses out there, but we hold them on a fairly light rein."

Employees say they are given a great deal of responsibility and, as a rule, no one is looking over a shoulder as they work. This sense of freedom produces a willingness to work long hours, including weekends, if a job has to be finished in a hurry.

There is considerable freedom in working hours. Each fall, all employees are allowed to "bank" extra time to put toward an extended Christmas vacation. In 1989, job-sharing was in place in one location and the success of this venture may lead to more of the same.

Construction traditionally is a male-dominated field, but PCL has started a more proactive approach to hiring women. They currently make up 21% of the salaried staff and 1% of management.

Employees agree they are given lots of support; if advice is needed, there is a wealth of experience they can tap.

One young worker: "If I am faced with a problem, I can always call someone who has more experience. In most cases, after two or three phone calls I have an answer to my problem. It's a tremendous feeling. You can always call on somebody who has knowledge you need."

Says another: "There is no limit to what you are allowed to take on. They will give you responsibility and a big work load, and yet the important thing is you are not alone here. It was made absolutely clear to me that I could contact anyone in the company for information."

Stollery, who joined the firm in 1949, spearheaded the purchase from the controlling Poole family in 1976. "I put everything I had on the line, and many millions of dollars that I did not have I put my bank on the line for."

Initially, ownership in the company was extended to 25 managers and old-timers, but by 1989 a total of 575 employees had bought a stake in the firm. Employees are required to dispose of 20% of their holdings each year from age 60, so control will remain in the hands of current employees.

No one is obliged to buy shares. In fact, the shareholder list remains confidential. Nor is a shareholder immune from firing. But as Stollery says, "It has been an incredibly good investment for them. We have many people retiring with significant benefits that they never dreamed of having."

PCL also has a bonus scheme for all salaried staff and hourly paid foremen to reward good performance. The biggest payouts don't necessarily go to the most profitable divisions.

"A few years ago the fellow with the highest bonus was on a job where we lost money," Stollery recalls. "It was weather that created the problem. He put himself in hospital because he worked so hard. It could have been a disaster. He got about 50% of his salary in bonus." Another factor in determining the size of a person's bonus is the amount of time he has spent away from his family.

By 1989, while retaining the chairmanship, Stollery was easing back on his daily involvement with the company and had handed the chief executive officer's role over to Vice-Chairman Bob Tarr.

PCL offers an unusual approach to benefits, called FLEX500. In addition to the usual coverage (life, accident, disability and dental insurance, extended health care and so on), a $500 flexible spending account is available to all full-time salaried employees. This sum may be used at the employee's discretion to offset uninsured medical and dental costs. Any amount unspent can be used to purchase an RRSP or additional vacation time.

If you enjoyed building with Lego as a child, you'll love the games the grownups play in construction — as PCL does it.

The Prudential

PRUDENTIAL INSURANCE CO. OF AMERICA
Canadian Operations

200 Consilium Place
Scarborough, Ontario
M1H 3E6
(416) 296-0777

Pay: **GOOD**	Atmosphere: **GOOD**
Benefits: **VERY GOOD**	Job Satisfaction: **VERY GOOD**
Promotion: **GOOD**	Communications: **VERY GOOD**
Job Security: **VERY GOOD**	Personal Development: **GOOD**

★ *The Canadian operations of the Prudential Insurance Co. of America sell a broad range of financial services across Canada. In 1988, the Canadian company had a net income of $56 million on total revenues of $1.1 billion. It has 1,107 full-time employees, plus approximately 1,500 full-time sales and field staff. It is a wholly owned subsidiary of Prudential Insurance Co. of America, Newark, N.J.*

"RON BARBARO CAME into the Prudential a couple of years ago to turn it around. He soon discovered it was a bit like trying to turn the Queen Mary around on a dime. It can't be done that fast," a Prudential executive says.

The Prudential has operated in Canada for many years, but with a much lower profile and market share than its parent, the largest insurer in the U.S. Barbaro, a chief executive with 32 years of insurance experience, has found the process of bringing about change slower than he expected.

Soon after taking over as president in 1985, Barbaro initiated a review of of the organization. And change is now under way. There's a new catch phrase circulating in Prudential offices these days: Step Out of the Square. In other words, be innovative and try something new.

Barbaro himself led the pack with his innovative "Living Benefits" policy. His concern over the plight of AIDS sufferers inspired Barbaro to find a way for Prudential to pay insurance benefits before death to terminally ill policyholders. This bold move has now been copied by a number of other major insurers.

"When you do something really new, when you Step Out of the Square, you often create a very strong reaction," Barbaro says. "It's funny, but most people are afraid of or resistant to change. After the change, they wonder why they hadn't changed sooner."

Barbaro hopes to instill that attitude into his employees. "I'm a people person, and I don't stand on ceremony," he says, explaining his approach to management. "I keep trying to make things better around here – and there's still lots of room for improvement."

Prudential employees are proud of their boss: "He's far more visible than our previous CEOs have been," says one woman secretary. "We now get a chance to know Barbaro as a human being, rather than a god," adds another employee. "There's two sides to him. He's friendly, but tough," explains a third.

Barbaro has made an impact on employees, at least on a personal level, but in many ways the company has a slightly old-fashioned air about it. "It's predictable, comfortable and well managed, not dynamic," a claims adjuster says. An accountant: "What I like about it is that Prudential has a habit of hiring such nice people."

Employees say the pay is competitive, although there are low pockets, particularly at junior hiring levels. One university graduate, recently hired, admits she's making $2 less an hour than her best friend at another insurance company. But she believes she has made the right choice, and will get promoted quickly at Prudential. Another employee adds: "The enthusiasm and respect for employees here are worth more than extra pay."

Opportunities for advancement seem numerous, even for secretaries (often rug-ranked and job-frozen elsewhere). One woman told of moving up five rankings in just three years. Another woman accountant said: "I've just been promoted into a manager's position, in spite of the fact that I'm pregnant, and just about to go off on maternity leave. They've been really good to me."

As in most insurance companies, most employees are women – 76% in the case of Prudential. And there's an encouraging 48% of women managers in this company.

The advantages for women working in this company include flexibility. For example, the company has installed a computer terminal in the home of one claims adjuster, and that's where she works four days a week. On the fifth, she goes to the office to discuss her next batch of work with her supervisor. There are also several examples of job-sharing at Prudential. And flextime makes life easier for mothers.

The company, while not paying high salaries, compensates with extra time off. In addition to a generous vacation allotment, each employee on staff for more than 18 months is allowed up to nine "personal absence" days a year. These days may be taken for any personal or family reason, with the consent of the employee's supervisor, and they are in addition to sick leave entitlement.

The flexible benefits package is also a big plus. Employees may choose between different levels of coverage for their dental and health care, for example. There have been a few problems in getting the recently up-graded plan rolling, but workers generally seem pleased with the options. Employees also get a 10% discount on home and car insurance.

Communication appears to be very good. In addition to an annual meeting for employees, there's a quarterly newsletter, a weekly news bulletin, a breezy one-page news summary distributed twice a week and an anonymous complaint program called "Speak-Up."

The quarterly Star Pruformers recognition program doles out four $250 awards to meritorious workers. Another program hands out awards ranging from $20 to $10,000 for labor-saving suggestions. Even so, there are gaps. One woman says: "In the underwriting department, there are times when we work really hard, long evenings and weekends, but we never get recognized for it."

Working at the Prudential is a bit like coming home and putting on your old pair of slippers. You slip them on easily, because they're predictable and very comfortable, and you know their contours well. Long-time employees like the sense of comfort and the job security at Prudential.

But if Ron Barbaro succeeds in turning this Queen Mary around, the Prudential may well become more dynamic and less comfortable, while still maintaining a caring atmosphere for its workers.

ROYAL BANK
OF CANADA

1 Place Ville Marie
P.O. Box 6001
Montreal, Quebec
H3C 3A9
(514) 874-2110

Pay: **EXCELLENT**	Atmosphere: **VERY GOOD**
Benefits: **VERY GOOD**	Job Satisfaction: **EXCELLENT**
Promotion: **VERY GOOD**	Communications: **VERY GOOD**
Job Security: **EXCELLENT**	Personal Development: **EXCELLENT**

★ *With 1,560 branches, 46,000 employees in 34 countries and total assets of $110 billion, the Royal is Canada's largest chartered bank and North America's fourth-largest bank overall. Approximately 36,000 people work for the Royal in Canada. Net income in 1988 was a record $712 million.*

THE ROYAL IS a bank where someone can start as a teller and still make it to the top. Allan Taylor is a living example. He started as a junior clerk at the age of 16 in Prince Albert, Sask., in 1949. He was made chairman and chief executive officer in 1986, following 37 years of internal training and promotions through the bank hierarchy.

Other examples aren't hard to find, either. "Education *per se* is not something we look at when we're looking to promote somebody," says Gordon Feeney, executive vice-president, operations and service delivery. "If they looked at education, I sure wouldn't be sitting in this chair."

But senior executives such as Taylor and Feeney get to the

top, partly thanks to the bank's emphasis on continual education, and increasingly through internal training programs.

Over the past few years, Canada's biggest bank has been undergoing a transformation, altering its business focus to concentrate on a retail banking base, while at the same time broadening its scope to offer a full range of financial services. The key to this change has been a determined effort to improve customer service. As Taylor explains it, "Business success can only be built on serving customers well."

This emphasis on service has renewed the focus on the Royal's Canadian employees. The bank realizes that it can only achieve its goal of serving customers superbly if its people are professional, well-trained and motivated. The Royal's corporate strategic plan states that one of its objectives is to be "a leading employer, committed to excellence."

Taylor explains the new human resource strategy as "empowering our people . . . giving them the means to get on with the job: the training, the resources, the authority and responsibility to serve customers as well as they can." As a result of this new thrust, Royal's staff are getting more training than ever. In 1988, more than 21,000 employees attended formal classroom training programs as the bank's spending on training soared to more than $50 million. (That's almost $1,100 per employee.) One employee describes the bank's training policy as "a continual investment in your career." Another worker comments: "The Royal Bank's commitment to training is phenomenal. I had the opportunity to take two years off and go back to school. It's astonishing."

A new initiative is the redesign of pay structures to focus more on performance and developing special remuneration awards for people not involved in incentive programs. The Quality Performance incentive program covers 8,000 executive and managerial staff, while 12 other pilot programs involve team compensation for non-managerial staff. A $2.5-million special achievement fund has been set up to allow area managers to reward outstanding achievements by workers in their area. These rewards can be paid out in cash, dinners, event tickets or weekends away.

In 1988, the new staff suggestion program accepted 371 suggestions that will save the bank more than $14 million over a three-year period. Fifteen of these awards earned the top

236

$10,000 prize in that year.

The extensive benefits package includes a generous savings and share ownership program, in which an employee can have up to 6% of salary deducted every two weeks. For every dollar the employee contributes, the bank adds 50¢ in the form of Royal Bank shares. The individual decides whether to have the money saved in a deposit account at high interest rates or put into bank shares, or a combination of both. The program has proved so popular since its introduction five years ago that 63% of Canadian employees are now shareholders – and the value of the shares (both employee and bank contributions) is almost $100 million.

Other extras included in the benefits package are a fitness subsidy, staff banking privileges, which provide most bank services free to employees, as well as reduced interest rates on loans and Visa balances. The noncontributory pension plan is also now accompanied by an optional contributory plan, by which an employee can augment the payout on retirement.

Not surprisingly, the personnel function at the Royal maintains its traditionally high profile. The head of personnel, who reports directly to the chief executive officer, also has a power rare in other organizations. He has the ultimate authority over dismissals; no one can be fired without his permission.

As an avenue of communication, apart from formal complaint procedures, someone from the personnel function visits every branch in Canada at least once every 18 months. Everyone is entitled to a private interview, to be given the chance to discuss problems with an objective outsider.

Another new communications initiative is the recently launched annual staff meeting. The first meetings were held in 1989, when 1,100 employees crowded into Montreal's Queen Elizabeth Hotel. A few days later, a further 2,200 gathered at Toronto's Roy Thomson Hall to hear about the bank's plans and to have any questions answered.

Because the staff is 74% female, the bank has a full-time equal opportunity co-ordinator, and significant strides have been made in improving the number of women in managerial roles. By 1989, 42% of managerial jobs were filled by women, and there are now four women classified as senior executives. Based on federal employment equity reports at the end of 1987, the Royal Bank ranks second among the Big Six chartered banks, in terms of numbers of women. Only the Bank of Montreal has a higher percentage — at 53%.

Employees like many things about their work at the Royal. In the latest opinion survey, 91% of employees said they were "proud to be associated with the Royal Bank." Other advantages include mobility: "You can stay in the organization and virtually switch careers as you move through it. That keeps it exciting," says one employee. A woman adds: "I think we can all look back on jobs that we possibly disliked or didn't like as well as others, but you always knew or had the confidence that it was only for a few years, that you'd be moving on."

The feeling of trust is high on employees' list of what makes the Royal special for them. "Honesty and integrity just have to be undoubted," says one. "We're taking care of other people's money. I like to think of us as the cream." That's not just an isolated sentiment, either. In the employee survey, 94% said they think the job they perform is important, and 88% feel they have a personal responsibility to make the Royal Bank a more successful company. With attitudes like that, it's hard to imagine them not succeeding.

Russelsteel Inc.

People making a difference

RUSSELSTEEL INC.

535 Bowes Road
P.O. Box 5009
Downsview, Ontario
M3M 3B5
(416) 669-6454

Pay: **AVERAGE**	Atmosphere: **VERY GOOD**
Benefits: **AVERAGE**	Job Satisfaction: **VERY GOOD**
Promotion: **GOOD**	Communications: **EXCELLENT**
Job Security: **GOOD**	Personal Development: **GOOD**

★ *With 25 locations across Canada and sales of more than $352 million, Russelsteel is the largest Canadian distributor of steel products. About 40% of the 900 employees are unionized, mainly by the United Steelworkers of America. Russelsteel is a division of Federal Industries, a diversified management company.*

"THE PROFIT sharing plan at Russelsteel is really an excuse to communicate," says Chief Executive Officer Wayne Mang. Touring a plant on one occasion, Mang tried to guess the upcoming profit performance before the figures were posted on the lunch room chart. "No, Wayne," one of the nearby workers said. "We did a bit better than that."

Comments Mang: "Here we were, before the figures were even out, and an employee knew how his division had performed the previous month. That's communication."

For lower-level employees, profit sharing represents an opportunity to earn up to $1,500 extra per year. This also applies to unionized employees, whose profit sharing falls outside of their negotiated contracts.

"The profit sharing plan will always be outside of the union contract," says Horace Ho, vice-president of human resources. "It is not something we have to do, but want to do."

Commitment to communication begins at the top. Mang, who comes across as a management evangelist, is the quintessential executive who manages by walking around.

A receptionist comments:"Whenever Wayne comes by our plant, he stops and takes the time to talk with me. Sometimes he will spend 15 minutes. In what other companies does that happen?"

"My job is to match talent and power with resources to empower individuals in the company," says Mang.

Empowering employees — "making everyone a manager" — is the aim of Russelsteel's three annual "core sample seminars," which bring together groups of 50 employees from different levels, divisions and plants for three-day sessions to discuss company goals, work in problem solving groups, and get to know one another.

Every employee will eventually attend a seminar. Mang participates in each one. Employees are overwhelmingly enthusiastic about the seminars, which foster a sense of equality and common purpose. But the program has not been effective in turning the company upside down, empowering employees to manage more directly their areas of responsibility. The program, however, is only in its first year.

Other schemes also encourage communication. Under the "bright ideas program," employees receive a cash award of 20% of the first year's net savings of accepted cost-cutting suggestions. Payoff ideas can be simple. One plant employee, for example, had to stop work four or five times a day to give truckers directions to the shipping bay. He received a $100 award for suggesting the company put up signs. More important to him than the money was the recognition that his ideas are important to the company.

The employee share ownership program allows employees who have been with the company for more than a year to contribute up to 5% of their pay toward buying Federal Industries stock. The company contributes $1 for every $3 employees put into the plan.

There is an atmosphere of trust in the company. Ho says proudly that on average he now negotiates union contracts in two or three meetings, compared with eight to 12 time-consuming meetings previously. Unresolved issues are sometimes set aside on the basis that Ho will deal fairly with any potential problem.

The company recently spent $30,000 on extensive improvements to an employee lunch room, even though only 12 people worked at that plant. A manager explains: "It was the philosophy that if we're going to do it, let's do it right."

A scholarship program has just been introduced for the children of employees. On the basis of academic standing, the company will grant annually up to 25 one-time undergraduate scholarships for the first year of university ($1,500) or community college ($700).

Compensation ranges from average to excellent. Shop floor workers' wages lag behind those of highly paid primary steel workers, but employees recognize that steel manufacturing and distribution are different industries. They feel their wages are average, and profit sharing and the employee share ownership program upgrade their compensation to good. For managers, profit sharing can increase their already competitive salaries by up to 40%.

Two unionized workers describe their pensions as "paltry," but Ho explains that the old pension fund was wound up in 1984 and a new fund was started. After the takeover by Federal Industries, employees received lump sum payments to invest in RRSPs. Therefore pensions for long-time employees are lower than the industry average, because employees have received part of their pensions already.

Employees feel their chances for promotion are good. One first-year employee had not only been promoted once, but had also attended a core sample seminar. It has been noted, however, that promotions will be few in the next while, because the management team is quite young.

Ho has discontinued rating employees according to their promotabilty. "Traditionally, 'promotable' employees are identified as an elite group with much more influence on company performance than others. This perception is inconsistent with what we wish to achieve as a people-driven organization," Ho says. "Our success depends on developing people with diverse management talents and the ability to 'expand' their responsibilities to their optimal potential."

SAMUEL
MANU-TECH INC.

195 The West Mall
Etobicoke, Ontario
M9C 5K1
(416) 626-2190

Pay: **AVERAGE**	Atmosphere: **VERY GOOD**
Benefits: **GOOD**	Job Satisfaction: **VERY GOOD**
Promotion: **GOOD**	Communications: **VERY GOOD**
Job Security: **VERY GOOD**	Personal Development: **EXCELLENT**

★ *Most of Samuel Manu-Tech's 869 employees process metals and plastics in 12 Ontario plants. In 1988, the company reported net earnings of $13 million on sales of $178 million.*

SAMUEL, SON & CO., a privately owned metals distributor based in Mississauga, Ont., incorporated Samuel Manu-Tech (SMT) on Aug. 30, 1985, to make some family shares available to the public. The new entity amalgamated three totally separate Samuel interests — Samuel Strapping Systems, Canadian Metal Rolling Mills (both of Mississauaga) and Nelson Steel (Stoney Creek and Nanticoke, Ont.).

Since then, the three divisions have expanded to seven, and five plants have swelled to 12, more than doubling the company in size. Apart from the financial affiliation and a metals orientation, the operations have only four things in common. First, the plants are relatively small. They have no unions. They're all innovative and markedly successful in mature markets.

The fourth commonality, as the SMT prospectus described it, is "excellent" employee relations. In other words, they're all good places to work.

To the people involved, none of this is coincidence. The four factors (as either causes or effects) are inextricably related. Profits, growth and a happy, highly-motivated work force simply go hand in hand.

"You cannot make money with unhappy people. I wouldn't know how to do it," says Karl Fox, vice-president and general manager of the Canadian Metal Rolling division.

While pay and benefit scales differ from division to division, the policy (not uncommon in non-unionized plants) had been to try to set them higher than others in similar local industries.At Nelson Steel, for example, wages are about 50¢ an hour below those of the nearby primary steel mills in Hamilton, but between $1-$1.50 above those in a typical steel service centre.

Though the divisions evolved independently, each has developed close, direct communications with its people. Each has been sharing its profits with employees for many years.

The SMT experience holds lessons for any low- or medium-tech industrial employer in Canada. In fact, the Nelson Steel division, a non-union shop in a highly unionized part of the country, makes a very clear case in point.

● In terms of people, Nelson is a small, capital-intensive operation with 200 employees working around the clock seven days a week "custom pickling" rolled steel sheets. Small, while not always beautiful, does have potential advantages. The people at Nelson all know each other, for example. Many newcomers tend to be friends of current employees, and that's a definite plus.

● Nelson has had profit sharing from the very beginning, and the proportion is large enough to give employees a real measure of their own effectiveness. The payout, distributed three times a year, has averaged between $300-$400 per quarter over the past couple of years.

SMT also offers its workers a chance to buy company stock. There are no direct incentives other than a payroll deduction plan and no brokerage fees, but in some SMT operations as many as two thirds of employees are now shareholders.

● The employees have a say in important matters such as pay, benefits and working conditions. At Nelson, for example, the hourly workers elect a committee to negotiate with management. "We've had our problems," says plant manager Ed O'Connor, "but the system works reasonably well." A number of unsuccessful attempts have been made local unions to organize the plant.

• From the outset, the atmosphere was established as informal, open and friendly, built on cornerstones of trust, and individual responsibility. Individual efforts are not only appreciated, but also openly recognized. Employee-of-the-month awards are given out, and cash rewards are made for labor-saving suggestions.

• The organization provides scope for individual development and enrichment. That automatically implies promotion from within, of course, but the process doesn't stop there. Lateral moves are encouraged from plant-to-plant. As one man puts it: "I don't think there's such a thing as a job description here. If you're genuinely interested in learning something, everyone around you will help you. All you have to do is ask."

• Although the steel-pickling business does have its ups and downs, job security has been very good recently. In fact, turnover at Nelson Steel in 1989 was only 2%-2½%, and that is without doubt the mark of an excellent employer.

SHOPPERS DRUG MART

225 Yorkland Boulevard
Willowdale, Ontario
M2J 4Y7
(416) 493-1220

Pay: **VERY GOOD**	Atmosphere: **VERY GOOD**
Benefits: **GOOD**	Job Satisfaction: **VERY GOOD**
Promotion: **GOOD**	Communications: **EXCELLENT**
Job Security: **GOOD**	Personal Development: **EXCELLENT**

★ *Shoppers Drug Mart (Pharmaprix in Quebec) is a subsidiary of Montreal-based Imasco Ltd., a holding and management company descended from Imperial Tobacco, an employer widely respected for its generous, people-oriented policies. As Canada's leading drug-store group, SDM had system-wide sales of $2.5 billion in 1988. The company has about 550 employees in offices across Canada. About 16,000 Canadians work full- or part-time in 630 franchised pharmacies.*

SHOPPERS DRUG MART is a master of communications — with its stores, with the communities in which it operates and within its own corporate offices.

You can almost say its business is communications. The stores operate independently, so if communications from SDM corporate offices aren't clear and well-received, standards could slip.

The company's light-handed approach to its stores is based on respect for the franchise owners (called associates) who run them. Although SDM provides the capital, leases the space and equips and stocks the stores, owners are their own bosses. They hire the personnel and establish themselves in the community.

SDM functions as a consultant and resource for the stores.

The approach seems to work. Sales rose 67% from 1985 to 1988, in part because the number of outlets increased. But sales also increased per store by an average of 50%. SDM credits the growth to the strong identity associates develop in their communities, combined with unique promotions and a good product mix. It's also the result of excellent communications between SDM corporate offices and the stores.

SDM sends its chief-executive team out on the road each year to visit as many of the 630 stores as possible. During the 1989 whirlwind tour, Chairman David Bloom, accompanied by President Herb Binder and Senior Executive Vice-presidents Fred Van Laare, David McDonald and Stan Thomas visited 52 stores from Vancouver to Gander.

In addition, each spring and fall, SDM gathers the stores' management teams for three-day buying shows and meetings — one east and one west. The company issues a monthly publication and quarterly newsletters. And SDM-TV puts out a video newsletter to all employees five times a year.

Communications is also important to the operation of individual stores. Not only are owners expected to communicate well with their employees, they are encouraged to be part of the community they're operating in. They are expected to be available to speak to high schools, seniors and other community groups. One interesting initiative is the "Adopt-a-school" program. School children are invited to the store and given a presentation on poisons and the use of medicine, followed by a question-and-answer session on drugs.

Good communications are also stressed in the corporate offices. Each quarterly staff meeting profiles a different department. Management uses the meeting to "bring us up to date," one woman says. "They tell you where the company is financially, and what their plans are."

In the Toronto central office, the PA system delivers a five-minute internal newscast to employees every Monday morning. "It's really a hatches, matches and dispatches kind of thing — who has joined us, who got married," one employee says.

SDM's operation is fascinating. It's neither a branch-store chain nor a true franchise operation. Some call the hybrid a "branchise" system, in which the company sets up pharmacists in their own businesses.

SDM hand-picks the associates, who must be licensed pharmacists with SDM experience (usually current employees in an SDM store) and hold a certificate from the company's associate-development course. The associate incorporates the business in his or her own name — Mary Jones Pharmacy Ltd., for example — and operates it as an independent store. Thirty percent-40% of the associates are now women vs about 10% in 1985.

Jones hires and pays her own staff, and buys her own merchandise and pays for it. There is no central purchasing although SDM sometimes negotiates with manufacturers for special prices.

If the store isn't profitable in the first year — statistics show new ones usually aren't — the pharmacist will get a guaranteed minimum income, much more than a pharmacist would normally earn as an employee elsewhere. Furthermore, SDM will make up the year's loss with a non-repayable grant, enabling the associate to start the second year fresh.

Once the store becomes successful, the pharmcist's earnings increase in line with the profitability of the store.

SDM doesn't manage or oversee the stores. In fact, it has specially designed terminology to describe the relationship, and the words don't include the term "head office." There is a "central office" (with branches), and its role is to co-ordinate and disseminate policies and procedures.

The assistance provided is impressive and on-going. It reflects the basic philosophy of the company — that the most important component of the job is the nuts and bolts of selling, which takes place in the store. The central office only provides the marketing expertise that gets the customer to the store.

A key component of SDM's assistance is Koffler Academy (named after SDM's founder, Murray Koffler), the company's training department, which offers about 30 courses on subjects ranging from marketing and purchasing to customer service. Some are one-shot sessions, while others go on for three to four months. They're open to full- and part-time employees and taken on company time. Some of the one-shot sessions are offered on the road to provide ready access to employees. The courses are not compulsory but virtually everyone takes at least one and most take quite a few.

The company also organizes special promotions. At any given time, there is at least one in all stores, and usually several.

SDM also has employee incentives, usually prizes or deep discounts on certain merchandise for employees who are discovered doing something extra.

At the company's corporate offices, there's a more formal employee incentive program. Bosses have instructions to catch their employees "doing something right." The orders are clear: "If somebody in your department goes beyond the call of duty, does something especially well and so on, write that down and send it in," one manager explains.

The names and deeds are announced at SDM's quarterly staff meetings. At the end of the year, the names of those who did something right go into a hat for a draw, and the winner gets a week's vacation.

The idea wasn't to get employees to do more, the manager says. "It was introduced more to get the idea through management's head to think about the people who were constantly doing things right who might be overlooked."

SDM pays responsible employees well, and there's a profit-sharing incentive program for those classified as management — 60%-70% of employees at the corporate offices. Salary scales for support staff (who are not entitled to the incentive but instead receive a cash Christmas bonus) are about average.

Other benefits include dental and orthodontic plans, and life and disability insurance for all employees (including store employees whose benefits are paid for by the associate). Pension is only provided for corporate office staff, although special retirement plans are provided for the associates.

Most of the key SDM employees came from the stores. While store employees technically work for the associates, they also make up the talent pool for SDM's management ranks.

A prospective employee may not need a diploma or degree to hold down a cashier's job in a drug store — if that's as far as he or she wants to go. "But we really want people to grow," says Ray Hallett, senior vice-president, human resources.

For anyone who would like to grow at SDM, the advice is simple: Go to college or university. Apply for a job in a store and take courses at Koffler Academy. SDM will be watching.

You can, of course, earn a promotion in one store, but there are mechanisms to enable you to move to higher positions in other stores, thanks to the open communication policy. And one day, if you're good, SDM may tap you on the shoulder.

WARNER LAMBERT

WARNER-LAMBERT CANADA INC.

2200 Eglinton Avenue East
Scarborough, Ontario
M1L 2N3
(416) 288-2000

Pay: **GOOD**	Atmosphere: **VERY GOOD**
Benefits: **GOOD**	Job Satisfaction: **VERY GOOD**
Promotion: **VERY GOOD**	Communications: **EXCELLENT**
Job Security: **EXCELLENT**	Personal Development: **EXCELLENT**

★ *Warner-Lambert Canada Inc., a manufacturer of pharmaceuticals, health care products (such as Sinutab and Bromoseltzer) and Chiclets chewing gum, records sales of about $280 million a year. The company has about 1,500 employees and plants in Metro Toronto and Brockville, Ont. It is a major international affiliate of Warner-Lambert Co., Morris Plains, N.J.*

WARNER-LAMBERT stands out as a company that cares for its employees and nurtures their personal growth. It has achieved public recognition for its pioneering affirmative action program, which is now being used as a model for other companies.

What is perhaps less well-known is that its treatment of other employee groups is just as remarkable as its treatment of women. This is the place to work if you want in-depth interest in your personal development.

The company embarked on its affirmative action program in 1975, International Women's Year. At the time, only 18% of its supervisory management were women. Fifteen years later, the proportion had increased dramatically to more than 45% — and women also occupied 17% of the executive offices.

Women comprise 41% of the Warner-Lambert Canada work-force. Without giving them an unfair advantage over men, the company has tried to create new opportunities for female employees and encouraged them to attend training programs designed to develop managerial skills. Two major awards, one by the Ontario government, the other by the YWCA, have acknowledged Warner-Lambert's success with this program.

Warner-Lambert has turned its attention to the disabled, who made up 3.4% of the company's workforce in 1989. It hires, for example, disabled students from a local school board's co-op program for 10-week work terms. A job fair held during the summer of 1989 attracted 21 disabled applicants, but none had been hired at the time of writing.

The general atmosphere in the company is warm, friendly and open. Communication is highly valued and encouraged in many ways. This is a company with very few secrets. Decisions affecting employees are discussed openly, feedback is requested, and honest dialogue occurs.

As the company's creed explains: "We are committed to attracting and retaining capable people, providing them with challenging work in an open and participatory environment, marked by equal opportunity for personal growth."

Another key component of the Warner-Lambert philosophy is the annual analysis of each employee's performance and personal development. This process is not just a rating system. It is a dialogue in which the individual employee identifies his or her plans and prime development needs. Goals, performance and the company's expectations are then assessed by the worker's department manager, the human resources manager and the president.

Because each employee receives a copy of this assessment, he knows exactly how he measures up to the company standard and what plans have been made to help him achieve his personal growth goals in the coming year. As one manager puts it: "Developing people is considered an integral part of your responsibilities here."

A good example of how the two-way dialogue works involved a secretary who took her boss to task during a performance appraisal. As she explained to him, the best way to improve *her* performance would be by making changes in some of *his* methods. The boss made appropriate changes, resulting in increased productivity and satisfaction on both sides.

The company does regular surveys to gauge employee attitudes and needs, and the results are published openly in the company newspaper.

So much emphasis is placed on individual training and development at Warner-Lambert that the company has more than one educational program. The educational assistance program will pay 100% of the costs of any training courses that will increase employees' ability in their current jobs, or qualify them for advancement. But Warner Lambert will also help those looking for a career change.

The second program, Post Employment Continuing Education Grants, gives increasingly large grants (linked to years of service, up to a maximum of $1,000 per year) to employees who leave the company for full-time higher education. The company tries to give them summer employment and rehire them after graduation. The company also has a scholarship program to help educate employees' children.

Pay levels are generally considered to be competitive. The benefits package has recently been upgraded with the addition of a fitness centre subsidy, weight loss courses, nutritional counseling, child care and eldercare programs, as well as a comprehensive employee assistance program. The company does not supplement UIC maternity benefits, but it does offer an unpaid extended leave with continued coverage under several benefit plans.

Employees seem content with their people-oriented management, and voice few serious criticisms. The only real concerns seem to revolve around workload and pressure. "The head-count has gone down, but the work-load has increased," says one long-time employee. Other workers chime in and say, "We're just rushed off our feet. Management recognizes the problem, but nothing's been done about it."

Don Henley, director of employee relations, doesn't disagree with this assessment, but views it both as a necessity of functioning in the new free trade era and in the face of increasing competition. "The competition is good, and getting better all the time. We are conscious of the absolute need to operate as effectively and efficiently as possible. It's a new burden for all of us. The price we have to pay is to do more with less people."

Being a subsidiary of a U.S. multinational corporation has its drawbacks too. Frustrations occur when decisions have to be referred to head office. Increased autonomy, it is argued, would solve this problem.

This aside, Warner-Lambert excels in developing the potential of its employees. As one sales manager says after two years with the company: "You really do get an excellent opportunity to grow here. They just throw responsibility at you, and encourage you to manage your own business. They really challenge you, and yet they coach you, too."

The caring way this company does everything — from employee appraisals to support for a summer camp for children with cancer — adds poignancy to one employee's sole complaint: "Warner-Lambert's name should be better known for all the society-oriented things we do. We should have a bigger profile and recognition for all these endeavors."

WEALL & CULLEN NURSERIES

4300 Steeles Ave. East
P.O. Box 4040
Industrial Park
Markham, Ontario
L3R 8G8
(416) 477-4475

Pay: **POOR**	Atmosphere: **VERY GOOD**
Benefits: **POOR**	Job Satisfaction: **EXCELLENT**
Promotion: **GOOD**	Communications: **GOOD**
Job Security: **AVERAGE**	Personal Development: **AVERAGE**

★ *Weall & Cullen Nurseries sells gardening products, both wholesale and retail, through a chain of garden centres. The company also owns and operates Cullen Country Barns, a retailing complex that includes a dinner theatre and four restaurants. The privately owned company has 250 full-time and 300 part-time employees. In 1988, the company had revenues of more than $35 million.*

"YOU HAVE TO demonstrate to people that work for you how you want them to work by working that way yourself, and by being as dedicated to them as you expect them to be dedicated to the company. And it really works."

That's the philosophy of 33-year-old Mark Cullen, vice-president of Weall & Cullen Nurseries (W&C). This down-to-earth style is one of the factors behind W&C's growth, helped by gardening's emergence as one of the most popular leisure activities of the past decade. The chain of garden centres now sells eight times more goods, in terms of dollar volume, than it did 10 years ago. And if expansion continues as expected under the company's 10-year plan, by 1998 sales will top $100 million.

W&C is doing a lot of the right things, according to its employees. Here are just some of the qualities they value in their workplace:

● " We're given the opportunity to choose the amount of responsibility we want to take on."

● "It's a relaxed and fun atmosphere — we're always joking with each other."

● "You're allowed to make mistakes here without being fired."

● "There are lots of opportunities to grow here, and to do things I never thought I could do."

● "Mark Cullen's operating style is very approachable. He's willing to listen and follow up on suggestions."

Workers also value the Cullen family's "roll-up-the-shirt-sleeves-and-get-involved" attitude. One supervisor tells of coming to work one morning and finding President Len Cullen picking up litter in the parking lot. "They're always on top of things," she exclaims, "even the garbage!"

Opportunities to advance are plentiful for those with drive and initiative.

Workers tell of an employee who started as a clerk and six years later was managing a garden centre. A woman adds: "I was here only two months. . . when I was made assistant manager."

Communication is good. Over a 24-month period between 1987 and 1989, Cullen invited all employees to a "breakfast with Mark" to explain the company's future course. Non-managerial employees from each store meet annually with Cullen or General Manager Barry Benjamin to discuss operations. Problems are later reviewed with their managers.

W&C has had a deferred profit-sharing plan (DPSP) since 1979, and the employees run it. Non-managerial representatives from every store and department are elected to the profit council, which Cullen says "serves more as a vehicle of communication between myself and staff than anything else."

Because the company doesn't have a pension plan, the DPSP is is all the more important. W&C sets aside 12% of pre-tax profits for all employees who work more than 1,000 hours a year. Since the mid-1980s, the average annual deposit in the plan has been about $1,200 per employee.

For some employees, the DPSP can be a real incentive. As one worker explained: "If you see a bag of fertilizer lying on the floor in your way, you move it, even if it isn't your job. If that bag of fertilizer gets a hole in it, it can't be sold, and that comes out of our profits."

Employees' main complaints have to do with pay and benefits. As is generally the case in retailing, the hourly wages are low.

"If pay is the more important factor, you shouldn't be working at W&C," one employee says. Another worker adds: "I'm making $5 less an hour than where I was before. But I have far less stress and greater job satisfaction." Workers, however, say they make more at W&C than at other nearby nurseries.

Salaries for skilled workers, such as store managers, floral designers and buyers, are significantly better, and in some cases augmented by healthy performance bonuses.

The benefits package includes a medical plan, vision care, and life insurance. But what employees want most is a dental plan. In 1989, the company was planning to add one.

W&C tries to show its appreciation to employees through pep rallies twice a year and monthly parties to honor employees with birthdays in that month. Each garden centre elects an employee of the season, who receives dinner for two and a plaque.

This is a great company for young, dynamic workers, keen to get ahead and prepared to work hard. It will grow and so will they.

THE
CLASSICS

Solid companies that demonstrate care for employees, but with a more traditional management flavor.

BOMBARDIER INC.
Motorized Consumer Products Division

55 rue de la Montagne
Valcourt, Quebec
J0E 2L0
(514) 532-2211

Pay: **VERY GOOD**	Atmosphere: **VERY GOOD**
Benefits: **VERY GOOD**	Job Satisfaction: **VERY GOOD**
Promotion: **GOOD**	Communications: **VERY GOOD**
Job Security: **EXCELLENT**	Personal Development: **VERY GOOD**

★ *Montreal-based Bombardier Inc., an internationally known manu-*
facturer of vehicles, engines and aeronautical products (with net sales of
close to $1.4 billion in 1988) is totally decentralized. Presidents run the
various divisions as separate companies with large degrees of autonomy.
The three plants at Valcourt have 2,300 nonunionized employees.

J. ARMAND BOMBARDIER founded his company in Valcourt, the village of his birth, to make tracked commercial vehicles for snow. In 1959, the company introduced the personal snowmobile, trade-named it Ski-Doo and gave the world a new perspective on winter recreation.

The Ski-Doo also gave Valcourt growing pains. The village quickly expanded to town size, but lacked many of the public services usually provided by a town, so the company assumed this responsibility. Bombardier built a rink, a golf course, a library and a cultural centre, owned by the company, but operated by the town, open to all residents of Valcourt.

(A fishing club, with its own lake, is restricted to employees.)

This kind of paternalism came naturally to a family business, centred on the father figure of the founder until he died in 1964. After that, growth alone forced the company to discard many aspects of paternalism, but it has tried to retain the best of them — including a true regard for its people.

Human needs and communication underlie the company's policies, says Marc Pelletier, vice-president of human resources, who knows all 2,300 employees by name. "We have a strong belief that human capital is important."

A new era in employee relations at Bombardier began in 1973, in the middle of the snowmobile boom. A wave of general labor unrest was rolling across Quebec, resulting in a rash of union organizing drives and demands for wage increases of 10%-15%.

The unrest hit Bombardier in Valcourt, and Pelletier reacted immediately. He recalls many occasions when he stood on an oil drum in the plant, surrounded by employees, trying to get at the root of the problem. The employees, he learned, wanted some kind of system to work out differences.

Pelletier considered it a logical request, because the payroll had grown to 2,000 by then and it was impossible for management and employees to deal with each other. There was only a goodwill committee, admitted to be very paternalistic, without any real framework for a dialogue.

The company proposed a work-relations committee — 11 delegates from the plants elected by the employees to represent them in discussions with management. There would also be a written compact on rights and practices, to be submitted to all employees in a referendum. The system was adopted, and later expanded to include a second committee of seven to represent the offices.

To discourage entrenched interests, the delegates change every year. Each August, the turnout runs as high as 99% when employees cast their secret ballots. The president of the plant committee is assigned an office and works full-time on committee affairs, paid by the company.

Pelletier hasn't been back on an oil drum since 1973. The communication is extremely good. As a female employee puts it: "If you talk to each other, you understand each other."

One man who worked for the company when it was small, left several times and finally returned to stay: "More and more, the company shows a deep interest in human beings as individuals. If managers [anywhere] respect their people, they won't have any problems."

The system makes compensation decisions using a base of eight other manufacturing companies chosen jointly by management and the committees for common characteristics. First, the companies must be unionized. The employees in them must work with metal, doing jobs similar to those at Bombardier. And the plants must be located in the surrounding Eastern Townships region.

Bombardier started the scheme with a higher average level of pay and benefits than the others, and maintains it by giving its employees the average increase paid by the six. When the annual comparison is completed the results are discussed with the staff. These dialogues take a week, but the idea is to obtain wider direct input from employees themselves, and they are considered well worthwhile.

Benefits, considered in terms of cents per hour, are improved in a similar way. The benefit package includes a noncontributory pension plan for all employees and substantial discounts on Bombardier products. Vacations range from two to five weeks, not uncommon, but the company tacks on a bonus — almost an extra day for each year's service.

This is an organization that emphasizes collective effort. But to encourage individual improvement, Bombardier recently launched a productivity involvement program, which selects the best suggestions made by employees each month. Outstanding suggestions are recognized with the award of a trophy at the end of the year in a gala ceremony.

Bombardier recently reorganized the more traditional assembly line operations into a work-group structure, and brought in new technology at the same time. To help employees adapt to the changes, a personalized three-year training program was implemented, allowing workers who voluntarily registered to upgrade their skills and attitudes on an individualized basis.

As a result of these training programs, La Commission de formation professionnelle de la main-d'oeuvre (the Manpower Professional Development Commission) awarded Bombardier the 1989 Optima prize in recognition of its work in developing the potential of its employees.

Job security has improved at Valcourt. Pelletier says this is a result of increased production. Instead of making snowmobiles for six months a year, Bombardier now produces year-round, making personal sea craft as well. "We have two products, one used in the winter, one used in the summer. Now people work close to 12 months a year; we stop only for the change on the assembly line." Since 1986, the division has grown by 300 employees.

Unions have tried unsuccessfully to organize the Valcourt plants since 1973. Each time, employees informed the company that an approach had been made, and management refused to take a back seat. "It's a right for any employees anywhere to have a union," Pelletier says. "It's also [management's] right to tell the employees that we believe our formula has proved to be the better. We let the employees decide which formula they prefer."

Employees describe a happy shop (the annual turnover rate is less than 1%, including retirements) with family touches. Early each July, the company unveils the next year's snowmobile models to employees at a wine and cheese party in the town arena. Open house for families falls on a Saturday in August. In September, the divisional head honors long-service employees at "The Evening of the President," a gala ball.

Pride in the company is enormous and more profound than many Canadians outside Quebec may realize. "For me and for many other French-Canadians, Bombardier represents something," a man in administration declares. "That big sprocket [the gear-wheel corporate logo] really means something."

In fact, many employees say the excellent relations stem from the shared goal of both workers and management — "to see Bombardier become bigger and more important."

CANADIAN PACIFIC HOTELS & RESORTS

1 University Avenue
Suite 1400
Toronto, Ontario
M5J 2P1
(416) 367-7111

Pay: **AVERAGE**	Atmosphere: **VERY GOOD**
Benefits: **GOOD**	Job Satisfaction: **EXCELLENT**
Promotion: **VERY GOOD**	Communications: **VERY GOOD**
Job Security: **VERY GOOD**	Personal Development: **VERY GOOD**

★ *Canadian Pacific Hotels & Resorts (CPH&R) has 25 hotels and resorts, making it Canada's largest hotel chain. There are 10,000 employees, 55% of them unionized (mainly in the Canadian Brotherhood of Railway Transport & General Workers and the Hotel & Restaurant Employees Union). In 1988, CPH&R reported a net profit of $23.5 million on a total revenue of $434.3 million.*

WHAT IS the hotel business? "It's meeting people, looking after their needs, making them happy, making sure they're kept smiling," says a catering manager who started out as a busboy in 1940.

A management trainee: "It's the energy, the show-business atmosphere. There are not many jobs where you can get that kind of feeling when you walk into work in the morning."

And what is Canadian Pacific Hotels & Resorts? "It's the best hotel chain in Canada, with the best image, the best people to work with. I fell in love with what I was doing, the people I met, the training I got. And it's gone on and on."

Hotel work isn't easy, particularly at the bottom of the ladder, and it's certainly not for everyone. There's shift work and the hours can be long. A hotel's busiest times often occur when the rest of the world is at leisure. In an field that averages 30% staff turnover, "we know we have the lowest turnover rate in the industry. And we have the largest percentage of long service employees," says President and Chief Executive Officer Robert DeMone. Half of all CPH&R's employees have been with the company for more than five years, and close to 25% for more than 10 years. In other words, people who like the work stay.

"Statistics show the cost to replace an hourly-paid employee can be more than $1,500; and more than $2,500 for a manager. So turnover is not only bad for morale and business, it's extremely costly," says Carolyn Clark, vice-president, human resources.

"Training is the secret for stability and employee loyalty. You've got to put money and time into developing employees. Otherwise they'll advance by going elsewhere to learn — to your competition probably." she adds.

The company teaches front-line employees interaction skills for dealing with customers. Managers learn hiring and interaction skills. And all employees are educated in safety practices. For employees who want to further their education, the company pays the tuition fees of work-related courses.

"We believe in pushing responsibility as far down the organization as possible," says DeMone. "We have a deep-felt belief that there is latent talent at all levels. The challenge of management is to bring that talent out. It is the front-line people who have guest contact, who can best service our guests' needs. We try to give them the maximum amount of responsibilty in dealing with situations as they arise. It is important to place responsibility and authority where it is most effective."

The work atmosphere and company reputation also play a part in employee satisfaction. An assistant reception manager with the chain says, "It's one big happy family, and it wouldn't matter if it were the Royal York [the largest] or any of the other hotels."

Another assistant manager who has worked for other large chains adds: "It gives you a lot of pride. I have never felt this pride working for any other chain."

One big difference, he finds, is that the organization is more personal, with a "living room" management style. He can approach top people for advice and guidance. Furthermore, other chains he has worked for are more structured "with a policy for everything." CPH&R, on the other hand, gives managers the freedom to make their own decisions.

A hotel human resources manager: "I enjoy having a comfortable amount of autonomy over the department I run." The mandate from her boss: " 'Do what you think is best, and if you need help let me know.' I enjoy that and try to let my staff feel that way also."

"The key today to a successful organization is being able to grow talent internally," Clark says. "The individual is never hindered when it comes to moving on, say, to another hotel. So everyone has a chance to do something else somewhere else," an employee adds.

A strong internal recruitment policy ensures this. A central list of the six employees at every hotel who are ready for immediate promotion to management is updated monthly. Employees on the list get the first available position for which they qualify. In 1988, 58% of supervisory-and-up vacancies were filled internally.

A vacant position will go to the best candidate at the same location. If no one there is qualified, the job gets posted company wide for two weeks. Only if this search fails is the job then posted externally. "Within the hotel itself, you can change from one department to another with blessings from the head of your department. They encourage individual growth," an employee says. Management promotes the feeling "that you're not stuck in a particular position."

While the pay at CPH&R (as in the hotel field generally) doesn't match the scales in some other industries, there are some compensations. For example, employees get complimentary rooms at Canadian Pacific hotels and resorts. The number of free nights depends on an employee's length of service, beginning at seven days after one year and increasing to 28 days after 20 years. Employees wanting to stay longer than their entitlement receive 70% off room rates.

During any stay, employees get a 50% discount off food and beverages. Supervisory and management personnel can have free laundry and valet service (in addition to free meals) while on duty.

Other employees are entitled to subsidized meals, such as a

full-course lunch or dinner for under $1.50. At the Banff and Lake Louise resorts, the company also offers subsidized accommodation in staff dormitories (paying $2.25-$3 a day for a room).

Employees also like the benefits package, which varies somewhat with the rank of the employee and with each hotel. They say the pension plan, tied to the original railway plan, is probably one of the best in the hotel industry in Canada.

There's also a suggestion plan with a $10,000 maximum award, and a tip-off plan that pays an employee 10% of the total bill (up to a maximum of $1,000) if a sales tip leads to a booking.

One of the greatest compensations of all for career people is the joy of the work itself. A food and beverage controller explains it this way: "I don't look on it as a job. It's a way of life. You live it the whole time that you're here. It gives you a great satisfaction to know that a guest is happy, that he feels safe and comfortable in your house, which is basically what it is."

Many employees who deal directly with the customer have a responsibility that can be rewarding. As a former front-desk clerk explains it: "Even though they're dealing within the structure of the company, it's how they treat the particular situation that dictates the outcome."

The chain also makes lateral transfers on request, and it pays the transportation and moving bills as well. "Those costs outweigh the high outside recruitment cost. We've transferred room clerks. We've transferred waiters from the Imperial Room [of the Royal York in Toronto] who wanted to go to Banff for the summer," says Clark.

The company draws most of its new career people from specialized college programs across the country. In 1988, more than 350 students of hotel and restaurant administration gained on-the-job summer training at five resort hotels, where the neophytes worked as busboys, maids and room clerks. On completion of their courses, these people will normally qualify for junior supervisory positions in a hotel.

CPH&R's management training program takes the process a step further. It selects "comers" from among the junior supervisors after they've had a minimum of a year with the company and puts them through a two-year, top-to-bottom immersion in hotel management.

Opportunities within the chain are going to multiply. "All the statistics confirm the fact that the tourism industry is the fastest growing industry," DeMone says. "It's already the largest employer in the world. One in every 16 people in the world is employed in travel and tourism, and by 2000 it will be the largest industry by any measure, including the largest generator of national income." CP Hotels & Resorts plans to seek a substantial share of that growth.

▄◣ Consumers Gas

CONSUMERS' GAS CO. LTD.

P.O. Box 650
Scarborough, Ontario
M1K 5E3
(416) 495-5000

Pay: **GOOD**	Atmosphere: **GOOD**
Benefits: **GOOD**	Job Satisfaction: **GOOD**
Job Security: **VERY GOOD**	Communications: **GOOD**
Promotion: **GOOD**	Personal Development: **GOOD**

★ *Consumers' Gas, Canada's largest natural gas distribution utility, is a publicly traded company, 83% owned by G. W. Utilities Ltd., a subsidiary of Olympia & York Developments. The company serves more than a million customers, mainly in Ontario. Revenue in 1988 was more than $1.8 billion. It has 3,300 employees, of whom about 56% are unionized, mainly by the Energy & Chemical Workers' Union.*

CONSUMERS' GAS is a solid, dependable, family-style operation with a paternalistic approach to its employees.

This company is not the place if you're looking for a dynamic, challenging, risk-taking atmosphere. If what you're after is solidity, reliability, the chance for controlled personal growth and above all, security, then Consumers' Gas will look after your needs very nicely.

It has established a reputation as a caring company. One employee says she joined Consumers' after months of extensive research into firms that treat their employees well. Good reports from several friends who worked at Consumers' convinced her to settle there.

A company whose employment reputation precedes it inevitably attracts good workers. But Consumers', not resting on its laurels, continues to improve working conditions.

Pay is competitive with other major Ontario employers. Benefits are quite generous. Part-time employees receive the same benefits as full-time staff with the exception of a pro-rated pension plan and a stock purchase and savings plan that is open only to full-time employees. The company promotes continuing education by reimbursing employees for 75% of tuition costs and books on the successful completion of a course.

One highly successful program is the Innovator's Circle, which pays cash awards for cost- or time-saving ideas. Consumers' works hard at promoting this form of participation. The minimum payment for an accepted idea is $50 and the maximum, $20,000. In 1988, one out of every five employees submitted applications.

The biggest innovation in 1989 came from gas technician John Selvaggio in the construction and maintenance department. His idea cut in half the time and cost of excavating city-centre gas mains, reduced traffic snarls and saved the company $31,600 a year. Selvaggio received $6,320 for his idea.

The company also recognizes an employee as Innovator of the Year, based on the number and value of innovations. The top 10 nominees for the award are honored at a special dinner. The winner in 1988 received the choice of a television set or a weekend away for two.

Consumers' has introduced new programs and benefits, while improving existing ones. For example, the successful employee voluntary assistance program was introduced in July, 1989. The program was designed and implemented by a committee of equal numbers of union and nonunion members that was given complete responsibility. It is committee members, not company representatives, who promote the plan among the employees.

Another example of management-union cooperation to improve the working environment has been the drive to improve safety. While Consumers' safety record is better than the industry average, "that isn't good enough," says Jim Simpson, vice-president of human resources. Through the safety committee, employees are encouraged to identify potential hazards then develop procedures to avoid them. All outside workers receive first aid training, and employees receive awards for accident-free records.

Consumers' allows long-service employees to retire early. Introduced in 1988, the early retirement enhancement lets employees over 57 whose age and length of service add up to 90 to retire on full pension. More than half of the employees retiring take advantage of the early retirement provisions.

Consumers' was one of five companies to win the Canadian Chamber of Commerce Fitness Canada Award for fitness and lifestyle programs in the workplace. Lunch-and-learn seminars on stress management, fitness, nutrition, first aid and family communication are popular.

Everything, however, isn't all roses within the company. Some employees can't get the promotions they feel they deserve, and inter-departmental shifts are hard to come by. It's a conservative company, trying to modernize gradually, and change is coming too slowly for some of the younger, ambitious workers. In addition, union rules on seniority makes it difficult to skip past anyone in the line.

As a utility, Consumers' has constant interaction with the public. Surveys have consistently shown that customers feel the company is quick to respond and concerned about their needs, and that it has warm and friendly employees. "One of the biggest motivators for employees is working for a company where customers think highly of you," says Simpson.

President Robert Martin developed a 15-year strategic plan. He recorded on videocassette his views on the direction the company was taking, described areas of concern and asked for feedback. The video was shown to all employees, who then discussed the issues involved and sent their comments back to the top.

"The experience was so positive," says Simpson, "that our managers are doing it again." The new project, called Leadership 2000, was launched in January, 1990.

Another communication forum is the annual employee meeting. "We owe employees a report in the same way owe shareholders. We present an overview of how the company has done and what the plans for the future are," Simpson explains.

Every year, the meeting brings together 150 employee representatives from all regions and departments. There is a no-holds-barred (with the exception of personal grievances) question and answer period, then representatives have the responsibility of reporting on the meeting to their fellow workers.

Women in management is an area the company is dedicated to improving. In 1989, there were only four women in senior management and none in the vice-presidential ranks. Earlier efforts to increase the number of women at senior levels weren't as successful as desired, so the human resources department has opted for a more aggressive plan, in which managers' performance will be partially measured by their ability to meet employment equity goals.

Consumers' is without doubt a reliable, stable, caring place to work. But it's still very much a middle-of-the-road company, and not yet the challenging work environment that it could be.

EQUITABLE LIFE INSURANCE CO. OF CANADA

1 Westmount Road North
Waterloo, Ontario
N2J 4C7
(519) 886-5110

Pay: **AVERAGE**	Atmosphere: **VERY GOOD**
Benefits: **GOOD**	Job Satisfaction: **GOOD**
Promotion: **GOOD**	Communication: **GOOD**
Job Security: **GOOD**	Personal Development: **GOOD**

★ *Equitable Life is an independent, Canadian mutual life insurance company. It has 291 nonunionized employees, and in 1988 total revenue exceeded $167 million, $114 million of it from life, health and annuity premiums.*

EMPLOYEES FEEL Equitable Life is such a good place to work that 18 of them wrote to The Financial Post to say why. They described the company as having:
  • "A caring attitude toward employees."
  • "A real family feeling."
  • "An air of friendliness."
  • "An open and honest communication from the top down and vice versa."
  • "A smiling culture where by and large people actually have fun as well as exercise the work ethic."
  And people really do care. The front desk receptionist makes an effort to greet everyone by name in the morning. Mail room

delivery people greet other employees in the hallways on their rounds. President Ian McIntosh sends each employee a handwritten note on the anniversary of his or her employment with the company.

While the insurance industry is by tradition conservative and characterized by rules and proceedures, McIntosh has tried to make Equitable open, flexible and responsive. When the company computerized part of its operation, although suggested, there was no feasibility study done. "We know we need to computerize," said MacIntosh. "Let's just do it."

His strategy is to shake up the organization a little bit, and implement new policies quickly. "We have been experimenting with a 'breakthrough strategy' — where rather than study a problem we just assign it to one or two people to solve. By building on little successes, you can get a faster result."

The company instituted flexible working hours in 1973, around the core hours of 9 a.m. to 3 p.m. Part-time employees who work 18 hours a week receive pro-rated benefits. And part-timers can job-share. One woman who has been sharing a job for nearly four years says it is ideally suited for her: "We both love the flexibility it gives us. Sharing the same position has worked well for both of us."

In addition to regular holidays, all employees at the company get five floating days off. These may be taken for any reason — from looking after a sick child to attending a matinee.

There is a strong policy of promoting from within. Says one new mail room employee: "Working in the mail room, you get to know a lot of people and see what all the departments do. I've already heard about a few openings."

The head of the mail room laments: "Over the last three years, 22 people who have started in the mail room have moved into other departments. It's terrible. I have to keep hiring new employees."

Equitable is not afraid of innovation. When the opportunity arose to develop some property behind the Waterloo head office, without any previous experience, Equitable designed and built its own condominiums, rather than assign the project to a property developer.

Another innovative program was GSP. "GSP is coming," announced the hallway signs. No one knew what it was. After employee curiosity and interest reached an all-time high, the

Gain Sharing Plan was introduced in 1987.

Under GSP, employees receive a day's pay for each half per cent increase in company-wide productivity, up to a maximum of 10 days' pay.

The success of GSP so far has exceeded expectations. Productivity increased by 7% in 1988. Because the program had clearly exceeded the maximum, senior management did not wait until the audited figures came out in March to give employees their bonuses, but instead had the cheques made up secretly.

When employees returned to work in January, 1989, signs directed them down to the cafeteria to have coffee and doughnuts. As employees arrived, they were each greeted by their divisional vice-president, congratulated on their effort, and given a cheque for two weeks' pay. Says one employee: "It was a wonderful way to start the year."

"GSP has been successful because it created an attitude that we can do things better," comments one-long serving employee. "Some of the best people are new ones, because they question the way we do things."

As at the end of June, 1989, the annualized productivity gain stood at 6.5% — so employees are headed for another 10-day pay-out.

H. J. HEINZ CO.
OF CANADA LTD.

5650 Yonge Street
16th floor
North York, Ont.
M2M 4G3
(416) 226-5757

Pay: **VERY GOOD**	Atmosphere: **VERY GOOD**
Benefits: **GOOD**	Job Satisfaction: **EXCELLENT**
Promotion: **GOOD**	Communications: **GOOD**
Job Security: **EXCELLENT**	Personal Development: **GOOD**

★ *Heinz produces more than 500 varieties of food product, of which the best known are tomato juice, ketchup and baby food. Head office is in Metro Toronto, while the main manufacturing operation is in Leamington, Ont. Employees of Heinz and its subsidiaries number 2,000, and 75% are unionized. Canadian sales top $400 million annually. The company is a wholly owned subsidiary of H. J. Heinz Co. of Pittsburgh.*

HEINZ'S HISTORY began in 1869 with an enterprising young man peddling freshly grated horseradish door to door in Pittsburgh. Today, the company is active on six continents, marketing thousands of products in more than 200 countries. Its Canadian operation has built a tradition of old-fashioned reliability, quality and permanence. Management style tends to be conservative, but with its reputation for looking after employees Heinz is considered an excellent place to work.

The company is modest about its very profitable history. Perhaps "understated" best describes the company's chief characteristic. As one employee explains: "We don't go around saying we're the greatest, but we do have [one of] the highest growth rates in the food industry in Canada."

Job security is not a concern. Heinz baby foods dominate the Canadian market, while the company's portion of the tomato-juice market has steadily grown, reaching record levels. Building on these strengths, Heinz continues to be a risk taker. The increasingly popular Weight Watchers products together with a line of frozen specialty baking may hold the key to future expansion.

Managerial and marketing staff say the company atmosphere is professional but friendly. "It's also entrepreneurial — we all work very hard to get the job done." Heinz works equally hard to retain good workers and make them feel valuable on the job.

The concern for people is evident at the Leamington plant. Although Heinz is virtually the only employer in town, labor-management relations are harmonious because the company runs a clean, efficient operation, placing emphasis on co-operation. Employee turnover is so low, it can hardly be counted. It takes three to four years of part-time, seasonal work to build up enough seniority to fill a vacant full-time post.

Workers are proud of both their plant and union, yet few problems result from this apparent conflict of interest. Most workers feel they are being treated fairly. Good will has left Heinz with an almost clean labor-relations record and few strikes. And the company's "total-quality management" program will give workers more responsibility for identifying and correcting problems in the plant.

Communications, once an area of concern for employees, improved with the appointment of Andrew Barrett as company president in 1989. Since then, a plant newsletter has been reintroduced, and a company-wide magazine keeps employees abreast of news and industry trends.

Salaries are good for the food-service industry, and although a worker might make more money in a big-city steel or car plant, most say they wouldn't leave. They enjoy their jobs and feel suitably compensated.

Benefits are generous and include a popular stock-purchase plan, to which the company makes a 10% contribution. Opportunities for promotion are good — although rare for women — at both the plant and head office. There are no female executives at

Heinz Canada.

Heinz takes its civic responsibilities seriously. It donated land and money to help build the Sherk Sports Complex in Leamington, and the company subsidizes about one fifth of employees and pensioners' membership costs.

In general, the company combines many of the elements that help create a happy work environment. It may not be the most dynamic company, but employees have good reason to be optimistic about their work. Heinz will likely be around for a long time.

Imperial Tobacco Limited/Limitée

IMPERIAL TOBACCO LTD.

3810 St. Antoine Street West
Montreal, Quebec
H4C 1B5
(514) 932-6161

Pay: **VERY GOOD**	Atmosphere: **VERY GOOD**
Benefits: **GOOD**	Job Satisfaction: **VERY GOOD**
Promotion: **VERY GOOD**	Communications: **VERY GOOD**
Job Security: **GOOD**	Personal Development: **VERY GOOD**

★ *Imperial Tobacco is the largest Canadian tobacco company, with a 56.2% share of a shrinking tobacco market. Imperial nevertheless enjoyed sales of $2 billion in fiscal 1988 and contributed operating earnings of $308 million to its parent holding company, Imasco Ltd. Roughly 65% of Imperial's 2,482 workers are unionized, mainly in the Bakery, Confectionery & Tobacco Workers.*

ONE OF THE measures of a truly fine employer is how it treats its workers in adversity. Imperial Tobacco, operating in a declining industry, looks after them very well indeed. Company stragegy, in place since 1983, has been to cut jobs gradually and voluntarily. Working with the unions, Imperial has came up with a very generous severance-pay offer that sometimes goes as high as four times salary. (The average severance pay is 2.7 times annual salary.)

The pay and tempting early retirement offers enabled Imperial to eliminate 59 head office positions in 1988, without any dismissals. Marius Dagneau, the company's vice-president of human resources, says the decline in numbers likely will continue, but more gradually.

"The projection we have is in all likelihood that the industry will continue to decline, but not at the same severe rate that we have witnessed since 1982-83. If you consider the value and the culture and the way of doing things here, it's a lot more difficult to reduce the number of employees, respecting our commitment to people. It requires a great deal more planning, not to be forced to lay off people. We have not laid off people for many, many years," Dagneau says.

Dagneau, who has been with the company 25 years, says staff reductions are not new. Jobs were eliminated in the 1960s and 1970s for competitive reasons and to accommodate technological change. Most recently, however, they have occurred because of strong opposition to smoking.

Imperial Tobacco does very little recruiting these days. However, when it does need staff its generous compensation package is an attractive magnet. And criticism of the tobacco industry doesn't seem to scare off potential employees.

Most employees at Imperial Tobacco are long-service workers and most are convinced they couldn't find better jobs anywhere else. Turnover rates are very low, averaging 3%-5%.

The pay scales are superb and the benefits superior. Salaries are between 20% and 30% higher than national averages for similar jobs. The midpoint salary for an entry-level clerk, for example, is close to $29,000 a year.

The quality of a job, however, depends on much more than compensation. Consider the views of a skilled worker at an Imperial cigarette plant, who attended a staff party of the company where his wife worked. The man shocked his spouse by trying to strike up a conversation with her boss of bosses.

"She said, 'You shouldn't do that. He's like God around there. Nobody talks to him except the big people,' " the Imperial man recalls, adding distainfully: "I wouldn't want to work for a person like that."

Clearly, Imperial's top executives are not persons like that. They take the time for simple acts of courtesy and recognition that make employees "feel as though you're important to the company." Furthermore, Imperial extends courtesy and dignity to the work itself.

"They know I can do my job, and they don't bother me," a plant man explains. "I don't see a foreman from one day to another sometimes."

A co-worker adds: "I worked for two other major companies, and there's no comparison whatsoever. [One of the other companies] was the pits right from the management to the foreman. They blew a whistle for coffee. As soon as your 10 minutes were up, they blew another one. Here it's not like that at all."

Imperial's plant people refer to a clean, friendly, almost family-style environment and bosses who work hard to be fair — sometimes more than fair. In one plant, management allots company time for employees to run the affairs of their credit union.

"They've been excellent," says a credit union man. "They give us every leeway they possibly can as far as that type of thing goes."

The company's sales and distribution people describe the same kind of cheerful, co-operative, no-hounding atmosphere, with the added spice of challenge and "endless opportunities."

"I've never, ever been bored," a sales supervisor says. "There's always something new coming down the pike — new products, new projects, always something to keep your interest high."

It's likely the company will be around for some time yet, despite the industry's critics. "It's very much a personal opinion, but I think we will continue to be a very profitable organization for the foreseeable future," says Dagneau. "The industry will be smaller, and obviously there will be less people involved. Traditionally, Imperial Tobacco has been a high-paying, profitable organization. Certainly our longer-term plans do not indicate any lowering of that. We will continue to be one of the very good employers in Canada."

KODAK
CANADA INC.

3500 Eglinton Avenue West
Toronto, Ontario
M6M 1V3
(416) 766-8233

Pay: **VERY GOOD**	Atmosphere: **VERY GOOD**
Benefits: **VERY GOOD**	Job Satisfaction: **VERY GOOD**
Promotion: **AVERAGE**	Communications: **AVERAGE**
Job Security: **VERY GOOD**	Personal Development: **AVERAGE**

★ *Kodak Canada produces and markets a broad range of photographic products and services. Its 2,300 employees work at the Toronto head office, regional offices in Vancouver and Montreal, as well as at sales and service outlets across Canada. The company, as a wholly owned subsidiary of Eastman Kodak Co. of Rochester, N.Y., does not disclose sales figures. The Employees' Association of Kodak Canada represents about 35% of the workers.*

"TEN YEARS ago, Kodak was God. Today the customer is God." That's how one employee describes the change in attitude within this one-time traditional company. Customer service, a greater response to the marketplace and a team management style have replaced complacency, caution, paternalism and set work patterns.

Increasing competition, particularly from Japan, has forced Kodak to become more *at*tuned to the marketplace. And its employees also are having to learn to adapt to constantly changing conditions within the company. The old-fashioned virtues of the one-big-happy-family concept have disappeared, a fact mourned by many long service employees. But they are realistic enough to accept that the company is still bending over backward to be fair to its workers.

Probably the most remarkable achievement has been the Canadian company's no-layoff record, which goes back to the Great Depression era of the 1930s. The record becomes even more astonishing when you realize that Eastman Kodak, its U.S. parent, has restructured itself four times since 1983, once paring 10% of its workforce. In Canada, Kodak maintained jobs by carving out its own market niche to remain competitive worldwide. Despite a plant closing in the late 1980s, the Canadian company's workforce has been stable at 2,300. Turnover remains a low 4%-5%.

The stability of the Canadian operation is certainly due in part to its president, Ron Morrison. "Ron's a fighter for Kodak Canada, and the management structure here is very, very strong," says one of his employees.

In 1985, when first appointed, Morrison set himself some impressive goals: reorganizing the company; establishing a pay-for-performance system; pushing decision-making down into the organization; and improving communication.

Some of these initiatives are well under way, others less advanced. The biggest problem area remains communication. The company has a generous compensation structure and benefits superior to those of many other companies, but the general perception among employees is that both pay and benefits are only fair or competitive. Clearly, the company has not promoted its own best qualities adequately to its employees.

In fact, salaries are very good. And the wage dividend (Kodak's version of a profit-sharing plan) makes the compensation hard to beat. Under the plan, any employee with five years or more of service gets a generous annual bonus, and workers with less service are rewarded in proportion to their length of employment. In 1989, the workers shared $6.6 million.

Some employees say communications are very effective in their area, while others believe communication is not good enough yet. It's improving, they say, but it has a long way to go.

Part of the problem, workers contend, is that their bosses aren't visible enough. "If I were a manager, I'd get down on the plant floor more often to find out what's happening down there," one woman says.

Training is another area of concern. While there appears to be quite a few optional courses (in everything from computer training to photography) for employees who wish to upgrade themselves, some workers believe there's too little job-specific training. "There are still too many people here who are not very good at their jobs," complains one worker. Another junior employee backs up this view: "There are too many bosses and supervisors who aren't sufficiently trained."

The benefits are up to date, and they include orthodontics, as well as an exceptionally generous sick pay plan that pays full salary for the first 52 weeks of illness. Employees would like to see the dental plan upgraded to pay more than the 70% of fees for routine dentistry.

Problems aside, job satisfaction is high at Kodak. Most employees speak very positively about the challenge, variety and opportunity in their jobs. Workers also prize their job security and the friendly, open atmosphere. And in a recent company survey, 72% of employees rated Kodak overall as an excellent place to work.

MARY KAY

MARY KAY COSMETICS LTD.

5600 Ambler Drive
Mississauga, Ontario
L4W 2K9
(416) 624-5600

Pay: **AVERAGE**	Atmosphere: **VERY GOOD**
Benefits: **GOOD**	Job Satisfaction: **VERY GOOD**
Promotion: **POOR**	Communications: **VERY GOOD**
Job Security: **GOOD**	Personal Development: **AVERAGE**

★ *Mary Kay is the second largest direct-selling cosmetics company in Canada, with sales of about $68 million. The company's 85 employees provide administrative, marketing and product backup to 10,000 independent beauty consultants, who sell 195 products at private parties.*

NOT SURPRISINGLY, for a company in the cosmetics business, Mary Kay has a very large female component in its workforce: 74% of its employees are women. About 58% of the managers and 40% of the executives are women, including two vice-presidents.

The company has what it calls a self-initiated affirmative action program. "Our basic company philosophy is to promote opportunity for women in areas of personal growth and income. We attempt to promote women in all levels," the company told us.

It's true to its word. Take, for example, Hannah McCurley who is vice-president of manufacturing, with a staff of six managers reporting to her. She is responsible for all aspects of

282

manufacturing — purchasing, planning, forecasting, inventory control and quality control. Her division oversees production done by sub-contractors.

She joined Mary Kay (with two chemistry degrees) in 1981, as a manager helping to set up a technical quality assurance group.

Even for the talented, rewards don't come easily. Between 1984 and 1986, she took on back-breaking studies for an MBA degree at the University of Toronto. She was given full financial support by Mary Kay, including pay for one day a week at the university. (She put in 90-hour weeks, juggling her studies, her job and responsibilities to her husband and two young sons.)

She says Mary Kay is one of a select few companies that sponsor employees in that kind of executive development program. "There's no doubt that Mary Kay is a very people-oriented company and we look to promote from within. We look at rewards for performance."

Employees say when they join Mary Kay they become part of a family. Some might find the cheerfulness and camaraderie almost cloying, but workers seem to adore the atmosphere. Inspired by a Texas grandmother who started this direct-sales company, Mary Kay's flock take seriously the corporate philosophy that people come first.

"That philosophy is no different from other service companies and particularly other direct-selling companies, like Avon," says President Ray Patrick, formerly an Avon executive. "What's different is that Mary Kay has formalized the approach to motivating people."

There are personal touches, such as birthday cards for employees, wedding presents and flowers in the event of a family funeral. There are company-sponsored picnics, Christmas gatherings and hockey teams, as well as departmental dinners with the president after a particularly busy period in the office.

Patrick denies it, but employees believe there is a Mary Kay stereotype: young, enthusiastic and co-operative. Conformity seems to be another ingredient. With perpetual smiles on their faces and dressed to the dictates of a company code, employees are prepared to fit the Mary Kay mold in order to succeed and enjoy the environment.

Most employees find Mary Kay a fun-loving and caring place to work. They expect their colleagues to pitch in when work loads get heavy. And they know co-workers will show concern for lives outside the office. An employee with a very ill child was grateful for the generous leave and the emotional support from friends at work. A single parent, who must sometimes come in late and leave early, gets some latitude, even though flexible working hours are not part of corporate policy.

Mary Kay's office procedures also show employees the company cares about them. Monthly department meetings, semi-annual meetings of small employee groups and the annual meeting provide employees with a chance to speak out and discuss what is happening in the company.

The company also seems prepared to take chances on people. Recognizing there are not as many opportunities for promotion in a small company, Mary Kay moves people around. Within a year and a half, a filing clerk was moved to accounts receivable clerk and then to consultant services clerk, with successive pay increments. A shipper who showed promise became the print co-ordinator.

Obviously, it's hard to do that with supervisors and managers. "We just have to accept the fact that some people outgrow this organization," Patrick says. "As we grow, hopefully we'll be able to accommodate more of them."

Although salaries were considered less than competitive in the past, they are now competitive with other companies in the Mississauga area. But Mary Kay employees get a lot of perks outside of straight salary. There's the deferred profit sharing plan, which increased from 5% of profits in the past to 10% for 1988. It was projected to rise to 12% for 1989. Managers (40% of staff) also receive an additional performance-based bonus. Then there's the Christmas bonus of 1%-2½% of salary.

The benefits plan is generous, and includes health care, a dental plan, accident coverage and life insurance — all 100% company-paid. Even unused sick leave days are paid for in cash at yearend. There is no pension plan, however.

For many employees, the price break on cosmetics is another valued benefit. Workers are entitled to $300 (wholesale) worth of company products in each calendar year at no charge. Additional purchases get a 50% discount.

It's also no wonder there are so many glittering hands to complement the smiling faces at Mary Kay. Employees can buy at cost sales-incentive items such as jewelry that were not awarded to consultants in the field for meeting sales goals.

MOORE®

MOORE BUSINESS FORMS & SYSTEMS DIVISION

130 Adelaide Street West
Suite 1600
Toronto, Ontario
M5H 3R7
(416) 863-6848

Pay: **GOOD**	Atmosphere: **VERY GOOD**
Benefits: **AVERAGE**	Job Satisfaction: **VERY GOOD**
Promotion: **GOOD**	Communications: **AVERAGE**
Job Security: **GOOD**	Personal Development: **GOOD**

★ *Moore's parent, Moore Corp., is the world's largest manufacturer of business forms. It has 139 plants in 53 countries. Moore employs over 25,000 people worldwide and has sales of more than US$2.5 billion a year. Moore's Canadian operations employ 2,200 people across the country. Four of the nine Canadian plants are unionized. Moore is publicly traded, and Canadians hold more than 87% of its shares.*

TO AN OUTSIDER, Moore's employees resemble their company: quiet, low profile and hard-working but also full of enthusiasm.

The company has been around a long time. It grew from a small operation in 1882, when Samuel Moore invented the Paragon Counter salesbook in Toronto, to become the world's largest manufacturer of business forms, with sales in excess of US$2.5 billion.

Business forms are the core of the company's operations, but

Moore also provides management services, including database retrieval, direct marketing and information distribution. Moore expects management services to be the fast-growth part of its business in the future. In 1988, the company redefined its "business mission" to reflect the shift from a forms manufacturer to a company helping customers manage business information more effectively.

Moore credits its success to its emphasis on serving the customer. "The company doesn't just fill orders, it's constantly suggesting new products for its customers," says David Carter, manager of human resources development. "Just recently, for example, we worked with Visa to switch to carbonless forms for their credit card sales drafts. These cost a little more, but they're much easier to use now that the messy carbons have been eliminated. Customers also benefit by being protected from confidential information on the carbon falling into the wrong hands."

A lot of emphasis is placed on the sales staff. Before going into the field, new employees complete a computerized self-instruction course at their own pace. Follow-up training includes a series of one-week training sessions in Chicago, at Moore's North American sales training centre. There are also refresher courses and frequent group presentations on everything from systems to form design.

Despite its success, Moore has been through some rough times. "The 1980s have been a decade of change and we're still adjusting as we move into the 1990s," Carter says.

Moore is in the process of streamlining and automating many of its systems and procedures, which has resulted in some jobs disappearing. Most have been eliminated through attrition, early retirement, transfers and retraining. Where that hasn't been possible, the company has worked hard to be compassionate and supportive to those who have to leave. Two- to three-months' notice and generous severance pay are usually provided. Moore also provides courses during work hours to provide help in looking for another job.

"The company's generosity and help to people who have to leave has been a great comfort through this difficult period," says an estimator who was squeezed out of his previous job in another company. "We've known that if we have to leave, the company would do everything to help, including providing good severance pay."

The employees are generally behind the move to more automation, in large part because of Project Tomorrow, a task force of employees set up in mid-1989. It's mandate was to find ways of cutting costs and improving systems and procedures, and workers were asked for their ideas. The task force concluded that more automation was required, particularly aimed at faster turnaround on orders. Moore has moved quickly on the recommendations. Some had been implemented by the end of 1989; the rest should be in place by the end of 1990.

Although concerned that their jobs might disappear or they might have to move to another location, employees are excited about the opportunities emerging from Project Tomorrow. The estimator is hoping to be transferred to the pricing division, which is revamping the pricing list to make it more cost reflective. And one salesman says: "It's very reassuring to work for a company that is so forward looking. You have an increased sense of security because you know the company will be able to survive and prosper even in tough times."

Union certification of the Trenton, Ont., plant in 1987 increased the number of unionized plants to four. The union called a strike during the second contract negotiation in 1989, but it was not a very acrimonious dispute. The union settled for the company's original offer after a two-week strike.

Pay levels are considered good, although entry level salaries are on the low side. Parts of the benefits package have been improved since 1985, but standards remain below those offered by the best employers.

The best benefits feature is the retirement savings plan, which is tied to the pension plan. Under the RSP, employees can set aside up to 5% of their salary. For every $1 employees contribute, the company adds 25¢. A profit-based supplementary contribution can add another 25¢ to every employee dollar.

Moore also pays recruitment bonuses. If a non-supervisory employee recommends someone hired by information services, the employee gets $2,000. The bonus for recruiting a sales representative is $1,000.

What's special about Moore is the atmosphere. People enjoy going to work. The estimator, for example, spends an hour each day traveling to work. Before he started at Moore, he thought this might be too much, but it hasn't turned out that way because he enjoys his job so much.

The management style is also excellent. Managers are demanding, but they're also reasonable about unavoidable delays. They also encourage employees to explore new ideas and they are accomodating about arranging schedules to allow employees to take courses that will update their skills.

Moore foresees continued growth in coming years, providing good chances for promotion, particularly for post-secondary graduates, as the company develops new markets in information management. With the company's traditional reliance on internal promotion, there will be lots of opportunities.

All in all, Moore remains a quiet, unobtrusive giant, which nevertheless has a longstanding philosophy of dealing with people in a positive way. "It's a tradition that many companies aspire to but few achieve," Carter says. "It's one quality that's not easy to put into a company. Moore's got it."

MOOSEHEAD BREWERIES LTD.

P.O. Box 3100
Station B
Saint John, New Brunswick
E2M 3H2
(506) 635-7000

Pay: **GOOD**	Atmosphere: **EXCELLENT**
Benefits: **VERY GOOD**	Job Satisfaction: **VERY GOOD**
Promotion: **AVERAGE**	Communications: **GOOD**
Job Security: **EXCELLENT**	Personal Development: **GOOD**

★ *Moosehead, the biggest private brewery in Canada (owned outright by the Oland family), annually markets more than $100 million worth of beer in Nova Scotia, New Brunswick, the U.S. and Britain. Most of the company's 367 employees work at the home base in Saint John. Sixty percent of the workers in the company's two breweries are unionized.*

IF YOU CAN get on staff, Moosehead Breweries provides one of the most secure jobs in the Maritimes. And the caring, family atmosphere will ensure that you won't want to leave. Turnover is less than 1%, , and Employee Relations Manager Mark Trask admits: "We certainly don't have to go looking for people."

The Olands have been brewers for more than a century, and through the years a tradition of genuine concern has built up for employees. Workers' needs, worries and concerns become the business of the Olands. Here are just a few examples offered by some of their loyal employees:

• "When I was off sick, the company offered my wife a car if she needed it."

● "I used to work nights, but then I had a medical problem. Now I work only days. The company really bends over backward to help you."

● "One employee had cancer, and the only effective treatment for that rare type was in Missouri. The company flew him down there."

Newly hired employees talk of the external reputation Moosehead has gained as an excellent work environment. One manager, who had previously worked as an auditor: "I saw many different companies, and as far as I'm concerned, Moosehead has to be one of the tops in the Maritimes."

The company looks after its employees in a material way as well. Salaries are high compared with others in the Atlantic provinces, and the benefits package is thoroughly up-to-date, containing such extras as vision care and orthodontic coverage. Christmas bonuses, turkeys and free beer count as additional perks. A formal employee assistance program, a recent addition to an already balanced benefits package, provides free confidential counseling for alcohol and drug abuse, as well as for personal problems of employees and their families.

In the company's Saint John brewery, employee activities centre around the Alpine Room, a convivial hospitality lounge where Phillip Oland, the 79-year-old patriarch of the clan, can be seen sitting down for a sandwich and a brew next to a production line worker most days of the week.

Moosehead is also very community-spirited. For instance, the company participates in a skateathon that raised $1,900 last year for a local psychiatric institution and in the restoration of the Marco Polo, a 19th century clipper ship built in New Brunswick.

Communications are simple and direct. You can just walk into the big boss's office, and talk to either Phil or son Derek Oland about your problem. Labor-management meetings are held once a month — so the union local is kept aware of problems and plans. (Moosehead has no Canadian expansion plans until it studies the effects of Canada-U.S. free trade on the industry, but it is looking farther afield. Says Trask: "We are looking at a world market in terms of direct sales for our product.")

Just about the only difficulty anyone considers serious is promotion — given low turnover and the Oland clan firmly in the top jobs (showing every sign of passing the mantle on to the fifth generation).

NBTel

NEW BRUNSWICK TELEPHONE CO. LTD.

One Brunswick Square
P.O. Box 1430
Saint John, New Brunswick
E2L 4K2
(506) 658-7355

Pay: **AVERAGE**	Atmosphere: **GOOD**
Benefits: **GOOD**	Job Satisfaction: **VERY GOOD**
Promotion: **GOOD**	Communications: **GOOD**
Job Security: **VERY GOOD**	Personal Development: **VERY GOOD**

★ *The New Brunswick Telephone Co. (NBTel) and its 2,469 employees provide 280,000 customers with up-to-date telecommunications services. NBTel (1988 operating revenue: $284 million) is owned by Bruncor Inc., which is publicly traded. BCE Inc. owns 31.2% of Bruncor; NBTel employees, 10.6 %; institutional investors, 16.7%; individual investors, 41.5%. About 40% of the employees are union members (Communications Workers of Canada).*

NBTEL PROVIDES a stable, no-layoff working environment in a province where such qualities are often rare. And its employees are well aware of their good lot.

"Working in the Maritimes, the quality of life here is better — and the cost of living lower. NBTel is one of best Maritime employers," one worker says. Another adds: "I could double my salary by moving to Toronto, but I like it here."

Management's style is conservative, but it's aware of the need to move with the times. NBTel employs state-of-the-art technology, and has been using productivity circles and stepped-up training programs to keep its workers up to date as well.

For example, the company has a program to retrain employees whose skills might become obsolete within 10 years. And it sends some employees to university full-time, and pays them 70% of their salaries while they're there. In 1989, 23 workers had completed their degree courses, and another 18 were enrolled as full-time students under the program.

The company also reimburses employees 100% for the cost of any work-related courses successfully completed. The reimbursement is 75% for courses not specifically job-related. In 1988, NBTel helped 350 employees enrolled in part-time studies at universities and technical schools. Another 110 workers took university-level courses given at corporate headquarters in Saint John.

Another perk is the home computer purchase assistance program (an interest-free loan repaid through payroll deductions) linked to computer literacy courses.

"We're small as telephone companies go, but because of that we have broad job descriptions," one worker says. "So we learn a lot more here than we would at Bell or B.C. Telephone."

Promotional opportunities, particularly in terms of career broadening positions, seem excellent, but the prospects for reaching the top levels are less sure. And women in managerial positions are few and far between.

The benefits package includes such extras as vision care, but the dental plan doesn't include orthodontics. The pension plan is non-contributory, and employees may enrich their pensions through NBTel's employee retirement savings plan. A share purchase plan gives workers the chance to invest up to 10% of pay in Bruncor stock at an average market price. For every $4 an employee invests, the company puts up $1.

To foster teamwork and improve productivity, NBTel has established a bonus plan for non-unionized employees, under which pay is linked to financial and customer-satisfaction objectives. In 1990, for example, if the year's objectives were achieved, the bonus would equal 4% of salary. If the objectives were exceeded, the bonus would be as high as 6%. The mix also contains an additional multiplier, based on personal performance.

In theory, an above-average performer could triple the basic bonus amount. This means an employee earning a $25,000 base salary would receive $1,000 for achieving the objectives, another

$500 for exceeding expectations, and another $3,000 for turning in an outstanding performance.

The company sends out monthly bulletins on the company's results so employees can keep track of their bonuses. As employee relations adviser Walter Carlson says: "There's quite a strong incentive to improve performance now."

NBTel celebrated its 100th birthday in 1988, and entered its second century with a new mission statement, which aptly sums up this traditional company: "A tradition of trust, a promise of performance."

Despite the middle-of-the-road corporate culture, NBTel comes across as a superior workplace where learning opportunities and career progression are excellent.

S. C. JOHNSON
& SON LTD.

1 Webster Street
Brantford, Ontario
N3T 5R1
(519) 756-7900

Pay: **GOOD**	Atmosphere: **VERY GOOD**
Benefits: **VERY GOOD**	Job Satisfaction: **GOOD**
Promotion: **AVERAGE**	Communications: **VERY GOOD**
Job Security: **EXCELLENT**	Personal Development: **GOOD**

★ *Better known to many as Johnson's Wax, S.C. Johnson & Son manufactures home and personal-care products at its plant adjacent to the Canadian head office in Brantford. Some of its brand names (such as Raid, Off!, Pledge, Bon Ami and Agree) are household words. This subsidiary of a multinational based in Racine, Wisc., had sales of about $100 million in 1988 and 325 full-time Canadian employees (110 hourly rated).*

JOHNSON'S WAX had the admiration and respect of almost everyone in Brantford in 1985. We were pleased to find that what we wrote then remained just as accurate in 1989.

To win envious glances in Brantford, a female employee told us, "all you have to do is say: 'I work at Johnson's Wax.' " The reasons were obvious then, and they still are:

- Good pay — maintained above the community average.
- Profit sharing — at between 20% and 35% of pay.
- Superb benefits — fully paid by the company.
- A 24-hour on-site recreation centre.
- A free vacation resort — winter and summer.

- A no-layoff policy.
- A four-day work week in the plant.
- Participative management.
- A real effort to take the boredom out of routine work.

And there's more than that. "The atmosphere is good," a male plant worker said. "The people you work with try to help you, whereas in other plants they say: 'That's not my job.' " A female worker added: "Everybody seems to try to boost each other's morale. It's just nice to know that somebody else in this world does care about you."

Another woman: "The people we work with are great — all of them. If you have a complaint, it's looked at right away. If you want to change jobs, all you have to do is mention it. We change jobs all the time. I've been trained for all those things. It makes everybody's job a lot [less humdrum]."

"I tended to get bored with my job," one long-service employee told us. "They gave me the chance [to do more responsible and interesting work]. At the time, she worked alone at night, changing over the production lines and doing some maintenance on the machinery. She prized the total lack of supervision: "I appreciate that, because I feel good about myself."

One of the reasons why Johnson is a great place to work is that the parent company, founded in 1886 by Samuel Curtis Johnson, is still owned by the same family. "And Sam Johnson runs it as a family," Robert Deacon, personnel director of the Canadian subsidiary, will tell you.

Family ownership is "a fantastic benefit to employees if the leader of that company is a people-oriented kind of person — someone who wants to build that company for the future. Sam Johnson and his family are building this for the future."

The no-layoff policy for full-time people, for example, went into force in the Depression and it still stands firmly in place. To make it work, the company handles its peak production requirements with temporary employees. Deacon: "Many of them are spouses who want extra money — but on their terms. They can work when they want to. It's a good relationship both ways."

The generous benefits package includes health-care and dental plans that continue for employees and dependents after retirement. The pension plan has provisions for passing on the pension to a beneficiary when the former employee dies.

The profit-sharing plan covers all employees, but operates on four levels from nonsupervisory workers up to the president. And seniority counts, too. After 10 years with the company, a nonsupervisory worker can get 20% of base pay. The plan pays the president 35%.

Cash profit-sharing awards are distributed to eligible employees in June and December each year. But each employee also has the option of putting the money into a deferred trust fund, which is invested and held until retirement.

The recreation centre managed by the Johnson Employees Association has a gym, exercise machines, basketball court, squash court, ping pong and pool tables. Even retired employees drop in to use it.

The Canadian company's family vacation resort for all employees, sited on Lake Joseph in the Muskoka Lakes region of Ontario, has seven cabins (three winterized), a sailboat and motor boats. There's no direct charge to the employee. Johnson allocates the use of the resort by a point system, whereby a younger person at the lower end of the pay scale, with a family, has a better chance than anyone else. An employee who vacationed there the previous year loses points, as does someone higher in the pay scale.

Johnson employees feel well informed, and so they should. In addition to monthly departmental meetings, the president conducts all-employee meetings up to four times a year. The company's "Managing to Win" program directly involves all employees in problem solving. Groups of 20, each group a complete cross-section of the organization, identify problems the employees would like to work on. Suggestions go directly to the management committee.

Employees also have a pride of association with Johnson's Wax, and not only because it treats them well. The Canadian subsidiary (like every one of its Johnson sisters around the world) also donates a fixed proportion of its profits to support local community projects — such as a women's fitness centre in the Brantford YMCA and a $350,000 nature centre for school children in a nearby conservation area.

In short, Johnson's Wax has *all* the qualities of a great place to work, without exception, though not on a huge scale. We hope it stays just the way it is far into the future.

SCOTT

SCOTT PAPER LTD.

1111 Melville Street
P.O. Box 3600
Vancouver, British Columbia
Y6B 3Y7
(604) 688-8131

Pay: **VERY GOOD**
Benefits: **GOOD**
Promotion: **AVERAGE**
Job Security: **VERY GOOD**

Atmosphere: **GOOD**
Job Satisfaction: **GOOD**
Communications: **GOOD**
Personal Development: **GOOD**

★ *At plants in British Columbia and Quebec, Vancouver-based Scott manufactures paper napkins, facial and sanitary tissues for household, commercial, industrial and institutional use. In 1988, its 1,681 employees generated sales of $313 million. About 81% of the workforce is unionized, mainly by the Canadian Paperworkers Union and the Confederation of National Trade Unions. Scott, a publicly traded company, is 50.1% owned by Scott Paper Co. of Philadelphia.*

ONE OF THE big attractions for workers at Scott is stability of employment. Employees like to boast that while they see friends in similar jobs in the forest industry laid off periodically or suffering through long strikes, their own paycheques are healthy and uninterrupted.

Scott has made money consistently, no matter how depressed the economy. By 1989, the company was able to point to an unbroken record of increases in sales and earnings over 23 years. It can't afford to be complacent, though. The paper tissue business is keenly competitive, and battles for market share are fought in every supermarket, drug store and convenience store in the country. To ensure its future prosperity, Scott spent almost $100 million between 1981 and 1985 modernizing its eastern and western operations.

The expansion came after intensive study and much agonizing. Scott is a conservatively run company, and management stresses old-time virtues: scrupulous attention to the quality of its products; a nonconfrontational approach to its employees; and a happy relationship with its customers.

Some employees find the conservatism hard to take at times, but they have to admit it works. One said: "You can't argue with success. I know there have been times when people have been frustrated."

A manager comments: "We don't rush into things. If we get an idea, we analyze it and sometimes over-analyze it. The downside is that we can get too comfortable. It happens sometimes and we address these areas."

Scott's caution extends to its hiring practices. When Scott recruits, it is looking for lifetime employees. In fact, 25% of its workforce has been with the company for more than 20 years. Interviews are rigorous and a candidate may see five different people in seven or eight interviews before he or she is offered a job. It is important that people not only have skills, but fit the corporate culture.

Whenever possible, Scott promotes from within. A salesman said: "I think the company looks upon its relations with its employees as a partnership, more than a traditional employer-employee relationship. I think the individual feels an important part of the whole organization."

Because they have worked together for decades in many cases, a strong camaraderie has evolved among Scott employees. Says one: "There are so many people who get involved in activities together within the organization. I can name 20 groups of guys who go hunting together, fishing together, playing ball together. People just don't leave, so you get to know the people who work here well."

Employees seem to have a genuine admiration for the skill of management. Said a long-term employee: "I have always felt that the future of Scott Paper is very secure, because of the clear, decisive direction of our executive people. They know exactly their respective functions, their markets and what they have to do to be profitable and successful."

Another says: "There's a lot of collective wisdom on the executive floor. It's like having a seasoned quarterback; he has a game plan and is not anxious to change it, since it's working."

While there are formal liaison procedures through various standing committees, union members say there is as much business carried out informally by union and management as there is officially. "You can probably hash out as many things over a cup of coffee as you can sitting around a table."

Jim Glanville, general manager of the western manufacturing division at New Westminster, B.C., says the company is not hung up on hiring specialists. His own career illustrates the point well. He has a degree in American History and English. He started in the distribution department, spent time in personnel, corporate planning and corporate services before moving to manufacturing.

Glanville says: "Scott does not strive to be the highest paying company or have the best benefits package. We are certainly competitive when it comes to salary and benefits, but we offer opportunity and stability. We don't lay people off. I don't mean as a policy, but as a practical measure we have not laid people off. We have expanded. We are a very strong company, with clear cut goals."

One popular benefits is the share purchase plan. Scott contributes 25¢ for every $1 a worker invests up to 5% of salary. Fully 45% of employees participate in the plan. As well as receiving regular dividends, shareholders have seen a steady appreciation in Scott stock. For example, a person investing $100 in shares in 1978 could have sold them for $1,100 by mid 1989, after stock splits.

Scott has two distinct operations, in British Columbia and Quebec. It has long-established plants at Crabtree and Lennox-ville in Quebec, and early in 1989 the Quebec workforce grew by 800 (bringing the total Canadian payroll to about 2,500) when Scott acquired the White Swan Tissue Division in Hull from E.B. Eddy Forest Products Ltd.

Apart from at the senior management level, there is little contact between employees in the two halves of the company and hardly ever a transfer between the company's two solitudes.

In spite of the geographic separation, Quebec employees bear out the success of the Scott management style. Workers at the Crabtree plant rate good working conditions and job security as the main reasons for their high levels of job satisfaction. In addition, as one plant worker put it, "the worker-boss relationship is particularly good here. They really try and resolve problems quickly when they crop up."

Meetings are held twice yearly to keep employees up-to-date on company issues, and spouses are invited to participate as well. Union officials are proud of their relaxed and easy rapport with management, and point to the fact that the last strike in the Crabtree plant, in 1953-54, predated Scott's 1957 takeover of the mill.

As the union president explained, "We have continual negotiations here. Although we've signed a three-year contract, we modify clauses within the agreement regularly."

At the White Swan plant in Hull, Scott proceeded slowly with regard to the employees who came with the acquisition. To ensure a harmonious marriage, Scott spent a lot of time getting to know the workers and telling them about Scott. Several months after the purchase, old policies regarding pay and benefits were still in place, and Scott appeared in no great rush to institute changes.

Scott provides a stable, traditional work environment for people who value job security highly.

Steelcase

STEELCASE
CANADA LTD.

P.O. Box 9
Don Mills, Ontario
M3C 2R7
(416) 475-6333

Pay: **VERY GOOD**	Atmosphere: **VERY GOOD**
Benefits: **VERY GOOD**	Job Satisfaction: **GOOD**
Promotion: **VERY GOOD**	Communications: **VERY GOOD**
Job Security: **GOOD**	Personal Development: **GOOD**

★ *Steelcase Canada is a manufacturer of metal and wood office furniture systems. It is a wholly owned subsidiary of privately held Steelcase Inc. of Grand Rapids, Mich. Steelcase Canada has 950 employees and sales of more than $100 million annually.*

EMPLOYEES IN this company have every reason to be highly motivated. Four times a year, the company hands each worker a cheque, which comes over and above the regular (and adequate) paycheque, as part of the profit-sharing plan.

In recent years, the payout has averaged 40% of each worker's pay. The higher your base salary, the greater your share of the profit pie. Since 1955, payouts have varied from a low of 26% to a high of 60%.

As one employee put it: "Is this profit-sharing plan unique? You want to believe it. People outside of here just don't believe the money we take home."

The U.S. parent company, a family operation, has been a strong proponent of profit sharing since the 1940s. The frequency of payouts really drive home the relationship between productivity and bottom-line results. When results for one quarter are down, leading to a lower profit share, the employees really put an extra effort into the next work period, according to Peter Wege, president of the Canadian operation.

Despite its international size and stature, Steelcase Inc. embodies many of the most admirable characteristics of the conservative, small-town business: entrepreneurial, yet cautious; extremely hard-working; high ethical values; concerned for its employees; and a strong social conscience. Most of this philosophy has been transplanted to the Canadian operation in a conscious way.

The emphasis at Steelcase Canada is on employee development. Management recognizes that given the opportunity, workers will try to do the best job possible. Promotions are made from within, whenever possible. Even if an employee does not have all the "paper" credentials, management is willing to take a chance on a highly motivated individual.

Open communication between management and staff is another area that Steelcase takes seriously. Managers are expected to use good judgment and common sense in making decisions that affect people. They are to consider people the most important asset the company has, and managers are to be accessible to everyone in the organization.

Employee-management relations in the company are so good that bringing up a question about whether they need a union brings shrieks of derision from staff: "If there were a union here, I think I would just quit. We've just got too much to lose. They couldn't do any better for us than we're already doing now. With a union here, you wouldn't have the same environment. You wouldn't be able to talk to management the way we do now. The president talks to the guys on the shop floor regularly — he even knows us by name."

Communications seem very direct and uncomplicated in this place. The president goes out of his way to talk to employees, and attends regular communications meetings held in different parts of the plant. His door is always open to anyone who has a specific problem that needs sorting out.

"I don't get too many employees approaching me like this — about one a month, but they know I'm there if they need me," says Peter Wege. "You can't get to know the business from top to bottom unless you get out there and meet the employees right on the plant floor."

Wege is the Canadian firm's third president, and he's continuing to run the place in the same style as his predecessors. As one of his employees explained it: "One of the good things about Steelcase over the years is that there is consistency throughout management. The corporate philosophy remains the same no matter who is president. The profit-sharing plan also helps to reinforce the team approach we have here."

The benefit program is wide-ranging and of high value, unusual for a relatively small firm. Tuition assistance for all employees is one of the extra perks available, as well as a group home and car insurance plan. The pension plan is noncontributory. A financially assisted confidential counseling service is also open to any employee who needs help with emotional difficulties, family concerns or drug/alcohol-related problems.

A recent innovation is the company's training and development program, which covers topics ranging from management by responsibility and leadership, to employee involvement training and effective presentations. Designed to develop a skilled group of employees who are "prepared to accept and excel in a changing environment," these constantly rotating in-house courses are presented by three specialists. More than 300 employees were expected to complete one or more of these courses during 1989.

Because of the promotions-from-within policy, many of the supervisory personnel started on the plant floor. Advancement for women seems to be encouraged as well, and several have reached management.

Quality clearly counts at all levels at Steelcase, and this commitment can be seen almost anywhere. The plant is kept spotlessly clean, and the safety program gets strong emphasis. The offices are a showplace of the company's wares and very comfortable to work in. The subsidized cafeteria is up-to-date, pleasantly decorated and a genuinely attractive place to eat superior-quality fare.

Most of the nonplant employees work a form of flextime. In any given month, each employee must work 152 hours, plus or minus 10. During the next month, the 10 hours must be taken off or made up, whichever the case. The employees are enthusiastic proponents of this system.

"It just takes the pressure off arrival and departure times. If I

get caught in a traffic jam, no one gets angry at me for being late
— I just make up the time another day."

"It means I can turn on my snooze alarm without worrying if
I'm having trouble getting up."

"If I need to leave early one day, I don't have to ask anyone for
permission. I stay later another day instead."

Steelcase takes its civic responsibilities seriously, too. Although it's not anxious to publicize the fact, the company is the
largest single contributor (corporate and employee donations
combined) to the United Way campaign in York Region, even
though it has only 950 employees.

Employees here know they've got a great deal at Steelcase,
but they still have a few suggestions on how the company could
become even better:

"It's a very conservative company. From a sales standpoint, it
seems to take us a long time to bring out new products, and that
can be frustrating. We also don't seem to get into new plant technology as quickly as we could."

Peter Wege is unperturbed by this criticism, agreeing the
company is highly conservative. "Because we're family-run, we
have a strong moral tone, along with a strong work ethic. We
don't believe in borrowing money. There are very few companies
in our financial position that don't use leverage at all. The point
is, we don't want to grow too rapidly and get into financial
trouble."

Although most of the employees express a strong commitment to the company, and many feel like shareholders because of
the profit-sharing program, they are disappointed at being unable
to buy shares in the privately held company.

Steelcase has established a good foothold in Canada since it
opened its first facility here in 1954, and it's expanding. It seems
to offer excellent opportunities to any worker who's prepared to
put in extra effort — and the rewards are certainly there.

TOYOTA

TOYOTA
CANADA INC.

1291 Bellamy Road North
Scarborough, Ontario
M1H 1H9
(416) 438-6320

Pay: **AVERAGE**	Atmosphere: **VERY GOOD**
Benefits: **VERY GOOD**	Job Satisfaction: **VERY GOOD**
Promotion: **AVERAGE**	Communications: **GOOD**
Job Security: **GOOD**	Personal Development: **VERY GOOD**

★ *Toyota Canada distributes Toyota vehicles, industrial equipment and related parts. Most of the company's 467 employees are in the Scarborough headquarters. There are also 237 dealers scattered across the country. Annual sales topped $1.3 billion in 1989. Toyota is 50% owned by Toyota Motor Corp. of Japan and 50% by Mitsui & Co. Ltd., a Japanese trading corporation.*

TEAMWORK is key to the Toyota management style. The company's emphasis on trust, fairness and co-operation have gone a long way in keeping employees loyal to the fold. Although the Japanese parent companies maintain firm control at the top, the corporate style is definitely Canadian.

The company makes an effort to keep communications open and informal. "Anybody can talk to any manager they want to," says Robert Marshall, vice-president, finance and administration. "We give people as much responsibility as they can take."

The atmosphere at Toyota's elegant, modern offices is professional but friendly; not surprising when you consider that about 60% of the workers have been with the company more than five years. Seventy-two people have been with the company more than 15 years. The low turnover can be credited not only to the company's winning performance but to the mutual respect and feeling of co-operation that binds the company. "We have an overall philosophy that everybody here is an employee," Marshall says. "The president is an employee and so is every other worker. There's a real feeling that we're in it together."

One Toyota Canada worker, who once worked at head office in Japan and has visited other Toyota companies throughout the world, says that "Toyota Canada's spirit of closeness and togetherness is unique. It doesn't exist in any of the other subsidiaries I have visited."

A monthly newsletter from the president keeps workers up to date on company events, and monthly birthday lunches give each employee an annual opportunity to speak with senior management in an informal setting.

Some departments hold regular communication meetings to give employees a say in decision making. An open-door policy extends throughout the company, and at least one employee is sent to Japan every year to remain current on head-office policies.

Toyota Canada is not the ideal environment for those who thrive on excitement or change in the work place. Although products have become more innovative and sales have set records in recent years, the management style remains conservative. Pay levels are average but competitive for the automotive industry, and not an issue at Toyota. "What I'm being paid is fair compensation for what I do," an employee says. "Security and peace of mind are much more important to me."

Toyota rewards its employees in many ways. The company is more than willing to share good results. In profitable years, employees receive a month's salary as a bonus. In April, 1989, Toyota was the first importer to sell 10,000 vehicles in one month. Management recognized the milestone with a $50 cheque to every employee.

Benefits are also generous. The company offers a comprehensive package, including 100% vision care, tuition coverage and partial reimbursement of physical-fitness costs. There's a 100% stop-smoking course subsidy, provided employees quit for six months. In-house training courses, aimed at improving not only job performance but daily life, include such programs as defensive driving and assault prevention. And each employee is eligible to collect a $50 bonus whenever a baby is born or adopted into the family.

Another benefit includes the opportunity to buy a Toyota car or truck at dealer cost, financed through payroll deductions at 8% interest.

And the rewards available to employees who have shown their loyalty to the company in years of service are also impressive, ranging from Royal Doulton dinnerware and Waterford crystal to name-brand watches and jewelry.

The company's stability may give most employees peace of mind, but the conservative style has its drawbacks. Women make up less than 30% of the company's workforce, less than 2% of management ranks and only one woman has reached the executive suite. Furthermore, there are no plans to correct this imbalance.

Although there are good opportunities for lateral movement and personal development because of expanding and changing job descriptions, the number of employees in long service to the company limits promotion.

Overall, a happy, family-like closeness prevails, and few morale problems are evident. A common frustration, however, stems from being a subsidiary with a head office thousands of miles away. Staffing decisions and many capital improvements have to be approved from Japan.

"This is my home," a supervisor says, summing up Toyota's importance. "I feel really comfortable here. Whenever I have a problem, there's always someone who can help answer it."

ULTRAMAR CANADA INC.

220 University Street
Montreal, Quebec
H3A 2L4
(514) 499-6111

Pay: **EXCELLENT**	Atmosphere: **VERY GOOD**
Benefits: **VERY GOOD**	Job Satisfaction: **VERY GOOD**
Promotion: **GOOD**	Communication: **VERY GOOD**
Job Security: **VERY GOOD**	Personal Development: **GOOD**

★ *Ultramar Canada refines, distributes and retails petroleum products. With more than 1,400 service stations, the largest network in Eastern Canada, Ultramar has 1,675 non-unionized employees. The company is a subsidiary of Ultramar PLC, a British-based international oil conglomerate.*

AT ULTRAMAR, customer responsiveness is critical. "Since we really work for the customer, *nothing* can be more important," says President Nick Di Tomaso.

Ultramar's mission statement drives the point home:

● We provide immediate attention to our customers, aiming to reduce the waiting period to zero.

● We strive to answer the telephone on the first ring.

● We endeavor to solve problems by phone, mail or in person within 24 hours.

● We promote continuous improvements to our service by convincing the proper authority every time we personally feel it is required.

These lofty goals are backed up by results. For instance, in March, 1989, 65% of all incoming telephone calls were answered on the first ring.

"Customer responsiveness means getting closer to the customer. We make a sincere effort to give satisfaction to the customer and get back to them within five minutes," says a manager.

Employees take a great deal of pride in working for Ultramar, the best-known service station chain in Quebec. "This company is a winner and everyone wants to work for a winner," a corporate planner says. "Everyone has a feeling that we are on the right track with the customer responsiveness campaign."

Introduced in September, 1987, as a pilot project in Quebec operations, the customer responsiveness campaign is one of the reasons Ultramar's market share is increasing. The campaign was introduced in the Atlantic and Ontario regions in 1989.

"Customer satisfaction really boils down to, 'Do you care?' And there is a real feeling of caring here," says a corporate planner. "You never get the response, 'Sorry, I can't help you. That falls just outside of my job description.' It is a real team effort. I care about other people and they care about me. That increases my job satisfaction."

Making the company more responsive to customers also has resulted in making management more responsive to employees. "Customer responsiveness at Ultramar is not only with customers outside the company. Requests from other departments are treated the same way," explains a financial analyst.

Ultramar purchased the Quebec and Maritimes division of Gulf Canada on Jan. 1, 1986. "When we were initially bought by Ultramar, I was afraid. But after three years, I am sure it was the best thing. We have more initiative in each of our jobs. Today we can take an action without having to send a memo to six people," says a former Gulf employee.

Former president Jean Gaulin (promoted in 1989 to CEO of parent Ultramar PLC) was, in the words of an employee, "someone who you could meet at any time. He was just like anyone else. Here, management is accessible. You can walk into anyone's office at any time."

After the takeover, Gaulin met three times with all employees of both Gulf and Ultramar and made an absolute commitment that no one would be laid off or take a pay cut. At the same time, he instituted a hiring freeze.

There was a lot of relocation, retraining and changing of job responsibilities, but no one lost a job. "Management was very fair. People who had worked out in the field came into the office and had to learn the computer system. For someone who had never worked with a computer, it was a scary experience. But people were given the time and consideration to learn," says one 17-year veteran.

Employee benefits were eventually made uniform, by adopting the best of both the Ultramar plan and the former Gulf plan. In this way, employee benefits actually improved.

"Gaulin recognizes that you are a human being," says a salesman and former Gulf employee. "He makes you feel like a somebody. After the takeover we had a golf tournament. Gaulin didn't play with the vice-presidents, but with a secretary, an administrator and myself. He sat in the cart and talked golf. He proved he was a human, and not some guy sitting on a throne and overlooking his subjects."

Ultramar is characterized by open communication. "The company makes a sincere effort to tell us what is going on. We are close to the board room," says an employee of 32 years. The highlights of executive committee meetings, which are circulated to all employees, are the most widely read documents in the company."

"I used to say I don't need all that information," a saleman says, "but if they stopped it now I would be the first to object."

Communications upward is good too, because there is very little middle management. Senior vice-presidents meet formally with all employees in their divisions twice a year, and they plan to continue the tradition begun by Gaulin of having monthly breakfast meetings with 14-20 randomly selected employees. An annual survey of all workers gives management a feel of the pulse of the organization.

The atmosphere at Ultramar is largely built on trust."My boss doesn't check up on me. He has confidence in me. If I don't succeed, then he'll tell me what to do, and have every right to give me hell. At Ultramar you're always right until you are proven the contrary," says a sales representative.

"You are given the flexiblity to do the job the way you feel it should be done. Results are what are important," adds another.

Chances for promotion are good. One financial analyst started as a steno became a clerk, then a sales rep and finally a commodity tax analyst. "My bosses were willing to give me the latitude to make mistakes and develop," she says.

There are few women in management, and it is not for lack of ability, as a former steno explains: "Many stenos know more than their bosses about the oil industry." The women-in-management situation is something they have to work on, female employees say.

"Remember, Quebec society is based on the Catholic church, which believed in women in the house and the men out working. We are now working to change that," says a sales manager.

One interesting educational benefit is that Ultramar not only pays the fees for both work-related and non-work-related courses, but also bonuses for successfully completed courses equal to the percentage marks attained multiplied by the tuition fees. There are also 50 annual $1,000 university scholarships for children of employees.

Pension plans are often a hidden benefit. Not so at Ultramar. "Savings Plus" which has replaced the pension plan, is highly visible. The company contributes the equivalent of 9% of every employee's salary to the plan. An employee has the option of contributing up to 6% of salary, which the company will match 50¢ per $1.

Each pay stub shows employees the equity building in the plan, which is completely portable. The first $3,500 in an employee's account is invested in a deferred profit sharing program, the next $3,500 in an RRSP. And for employees who make more than $38,900 and participate to the maximum, the remainder goes into an employee savings plan that is not tax sheltered.

Not everyone is happy about the plan. When the pension plan existed, employees who wanted to be better off in retirement could have an RRSP as well. But Savings Plus uses up most, if not all, of employees' allowable contributions.

Part of the problem arises from the federal government's not increasing, as promised, allowable contributions to combined DPSP/RRSP plans. To explain the situation, the company is holding financial seminars for all employees.

Ultramar, we feel, exemplifies a management touch seemingly particular to modern Quebec business, and it may stem from the superb executives being turned out by the province's universities. We found similar atmospheres at Bombardier and Lavalin (both in this book).

⚘NION GAS

UNION GAS LTD.

P.O. Box 2001
50 Keil Drive North
Chatham, Ontario
N7M 5M1
(519) 352-3100

Pay: **GOOD**	Atmosphere: **VERY GOOD**
Benefits: **AVERAGE**	Job Satisfaction: **VERY GOOD**
Promotion: **AVERAGE**	Communications: **AVERAGE**
Job Security: **VERY GOOD**	Personal Development: **GOOD**

★ *Union Gas is the second largest natural gas distributor in Canada, serving more than 550,000 customers in southwestern Ontario. Annual revenue is more than $1.2 billion. Its 2,272 employees work in four regional offices and the Chatham headquarters. Forty percent of the workforce belongs to the Energy & Chemical Workers Union. The company is a subsidiary of Union Enterprises Ltd., controlled by Unicorp Canada Corp.*

"MY DAD told me, get a job with a utility and you'll earn a lot of money, and have a job for life." That kind of advice has brought many employees to Union Gas over the years.

Even after deregulation of the gas industry in 1985 and a takeover by Unicorp Canada the same year, employees still feel their jobs are secure. As one worker says, "You don't ever have to worry at Union Gas as long as you do a good job."

Of the two changes to hit Union Gas, deregulation has had the greatest impact. Unicorp maintains a hands-off policy. No significant changes have been made in the day-to-day management or direction of the company. "Although it has been very supportive during the adjustment to a deregulated market, Unicorp has basically left us to get on with the job, using our resources and expertise," Union Gas President Stephen Bellringer says.

The impact of deregulation, on the other hand, has been significant. The company is operating in a very different environment. Customers can now buy direct from suppliers, so Union Gas has had to change its approach to buying, selling and marketing. Its engineers have been busy building new storage and transportation facilities to accomodate those customers. A new pipeline was built under the St. Clair River in 1989 to improve gas sales between Canada and the U.S. Construction schedules were accelerated and total capital budgets have increased from an average $76 million annually to $155 million. Three new plants and about 80 kilometres of pipeline have been built. One plant requires about 35,000 manhours of planning and design plus 100,000 manhours to construct.

"There's no doubt it's a more demanding environment," Bellringer says. "Things move at a much quicker pace now that there are other suppliers ready to step in if you don't do a good enough job." One innovation, introduced in 1988, is in-truck computers, allowing service personnel to respond quickly to customer-service requests in the field and to maintain service commitments.

Union Gas has weathered the transition to a more competitive market without having to reduce staff. With steady growth, the company continues to provide very good job security.

For many, Union Gas is an ideal employer. There's room for promotion if you're qualified or prepared to upgrade your skills. Although there are complaints among unionized employees about promotion, benefits, communications and wage levels, most say it is a good place to work. Low employee turnover supports the claim.

Management recognizes the need for good communications. Teams of senior managers visit all locations once a year, and a forum is held to allow employees to ask questions and air their grievances. But problems persist. "Employee relations at clerical levels are not very good," one long-term employee states. Complaints and concerns at lower levels rarely reach senior managers capable of improving conditions.

Employees say it's tough to rise through the ranks without a university degree. Some also feel too many people are brought in from outside the organization, limiting opportunities for promotion. "Experience means nothing anymore," one woman says. "The only thing that counts is education. And if you haven't got it, they bring in somebody with a degree from outside."

Union Gas does, however, provide every opportunity to get a degree. It has increased its tuition reimbursement to 100% from 75%. In 1988, it introduced an extended educational-leave program of up to two years. Two employees immediately took advantage of the program and are now pursuing Masters degrees. The company also offers in-house training programs.

For those who are keen and prepared to further their education, opportunities for promotion exist. "If you want advancement, and you're not afraid to move, the chances are available," one worker says.

Ida Goodreau's climb up the corporate ladder is an example of how the process works. Goodreau first worked as secretary to the executive vice-president. A few years later, she took a leave of absence to obtain her MBA and returned to the company as a budget analyst. She then moved into operations and later to human resources. After several promotions, she is now vice-president of human resources.

Goodreau's rise serves as a model for other women in an organization dominated by men. Women constitute only 32% of the workforce, although an encouraging 17% are supervisors. A few, like Goodreau, are showing up in senior management.

Pay at Union Gas, at least among salaried workers, is good. Employees seem content with the compensation, which they feel is competitive and allows them to live comfortably in southwestern Ontario.

Employees can also buy a stake in the company through a share-ownership plan. The company adds $1 for every $3 contributed by the employee, who is eligible to put up to 10% of his salary a year into the program.

Benefits are improving. Since 1985, Union Gas has extended maternity leave to 10 months, set up employee development and job coaching for clerical staff, added career planning for non-management employees, and introduced wellness programs. In 1988, Union Gas provided a supplementary payment to survivors of pensioners.

In 1989, Union Gas started organizing a day-care program. In partnership with a community college (and partially funded by the government), the company is financing an employee-run day-care centre, expected to open in mid-1990 with space for about 65.

Union Gas continues to be a good place to work for the qualified worker looking for a steady job at good pay with what employees describe as "a fair degree of job security at the moment."

WESTCOAST ENERGY INC.

1333 West Georgia Street
Vancouver, British Columbia
V6E 3K9
(604) 664-5500

Pay: **VERY GOOD**	Atmosphere: **GOOD**
Benefits: **VERY GOOD**	Job Satisfaction: **GOOD**
Promotion: **AVERAGE**	Communications: **GOOD**
Job Security: **VERY GOOD**	Personal Development: **GOOD**

★ *Westcoast Energy (formerly Westcoast Transmission Co. Ltd.) owns and operates a pipeline system that gathers, processes and transports natural gas from the northeast corner of British Columbia to markets in the province and the western U.S. Through subsidiaries, it also retails natural gas and explores for and produces both natural gas and crude oil. Westcoast has 839 employees, about 330 working at the head office in Vancouver and the rest at gas processing plants and compressor stations along the 1,040-kilometre pipeline. About 38% of the workforce is unionized, mainly by the Canadian Pipeline Employees Association.*

THE START of the 1990s coincided with a new excitement at Westcoast, long regarded as one of British Columbia's superior, although perhaps duller, employers.

Three things were happening at once. The company was helping to build a new pipeline to supply natural gas to Vancouver Island. It was in the process of buying a big share of Ranger Oil Ltd. of Calgary, which has important petroleum interests in the North Sea. And it was just completing a deal to acquire the utility division of Inter-City Gas Corp. of Winnipeg. The deal would, in effect, give the British Columbia company a high-profile national presence. Whether ICG and its 1,600 employees would be fully integrated into Westcoast, however, was being studied as the final regulatory approvals were sought and financial arrangement completed.

A rise in demand for natural gas, especially in the U.S., held out the prospect of new career opportunities in major expansions to pipelines and pumping capacity. Through subsidiaries, Westcoast was also stepping up its own search for oil and natural gas.

From the employees' viewpoint, the most immediate tangible satisfaction in all this was a significant rise in the price of the company's shares. Many employees are shareholders. "There's a great deal of excitement among the staff, because they can see the company growing," says Harvey Permack, vice-president, administration.

Employees say Westcoast is a solid, secure company with which they are happy to plan a lifelong career. Almost a third of the workforce has been employed for more than 10 years. About 11% have been with Westcoast at least twice that long. Employee turnover is low, at 5% a year.

Westcoast looks after its employees in many special ways and sometimes goes to extraordinary lengths to earn their loyalty. The experience of Eugene Barton is an example. He is a technician employed in Fort St. John in the northeast corner of British Columbia, whose job it is to ensure that corrosion does not build up inside the gas pipeline.

When he suffered an injury to his back requiring surgery in Vancouver, he was told by his doctor he had to remain on his back for six weeks. This posed a major problem: how was he to return home to Fort St. John, 800 kilometres away by air? While lying in hospital, he pondered the cost of buying three seats on a commercial airline flight so he could travel on a stretcher. But he needn't have worried. His boss, hearing of his plight, quietly arranged to commandeer Westcoast's corporate jet as an improvised air ambulance. Barton was back home within a couple of hours after leaving hospital.

Although Barton's back problem didn't result from an industrial injury, he received full pay for the six months he was unable to work.

This wasn't an isolated incident. A young employee at Fort St. John said he received full pay during six weeks he was off work after breaking four ribs in a snowmobile accident.

With a big percentage of employees at remote locations, Westcoast takes special steps to keep them happy. The company owns houses, condominiums, apartments at numerous places along its right of way. Rents are heavily subsidized. For instance, it charges only $70-$90 a month for an apartment, and an employee pays only $100 for a townhouse or a four-bedroom house.

Sharon Woloshyn says joining the company was the luckiest move she ever made. She moved to Vancouver to avoid Alberta winters, and although hired in a junior capacity, she brought with her some useful oil industry cost-control experience. "I came to this company from Calgary more or less as a junior clerk, but within three weeks they were saying, 'Here's a plane ticket. Go and fix things at a gas plant.'"

She was sent to do a two-year stint at Fort Nelson in the far north of British Columbia. "I thought it was just great. I really enjoyed it. I had a wonderful time in Fort Nelson, and I met my husband there."

Westcoast helps its employees save by matching savings dollar for dollar after six years of service (to a maximum of 5% of earnings). And company contributions are vested immediately, meaning workers have full entitlement to the the company's contributions.

The company also has forgivable loans of up to $2,200 annually to help the children of employees pay for their post-secondary education. Its medical plan covers such expenses as hearing aids, orthopedic shoes, speech therapy, clinical psychology, acupuncture and the services of chiropractors and naturopaths. There's also a non-contributory pension plan.

Westcoast encourages suggestions from its employees relating to increased efficiency, safety or cost cutting. Gifts range from snow shovels, radios, camping equipment to travel vouchers. For major suggestions, the company offers cash awards of up to $15,000.

Westcoast is a solid company with an exciting future.

IN A CLASS
OF THEIR OWN

This is a classification for companies that don't fit easily into any other category, or for unique situations.

THE BODY SHOP
CANADA LTD.

15 Prince Andrew Place
Don Mills, Ontario
M3C 2H2
(416) 441-3202

Pay: **POOR**
Benefits: **AVERAGE**
Promotion: **VERY GOOD**
Job Security: **GOOD**

Atmosphere: **EXCELLENT**
Job Satisfaction: **EXCELLENT**
Communications: **GOOD**
Personal Development: **VERY GOOD**

★ *The Body Shop Canada is a retailer of naturally based skin and hair care products with the exclusive Canadian franchise from The Body Shop International PLC of Britain. Of the 72 stores across Canada, 16 are company-owned and 56 are franchises. The corporate stores have 90 full-time and 75 part-time employees, while franchises employ 160 full-time and 168 part-time employees. Revenues in 1989 were more than $40 million.*

"THIS IS A very womanly company which operates on the principles of nurturing, caring and developing others," says President Margot Franssen. Worldwide, 95% of Body Shop franchises are owned and operated by women. "It is being surrounded by these women that is possibly the greatest joy in running this company," Franssen says.

The Body Shop's philosophy and operation is unique among retailers for many other reasons. Among them is a sincere concern for the environment. Says Franssen: "We really work toward our goal of being an environmentally friendly company every day of our lives." As a result, the Body Shop will not sell or

use products that:
- Consume a disproportionate amount of energy during manufacture or disposal.
- Cause unnecessary waste.
- Use materials derived from threatened species or from threatened environments.
- Involve cruelty to animals.
- Adversely affect other countries, particularly in the Third World.

All products are biodegradable, and the company will not deal with suppliers whose practices do not conform to the Body Shop's ethical and environmental standards. The organization uses only recycled paper. And wherever possible, the Body Shop obtains its ingredients from Third World countries. Says Franssen: "It is a simple measure to direct our purchases toward people who desperately need the trade."

In India, there are two Body Shop boys' towns that take in children at age four. The boys receive food, shelter and education, and remain in the home until age 14. Then they return to their villages with two oxen and skills in carpentry, agriculture and management.

In return , these children make Body Shop foot rollers and grow bananas for hair conditioner. "We could quite easily purchase these products from a First World country, but prefer to pay First World price to Third World children. To date, we have pulled two villages out of abject poverty," says Franssen.

There was little hope in the slums of Easterhouse, Scotland, until Body Shop purchased a soap factory that had been idle for 10 years. The residents have jobs again, and 25% of the profits go back into the community to build playgrounds and daycare centres.

The Body Shop is also working on a project with some New Brunswick Indians to supply fancy gift baskets. This may alleviate the 95% unemployment on the reserves.

The Body Shop's philosophy also extends to the local community. "We must put something back into the community from which we derive our profits," Franssen says. Each store donates four hours a week to a community project. It might be a home for battered women, a food bank or "meals on wheels." Employees, who are paid for the time, take turns doing the community work. All damaged products that can't be sold in the stores are given to homes for battered women.

Because of this philosopy, employees feel a deep sense of personal commitment to the company. Says an assistant manager: "All of us work here because our ethics are like the company's. All of us have a real passion for these issues."

Adds another employee: "It makes you feel proud to work here. There is so much more to the company than meets the eye. They really care about all these things." A recent survey showed that more than 84% of employees felt their values were those of the company. As a result, employees just ooze pride in working there.

There is a feeling of teamwork. "Here, everyone sweeps the floor," says a new employee. It is not uncommon to find a manager helping in the stock room. And handicapped persons who work in the stores and warehouse are "a necessary part of the team," says one saleswoman. "They get a lot of support."

New employees take a two-week training course, in which "what you learn is of benefit for your whole life," a part-time employee says. The course concentrates on corporate philosophy, human anatomy and company products. "It was incredible. Out of this world. It taught me about a healthy way of living. It was so good I would have paid to take it," adds another employee.

Product knowledge is an integral part of customer service at the Body Shop. "Our relationship with customers is built on trust," says a sales rep. "We know our product inside out."

Customers develop close relationships with sales people. One customer dropped by a store to talk about the birth of her twins. Another employee recalls walking around a store for half an hour with a customer's baby while explaining products. The commitment to the customer service is tied to the employees' commitment to the company. Says a store manager: "Customer service really comes from within."

Four months a year, Body Shop windows are used for information campaigns. In 1988, these included displays, pamphlets and petitions on ozone depletion, amnesty international, pesticide control and the rain forests.

Companies that espouse such high ideals have high standards to live up to, and that's why some employees are disappointed by their pay and benefits. Salaries in retailing are traditionally low, but long-time employees feel they are underpaid relative to new employees.

Benefits are average, but employees get 30%-50% discounts on products. The company pays for self-improvement courses, as well as for ones directly related to business.

There are two bonus systems. The first, the Bravo Recognition Program, rewards employees with "points" for special service "above and beyond the call of duty." These points can be traded in for cash or prizes. The second bonus plan gives staff a share in a percentage of the gross sales after tax. Each store is given annual sales targets, and the greater the sales over target, the higher the percentage goes — to a maximum of 2%.

The company has a user-pay maternity benefits program. An employee can elect to pay into an account and the company will match her contributions. The employee can withdraw the cash when on maternity leave.

The disadvantages of rapid growth are evident at the Body Shop. Employees have lost the personal contact they once had with Franssen. Longer-service employees miss the way it was. The growth of the head office staff hasn't kept pace with the growth of the company. New products lines often sell out before production can meet demand. Product launches, announced to an eager staff, have been delayed for up to two years.

Despite these shortcomings, most employees don't leave. For a retailer, the Body Shop's 15% staff turnover rate is very low. Franssen attributes it to the fact that "our employees want work that will make a difference," Franssen says.

"There is a tremendous difference between marketing to the environmentally conscious consumer and being environmentally conscious yourself," Franssen adds. "If you do both, fine. But to merely market green products is a bit like benefiting from the spoils of war. Marketing without morality is criminal.

"We cannot go into the '90s thinking that business is merely a machine for grinding out profits. Profit is not our main objective. We are certainly not against making a profit. But I also want to sleep at night and know that I'm building a future for my child. In order to do that, we must operate on the principle of sustainable development. We must conduct ourselves in a holistic fashion.

"You can have profits with principles, be successful and soulful, be economical and ecological."

CANADIAN TIRE
CORP. LTD.

2180 Yonge Street
P.O. Box 770
Station K
Toronto, Ontario
M4P 2V8
(416) 480-3000

Pay: **GOOD**	Atmosphere: **GOOD**
Benefits: **VERY GOOD**	Job Satisfaction: **GOOD**
Promotion: **GOOD**	Communications: **GOOD**
Job Security: **GOOD**	Personal Development: **GOOD**

★ *Canadian Tire Corp. Ltd. is Canada's largest auto accessory and do-it-yourself retailing chain, with 410 stores in Canada and sales of $2.64 billion in 1988. It has 4,727 direct employees (grouped mainly in its Toronto head office and two distribution centres) and about 22,000 workers employed by its franchised stores. Most CTC stores are operated by franchises or "associate dealers," but the corporation owns the buildings and land.*

"YOU GET BACK the seeds you sow," says Alfred Billes, the 87-year-old co-founder of Canadian Tire, who is affectionately referred to as A.J. by employees. "If you want to be successful, you have to benefit the people who benefit you most."

He's referring to the company's commitment to its employees. And profit sharing is a perfect example of that commitment.

Canadian Tire was started by A.J. and his brother, John, in the 1920s. Even in the company's infancy, employees received cash bonuses based on their contribution to the bottom line. The existing profit sharing plan dates from 1957, when CTC was one of the first companies in Canada to introduce such a program for all employees. The plan has undergone many changes over the years, but the basic philosophy remains the same.

Many companies have profit sharing plans, but few can quite match Canadian Tire's. Employees feel they have a personal share of the action, and that they're working to better themselves as well as the company. "I don't know of any other company where every employee has a stock broker," says a shift manager.

For more than 30 years, all full-time employees have received an amount that has varied between 11% and 20% of their annual salaries in Canadian Tire shares. In 1988, for example, an employee earning $35,588, which was the average salary at the corporation, had $5,658 worth of Canadian Tire shares put aside into his profit-sharing account.

This account can be run in several different ways, including a tax-deferred plan similar to an RRSP. Other options allow withdrawals from the plan to pay off a mortgage, say. Every employee is fully vested after two years. In 1988, the company paid out $17 million to employees.

More than 400 associate stores have profit sharing, as well. In 1988, 13,000 employees who worked more than 1,000 hours in the year received a profit share equal to 12% of their pay.

There is one caveat. Unlike some companies that combine some form of profit sharing with a pension plan, CTC has no other retirement plan. But as long as the company's shares continue to do well, long-term employees can be assured of a substantial nest egg at retirement.

This applies in particular to those who started with the company more than 25 years ago. Over that time, there have been share splits, some as large as five-for-one, which have increased the value of shares immensely. There are stories circulating among Canadian Tire staff, perhaps exaggerated, of janitors going to their well-earned retirement with close to $1 million in savings. CTC's workers feel they are far better off under profit sharing than those who work for other companies with pension plans.

There is also a company assisted stock purchase plan. An employee may contribute up to 10% of his salary, and for every

$2 he or she contributes the company will add the after-tax equivalent of $1. Thus company contributions are larger for higher income employees in higher tax brackets. In 1988, 74% of corporate employees invested $5.6 million in CTC stock under the plan.

There is a problem, though. Employees, with the company for more than two years, get all the cash they invested in the plans if they quit. Large increases in the stock price — such as the 50% rise between December, 1988, and July, 1989 — mean some employees' portfolios are worth plenty. And this can act as an incentive to resign.

As a disincentive, CTC rules say employees who quit and rejoin the company may not participate in profit sharing for three years after their return. "The problem is that people see this [profit sharing] as cash in the bank, not a saving for their future, like a pension," says one manager.

"At Canadian Tire good employees are extremely valuable. I didn't get that feeling at other companies I've worked for. Canadian Tire develops people so they will be happy and stay in the company. When I came here, I was struck by the number of young people in their 20s and 30s who had been here for 10 and 15 years. They have found their niche and don't want to move on," says a human resources consultant.

Canadian Tire is not one business, but many. This diversity allows employees the opportunity to move from one division to another. But as one long time employee points out: "If you want a promotion, you have to make yourself known. There are too many bright, competitive people." A career path is no longer directly upward, but a spiral through different departments.

The company has a flexible attitude and encourages workers to take the initiative. As one fairly new employee who came from a far more structured work environment puts it: "At first, I used to worry about whether I should be doing a specific job or not. My supervisor kept saying, 'Don't worry about it. Go ahead until I tell you to stop.' People just take on as much responsibility as they can."

"There is the scope to be your own boss," says a buyer who proudly runs her division as if it were her own business. The experience has been invaluable: "It allows entrepreneurial spirit to show. Spending one year here is like spending five years with another retailer. I look at the age of buyers in other companies and they are all 10 to 15 years older."

One young employee feels that CTC's up-to-date computer equipment and training have increased his skills. "If I couldn't stay market-worthy, then I wouldn't be here. If they are willing to train you — make you worth more — that's important to me." Many employees agree that leading edge technology is essential to CTC's success.

Some employees, however, feel the corporation is becoming very lean. "You are often doing three jobs," says one manager. The company has changed from the small family business it once was, and one buyer laments: "I'm so busy that I don't have the chance to stop and talk to new people sometimes. I just have to get my work done. The company is as family oriented as it can be for a company its size."

But the family focus is apparent. For instance, many employees have relatives working for the company and every year, the company awards 12 renewable $2,000 university scholarships and 12 renewable $1,000 college scholarships to children of employees.

And despite the increased pace, the company takes time out to recognize service. Employees of five years or more attend a pin party every other year, and 25-year veterans are the VIPs of the evening.

As for communication, warehouse employees elect representatives who attend monthly meetings to discuss problems and company plans. Head office workers hold monthly meetings, while managers attend quarterly "contact forum meetings," where top management is queried on operating policy and the company's progress. "The questions can be really detailed and the executives really are on the hot seat," says one manager. Despite these efforts, employees feel communication could be better.

The company has been slow in bringing women into senior management positions. And women complain about rigidity in areas such as flex-time. (At the time of writing, there was limited flex-time only for the 1,000 head office staff.) Of the 410 associate dealers, only one is a woman and just 10% of directors in the company are women.

There also has been a great deal of uncertainty over the issue of control of Canadian Tire. A.J.'s children, Martha, David and Fred, control 61% of CTC's common stock. The associate dealers collectively own 17%, employees 12.5% and the remainder is widely held.

Under an Ontario Securities Commission ruling, if control of the voting shares changes hands, all nonvoting shares will convert to a voting status. Through the profit sharing and stock purchase plans, employees control the largest single block of nonvoting shares and therefore will have a significant say in any ownership change. Perhaps this is why they are unconcerned about the issue. Says one manager: "It doesn't affect what we do."

But the ownership dispute has left employees with a jaundiced view of the second generation Billeses and the dealers. The Billeses, one employee says, "don't even know we exist."

Corporate employees are tough critics of CTC stores. They say some dealers do not hire enough staff or provide enough training to meet the high standards they as employees expect. Conditions within the 410 stores across the country vary from location to location. There have been stores where student labor has been underpaid, overworked, not given much initiative. CTC's corporate management, however, tries hard to promote profit sharing and people-oriented values in the dealerships. Only a half dozen now do not share profits.

For employees, the positive elements at Canadian Tire far outweigh the drawbacks.

CITY OF

Waterloo

THE CITY OF WATERLOO

100 Regina St. South
PO Box 337
Waterloo, Ontario
N2J 4A8
(519) 886-1550

Pay: **GOOD**	Atmosphere: **VERY GOOD**
Benefits: **VERY GOOD**	Job Satisfaction: **VERY GOOD**
Promotion: **GOOD**	Communications: **VERY GOOD**
Job Security: **EXCELLENT**	Personal Development: **VERY GOOD**

★ *The Corporation of the City of Waterloo provides municipal services to the 73,000 residents of Waterloo, Ont., within a regional government structure. The corporation employs 307 full-time and 125 part-time workers, and operates on an annual budget of $38 million. About 56% of the workers are unionized.*

IN 1984, ENGINEER, management consultant and municipal administrator Don Roughley took up a challenge to try to turn a public sector organization into the kind of forward-thinking, dynamic and goal-oriented group any company in the private sector would be proud to be associated with.

Setting himself an exact timetable to achieve this transformation, Roughley took over the chief administrative officer's job with the City of Waterloo, and went to work breathing additional life and vigor into a basically sound, but slow-moving organization. Within three years, Roughley had initiated changes that took root and flourished in the southern-Ontario community, and he moved back to the private sector.

An "In Search of Excellence" program was initiated within the

329

corporation. Employees were bombarded with seemingly new concepts, and were expected to translate them into action within their own departments: team-building, participation in decision-making, goal setting, establishing mission statements, recognition programs, clarifying management techniques and more.

A senior manager says the change to a more businesslike environment has had an unexpectedly positive effect on his frame of mind. He was asked to be a member of one of the numerous interdepartmental task forces that were established to facilitate new approaches to problem-solving. "I went in with a closed mind. I didn't want to be bothered with this. But slowly I realized I didn't know everything. Other people can help to make any project even better."

In redefining work structures within the organization, the corporation decided to use the premise, "our employees are our most valuable resource" as a springboard for change. According to Terry Hallman, commissioner of personnel, that concept was "a big change. And getting city council to see that took a lot of persuading. But once we got them onside, they were very supportive."

A senior clerical worker was delighted when her input was asked for before a move into a new municipal building. "We had to implement a central counter on the ground floor when we moved into this new building. All the staff were involved in how that should be done, so that it would be efficient to work in. Staff really appreciated that."

The changes have been so positive, in fact, that when the administration approached council for a 600% budget increase for training and development programs for city employees, their response was, "Do you have enough money to accomplish your goals?"

In addition to the emphasis on a team approach, training was also emphasized. This included everything from assertiveness and creative thinking to better telephone techniques. The kinds of programs developed in Waterloo that set this municipality above the public sector norm include: rigorous corporate planning; pay for performance; annual job evaluations; employee recognition programs. There is a comprehensive mission statement and management philosophy, available for any member of the public to scrutinize.

And it seems to work. Not only do employees like to work for

330

the city, but the level of service offered to the public has improved as well, a fact most workers take great pride in pointing out.

One of the most effective programs has been the interdepartmental task force. As one employee explained: "It gives everyone an opportunity to share their ideas." These task forces have increased employees' knowledge about other departments and been an effective communications tool as well.

Other forms of communication used efficiently in this organization include monthly departmental and divisional meetings with all employees. Labor-management meetings are also held monthly.

As one employee explained: "I come out of a union environment. Before, we used to deal with problems through normal grievance procedure. Now, we have set up a union-management committee, and they meet regularly to discuss any problem before it gets to the grievance level."

Benefits are generous and almost totally employer-paid. They include vision care, orthodontic coverage, a subsidized personal computer purchase program, and extended maternity leave.

Salaries are competitive for the area, but many employees admit they could make more in the private sector. They stay in Waterloo because they believe the quality of life is superior there. "We know we're getting less than other people in other municipalities in similar positions," says one employee. "But money isn't everything. And our other benefits are really good."

Chief Administrative Officer Robert Byron, a municipal administrator with 30 years' experience in the field, is committed to continuing the people-oriented programs Don Roughley began. Byron says the employees in Waterloo are the most appreciative of the importance of the individual of any group he has ever worked with. "And I've never seen the level of team-building achieved so far in any other municipality."

As for the future, Byron says, "Communications are number one. It's the key that motivates me the most, and I want to improve communications here, not just internally, but externally as well. The whole secret to advancement in society lies in communicating better."

For those who want a private-sector pace in the public arena, The Corporation of the City of Waterloo is an exciting place.

CleanWear

CLEANWEAR PRODUCTS LTD.

705 Progress Avenue, Unit 7
Scarborough, Ontario
M1H 2X1
(416) 438-4831

Pay: **AVERAGE**	Atmosphere: **VERY GOOD**
Benefits: **POOR**	Job Satisfaction: **VERY GOOD**
Promotion: **VERY GOOD**	Communications: **GOOD**
Job Security: **GOOD**	Personal Development: **VERY GOOD**

★ *CleanWear manufactures and distributes disposable protective gar-
ments and accessories for hospitals and industry. Started in 1976 as a
part-time operation, the company now employs 36 people and has
annual sales of $2 million. Its offices are located in Scarborough, Ont.*

"SMALL IS beautiful" really applies to CleanWear Products.
From a beginning start in President Barbara Caldwell's basement, she has built a thriving small business, staffed by an
enthusiastic and satisfied group of workers, made up mainly of
immigrant women.

Caldwell is committed to improving conditions for her workers, despite increasing competition, low margins, economic
volatility and slim profits. Two measures of this dedication are
her commitment to sharing profits with her workforce and a
benefits program (including group life and health insurance and
long-term disability) that is costly to administer for only three
dozen employees.

Caldwell believes contented workers are the foundation of her
success, and she goes out of her way to keep employees satisfied.

"People care here," she says, "they really go the extra bit." If an employee is having trouble with immigration authorites, for example, the company will intercede on her behalf and try to sort out the problem. Employees are also urged to take English classes to improve their communications abilities.

Regular meetings are held to keep employees fully informed about developments within the company. A quarterly newsletter gives additional news, both good and bad. The good might be official recognition of an employee's suggestion that will save the company $7,000. The bad might be a detailed analysis of a job returned because of poor quality that resulted in increased costs and lost sales. The company stresses quality and customer service, emphasizing how to do the next job better.

Social events such as a Christmas party and the summer picnic help to cement the company's convivial atmosphere.

Wages are not high for this unskilled work, but the base pay is augmented by an incentive program that enables a productive worker to earn more. The profit-sharing program, which divides 15% of the company's earnings among the workers under a formula based on a combination of pay and years of service, offers an additional incentive to improve productivity.

The company also stresses training and education, paying half the cost of any skills-related course successfully completed by an employee, but upgrading its share to 100% if the employee attains a grade of 70% or better.

CleanWear has a mission statement (unusual for so small an operation) that appears on the first page of the employee manual. This straightforward philosophy revolves around quality, customer service and employee participation in both decision-making and profits.

CleanWear isn't the most outstanding company in Canada, but it does shine in its caring, understanding attitude to its employees. They work in a factory environment that is bright, clean and congenial, decorated with hanging plants. Management works closely with workers to ensure they have a pleasant, flexible and happy work environment.

As one worker's husband told Caldwell: "My wife has never worked anywhere where the boss really cared for her before. She's so happy at work that it had a positive impact on her home life. She's happy and it really shows."

CLUB DE HOCKEY CANADIEN INC.

2313 St. Catherine Street West
Montreal, Quebec
H3H 1N2
(514) 932-6181

Pay: **GOOD**	Atmosphere: **EXCELLENT**
Benefits: **GOOD**	Job Satisfaction: **GOOD**
Promotion: **GOOD**	Communications: **GOOD**
Job Security: **EXCELLENT**	Personal Development: **AVERAGE**

★ *This subsidiary of Molson Companies Ltd. owns the Montreal Canadiens (who still hold the record of five Stanley Cups in a row), and a several teams of smaller stature. An affiliate runs the Montreal Forum and a new souvenir merchandising arm. Apart from players, the organization has about 170 full-time employees (most of them organized by the Teamsters) and up to 600 part-timers who work only during events at the Forum.*

AFTER CAMIL DesRoches' 65th birthday had passed, he kept coming in as usual to his office at the Forum, where he's director of publicity. When DesRoches turned 70 he started to work a three-day week. As he neared 75, the club said it still intended to employ him, but on a part-time basis. Making use of DesRoches' phenomenal knowledge of the organization, the Canadiens want him to compile a written history of the club. He'll probably still be around when number 80 rolls by.

Treatment like that is routine, DesRoches says. He adds: "Even if you searched, I don't think you could find two or three bad things to say about the organization — things they did wrong, shabby treatment."

The excellent way employees are treated in this organization accounts for the virtually nonexistent turnover. People in this organization just don't leave. The average turnover rate for the past five years has been 1%.

Players who left the team have told employees they regretted the moves and wished they were back. "It's not the same on the outside," they said.

The employees agree. All of them are entitled to a pair of tickets to a number of events each season. Four times a year the club throws parties (such as spaghetti nights and corn roasts) for all the employee to bring them together "just to enjoy themselves."

There are skating nights for workers and their families, attended by the president. At the annual Christmas party, $60 is allotted per child for gifts, which in 1988 included Nintendo computer games. And everyone is intensely proud that people as far away as Europe call the Forum the Shrine of Hockey.

The organization's treatment of former players (whose pensions come from the National Hockey League, not the club) is legendary. In fact, many of them are still working for the Canadiens.

All former players are entitled to 10 pairs of tickets a season, and they can gather before games in a private room provided for them by management. There's an annual golf tournament to maintain the contact.

Jean Beliveau, the club's vice-president, corporate affairs, was the captain of those great teams. He recalls fondly the club's Stanley Cup victory receptions, to which all employees — 500-600 people, including ticket takers, ushers and others the public never sees — were generously invited.

In his 18 years as a player in the red, white and blue uniform, Beliveau and his teammates were always "treated first-class" in every way, including travel and hotels. Since 1971, when he hung up his skates and joined management, it has been the same, he says.

The atmosphere has probably been the same since the very beginning in 1909, he and many others believe. "The ownership of this organization has always been in the hands of great people, great families," Beliveau explains. "I've always said it starts right there — with your ownership."

The organization, in Beliveau's view, has been "a combination of good hockey players and owners who ask their management to run the organization as they run their own lives."

While the club is corporately owned today, the brewing company gives it total autonomy, and the Molson family (former owners) still takes a strong interest in it. Employees say the current president, Ronald Corey, has the charisma of a John Kennedy. "Everybody loves him."

Unlike the majority of major league teams, the Canadiens really do provide job security for their players, due to a consistent manpower planning strategy. According to Personnel Vice-President Louis-Joseph Régimbal, Corey and General Manager Serge Savard develop young, promising players on their farm team, the Sherbrooke Canadiens, for specific slots with the Montreal team. When veterans retire (in many cases taking up backroom positions with the organization), replacements are groomed and ready to take their places. "We have had fantastic success with this system. It's really exemplary when compared to other sports franchises," says Régimbal.

Opportunities for advancement within the organization also seem to be expanding with the establishment in 1988, of the souvenir merchandising scheme. Les Boutiques Les Canadiens now have 25 outlets in Quebec, selling Canadiens souvenirs, ranging from sweatshirts to key rings. "The response and sales have been phenomenal," Régimbal explains. The division grew from three employees to 48 in just 18 months, she adds.

The strong sales of Canadiens souvenirs to a supportive public seem to demonstrate that whatever the organization does, it does well. And it offers a steady and caring environment for anyone lucky enough to work there.

D. W. FRIESEN
& SONS LTD.

Altona, Manitoba
R0G 0B0
(204) 324-6401

Pay: **AVERAGE**	Atmosphere: **VERY GOOD**
Benefits: **AVERAGE**	Job Satisfaction: **EXCELLENT**
Promotion: **POOR**	Communications: **AVERAGE**
Job Security: **EXCELLENT**	Personal Development: **VERY GOOD**

★ *D. W. Friesen & Sons specializes in high-quality printing, book manufacturing, packaging, wholesale stationery, school supplies and business machines. It has 358 full-time and 92 part-time employees, most of whom work in Altona, where the company was founded in 1907. It has a stationery office in Edmonton and sales offices across Canada. It owns some retail outlets and publishes a weekly newspaper.*

THE PREDOMINANTLY Mennonite community of Altona (pop. 3,000) on the flat tableland of southern Manitoba, 100 kilometres south of Winnipeg and just a stone's throw from the U.S. border, calls itself Canada's Sunflower Capital. It is also the home of an unusual enterprise that ranks among the top book manufacturers in Canada.

Friesen manufactures top quality books for Canada's major publishers. It also produces year books for more than 1,000 high schools and colleges and a line of successful community histories. Friesen has some of the most modern four color printing equipment in Canada in a plant as spotless as a printing facility is ever likely to get. To promote business, it runs workshops and seminars across the country for yearbook editors, local historical societies and the publishing trade.

The location of a sophisticated operation of this kind in rural Manitoba surprises visitors. The company's president, David Friesen Jr., repeats a local joke: "This is not the end of the world, but you can see it from here."

Friesen's sales grew from $30 million in 1984 to about $50 million in 1989 and could reach $100 in another five or six years if the company's ambitious projections are on track. The company is located in Altona not because of any natural competitive advantage, but despite a number of significant disadvantages. It is remote from its customers and suppliers and has a limited labor pool to draw on. It is there for perhaps the best of all reasons: Altona is where the owners and employees want to live and work. They enjoy life in the close-knit Mennonite community and have no desire to work in a big city. Friesen is the major community employer.

David Friesen says: "People continue to ask us, 'Why don't you consider moving closer to the market?' If we pulled out of Altona there might not be an Altona, and I am not sure we can duplicate [elsewhere] what we do here."

A chamber of commerce publication says succinctly: "People who work in the community are always within walking distance of their place of employment. The only time there is a traffic jam is at the post office at lunch hour."

One employee said: "You are working for a big time company in a small town. That definitely has to be considered a benefit. For me it's just a five minute bike ride to work."

D. W. Friesen is characterized by friendliness and informality much valued by employees. Everyone uses first names and the boss's door is always open to employees.

Since it is impossible to find skilled employees locally, Friesen recruits unskilled workers in Altona and neighboring communities and trains them to meet its standards, which are high. While the attractions of Altona are important to its natives, they hold less allure for outsiders, and Friesen has not had much success in recruiting talent from bigger centres. Despite the small labor market, the company's treatment of its employees ensures a supply of staff.

Friesen boasts many long term employees; 38% of its workforce has been with the company more than five years; 23%, for more than 10. One worker, who rose from floor sweeper to purchasing agent for the printing division, retired just short of his 50th anniversary with the company. Honorary Chairman Ray Friesen says: "We said to our employees, 'If you give us your working life, you shall have as much expendible income when you retire as when you were working.'"

In addition to its own workers, Friesen supports a cottage industry by putting out overflow business to about 36 contract workers, mostly women, who can work at home and earn about $5,000 a year by setting type by computer or by masking negatives.

The company earns loyalty in many ways. Says one employee, whose wife was stricken with cancer: "Management called me into the office and said, 'Stay home and spend the time with her.' I stayed home for a little over two months and was paid for every hour. On top of that there was a lot of encouragement and support from staff and management. It meant a lot to me."

The company has co-signed employees' mortgages. It also boosts basic earnings (not especially high) by sharing profits. Each year, it distributes 10% of gross pre-tax earnings, which can amount to an additional four to six weeks pay, employees say.

Says a supervisor: "Everybody is very conscious of waste. You will hear: 'Hey, don't waste that. That's profit-sharing money.'"

There is a rule that any of the 150 employee-shareholders who leaves the company must sell his or her shares to co-workers. If there are no willing buyers, a trust fund buys the shares at net book value. The rule has reduced the Friesen family's equity from 60% to 25% in recent years as family members left the business. Only David Friesen remains from the founding family.

The company shares its plans with employees to a degree not found in many companies. It circulates its annual goals and objectives and discusses freely management's analysis of the business.

Employees say part of the company's success can be attributed to the Mennonite work ethic. These same beliefs also translate into a moral approach to suppliers and customers, not often articulated, but embedded in Mennonite business culture.

Employees say the company's vacation policies could stand some improvement. Workers get two weeks' vacation after one year's service (three weeks after five years and four weeks after 15 years), but they are expected to take one week's vacation when the company closes down at Christmas time. Summer holidays can't always be taken when employees choose, because Friesen is hostage to the deadline demands of its customers.

However, the company does allow six weeks' unpaid paternity leave for natural fathers. Mothers get 17 weeks of unpaid leave, as dictated by provincial policy, but the company is flexible. Employees have returned after a year at the same rate of pay, and missed pay increases have been given immediately upon their return.

Friesen has been expanding rapidly and recently opened a new 40,000-square-foot stationery warehouse in Altona. "Growth is very much on our mind," says David Friesen. The company's sales grew by close to 20% in 1989, and it expects growth to continue in the 10%-20% range. The company could have close to $100 million in annual sales within five or six years. And that, Friesen says, will be a far cry from the modest business his great grandfather had in mind when he started the company on Christian principles in 1907.

Because his grandfather wanted to live in and serve his home community, David Friesen has a future to believe in. So do those people who share these beliefs and values.

Four Seasons
Hotels·Resorts

FOUR SEASONS HOTELS INC.

1165 Leslie Street
Don Mills, Ontario
M3C 2K8
(416) 449-1750

Pay: **GOOD**	Atmosphere: **VERY GOOD**
Benefits: **GOOD**	Job Satisfaction: **EXCELLENT**
Promotion: **GOOD**	Communications: **VERY GOOD**
Job Security: **VERY GOOD**	Personal Development: **VERY GOOD**

★ *Four Seasons Hotels, a publicly traded chain based in Toronto, operates 22 hotels in the top-dollar-for-top-quality markets of Canada, the U.S. and Britain, and is currently expanding into Japan, Europe, the Far East and Latin America. In 1988, five Four Seasons Hotels were ranked among the top eight in North America by Institutional Investor magazine. And 1988 earnings were $13.1 million on total revenues of $603 million. The company employs more than 10,000 people with 3,000 in Canada, 25% of whom are unionized.*

FOUR SEASONS cares about its employees and their families. The food and beverage manager's daughter had cancer. Management at Four Seasons' Inn on the Park in Toronto gave him time off and a promise to hold his job until he returned. After the child died, staff members chipped in to send the bereaved father on vacation.

"Everyone knew and everyone was involved in arranging it, from the top level down," a marketing executive says. "It is nice to know that if someone in my family is sick or in the hospital, management will say, 'Take as much time as you need.' "

Stories of corporate caring are common at Four Seasons. The company's generosity extends into the community — it sponsors the annual Terry Fox Run. After Hurricane Hugo, executives organized other hotels and food companies in a relief effort. "We went to home office to help, and when we got there, the vice-president came out with his shirt sleeves rolled up and said, 'Okay, we've got to get boxing these things,'" one manager recalls. "Here we are with two of the senior vice-presidents, out on the lawn, packing up boxes. And this was their third or fourth day at it."

The all-hands-on-deck team approach is typical and was illustrated when water to one of the hotels was cut off. "This was a serious crisis, but while we were working on it, it was almost fun," one manager says. "Now its one of the things we laugh and talk about. Even then there was a sense of humor; everyone was pulling together."

Employees like to work for Four Seasons. "It's a good place to work, I love it here," one waitress says. "When I'm on holidays, I miss the place. When I first came here for a drink, it was like falling in love with the hotel. I quit my job the next day and I've been here 22 years." Employee pride is evident. A reservation sales agent who has been with the company since 1968 says: "I feel like a bit of a snob when I tell people where I work."

Four Seasons employees have certain qualities. "You really need to be a team player," one manager says. "If you aren't, you won't last. It goes back to Chairman Isadore Sharpe's ideals of the company: people, product and profit. That summarizes Four Seasons."

Flexibility is also essential. "You have to be able to cope with change," the manager says. "You never have the same day twice here, and that's for everyone. There's not one routine nine-to-five job."

Four Seasons is known for basing its hiring on personality and attitude rather than skill. "The reasoning is if someone has the right outlook, they can easily be trained to our job standards," says William Pallett, director of management development.

Many employees who started at entry level positions have worked their way up. Career planning in the company is thorough. "They really develop their people; I came up through the ranks," a marketing director says. "They'll promote you, and their training is focused on that."

This is the reason behind Individual Development Plans, started in 1988. "The plans are outstanding because the company is committed to sit down with you and design a progression chart suited to your abilities, skills, and desires," a manager explains. "They say, 'Where do you want to go; how are we going to get you there?' and then they put a commitment on paper to get you there by a certain time."

The plan is put into a database at head office and vacancies are then matched with qualified candidates. The database lists the employee's next three career moves and a projected date when they should be qualified for those positions.

Recognizing achievements is another way Four Seasons makes employees feel special. They have awards for employee of the month and year. In 1988, the employee of the year won a trip to California.

An assistance program, started in 1988, gives employees access to drug and alcohol treatment and counseling. And the company foots the bill.

Four Seasons is committed to good communications within the organization. The direct-line committee gives employees access to the general manager, who meets regularly with department heads. And suggestions are quickly acted upon. "Once employees said they'd like to see a certain kind of salad dressing in the cafeteria," a manager recalls. "By afternoon, it was there."

And Four Seasons' growth hasn't disturbed the atmosphere. "I think this is the best hotel company, and we all have a sense of pride in working here," a sales manager says. "No matter how much you grow or the company grows, you still have that small, family-type feeling."

Expansion brings benefits, Pallett says. "We are now moving out of North America into hotel and resorts in Maui, Nevis, Tokyo, Singapore, Mexico City and Paris. It opens career opportunities within the organization. For instance, the concierge from here will be going to Maui." Another incentive to join an already attractive company.

⬐ Lindsay

J.W. LINDSAY
ENTERPRISES LTD.

22 Fielding Avenue
Dartmouth, Nova Scotia
B3B 1E2
(902) 463-5000

Pay: **GOOD**	Atmosphere: **EXCELLENT**
Benefits: **VERY GOOD**	Job Satisfaction: **EXCELLENT**
Promotion: **VERY GOOD**	Communications: **EXCELLENT**
Job Security: **GOOD**	Personal Development: **EXCELLENT**

★ *Lindsay Enterprises provides building construction services and products to clients in the industrial, commercial and institutional sectors in Nova Scotia. With 50 full-time workers and a field force varying from 35 to 135, Lindsay has healthy business revenues of $63 million annually.*

LINDSAY ENTERPRISES has gone from 35 full-time employees in 1986 to 50 in 1989, and in that time has increased revenues to $63 million from $30 million. This is a growing company that offers a good future in the Maritimes.

When John W. Lindsay started his business in 1959, he visualized a dynamic, relatively unstructured organization where people could derive real enjoyment from their work. Although the founder himself no longer runs day-to-day affairs, he left his mark.

"The first thing he didn't want us to be was a big organization," comments President Bob Todd. But Todd finds it harder and harder to maintain the small-firm spirit. There has been increased staff turnover in the past few years, and younger people are coming on board. In Todd's words, the company is "evolving."

Given the firm's gilt-edged list of repeat clients, employees have good reason to boast that Lindsay's reputation is second to none. A common theme in the organization: "Lindsay does what it says it's going to do — on time, on budget."

In fact, the Lindsay construction-management group has been awarded contracts ranging in value from $3 million to more than $30 million, based solely on the company's reputation. In these deals, instead of bidding, the company sells its professional services for a fee.

There is, the company believes, what Todd calls "a Lindsay person." The characteristics of that individual are high energy and lively intelligence, and the organization has been designed to challenge both qualities to the utmost.

"I've never worked for another place that does what this company does for its employees," a woman says. "There's no caste system here. Everybody is given an equal amount of respect, and everybody is treated the same."

The Lindsay structure consists of a number of small groups or profit centres — the smallest having one full-time person and the largest, four or five. Each group, which can call on the company's entire pool of talent, has a special focus of interest.

The core unit, for example, is the design-build group which specializes in one-source, pre-engineered buildings. The group has four members — three sales estimators and a company director.

Quite literally, happy clients of the design-build group inspired an entirely new unit — the small-jobs group. As Todd puts it: "We had a lot of repeat customers who wanted us to fix their kitchens or do all sorts of odds and ends of things."

With typical flexibility, Lindsay established a new unit whose original goal was to look after the wishes of good clients and break even doing so. Instead, as the idea blossomed, the group began to make money hand over fist. Today, small jobs represent the third largest and most stable source of revenue.

Employees move among groups, and the mix of groups is in a constant state of flux. The organization now is not what it might be in a year's time, and that implies opportunity as well as variety for employees, Todd emphasizes.

"If a new market area becomes evident to us, we'll find

somebody [within the firm] who has an interest in it," he says. "The ideal situation is for somebody who now works for us to come to us and say, 'This [idea looks as though it has potential]. I'm interested in that. Let's see if we can work something out.' "

As for pay, Lindsay tries to be competitive. And the benefits package is better than those in some large national firms. As with most other aspects of Lindsay, the profit-sharing arrangement is totally informal. At year's end, the company's 10 directors set aside a portion of after-plowback, after-dividend earnings for employees — including field workers who might be gone a few months later.

The pot is "substantial, not token," Todd says. "The formula, if any, is based on how well the company does, with some recognition of special contributions by individuals. And it's arbitrary. Ten of us sit around and decide who's going to get what. There's no rule book, but with 10 people in consensus, it's usually fairly equitable."

Since 1985, there has been an increase from six owner-managers to 13 shareholders and 10 directors. As they near retirement, the senior owners and managers sell their equity to younger managers.

With this incentive in place, Lindsay Enterprises is even more of a mecca for enthusiastic young people who want freedom, fun, variety, challenge and opportunity in the Maritimes.

PARKRIDGE CENTRE

110 Gropper Crescent
Saskatoon, Saskatchewan
S7M 5N9
(306) 978-2333

Pay: **GOOD**	Atmosphere: **EXCELLENT**
Benefits: **GOOD**	Job Satisfaction: **EXCELLENT**
Promotion: **AVERAGE**	Communications: **AVERAGE**
Job Security: **GOOD**	Personal Development: **EXCELLENT**

★ *Parkridge Centre is a modern 238-bed home for residents needing nursing care, therapy and rehabilitation. The staff of 401 (203 full-time, 117 part-time, 81 casual) provide year-round 24-hour service. Most employees (86%) belong to either the Service Employees International Union or the Saskatchewan Union of Nurses. Parkridge is a non-profit organization funded by the Saskatchewan government.*

WHILE SASKATOON is shivering in winter's grip, inside the Parkridge Centre there's a warmth that has little to do with the facility's heating system. There is an unmistakable air of cheerfulness and enthusiasm among the centre's staff, who clearly enjoy caring for the elderly and the sick.

Nurses and therapists who have previously worked in hospitals and other institutions say they would never willingly go back. They applaud a lack of bureaucracy and the opportunity to assume greater professional responsibility than they would elsewhere. They say they are able to give superior care and are proud of it.

Because the emphasis is on long-term care, staff develop friendships with residents that just do not happen in short-term facilities. This friendliness extends to the families of residents and to community volunteers — about 150 of whom drop by to help out. Parkridge, they say, is well managed along modern lines and they are envied by colleagues at other institutions.

Issues such as atmosphere, personal satisfaction and professional development distinguish Parkridge Centre as a superior place to work. Pay levels and benefits are comparable to those at other health-care facilities that negotiate collective agreements with the provincial government, and staff say they work within a state-of-the-art facility with an easy-going atmosphere.

A female employee remarks: "One of the things that makes it attractive for me is that this is a very progressive place. Administration is always looking for ways to make things better. In our department, we are always having the opportunity to try new equipment. There is a pride about what we are doing here and people should know about it."

Yet Parkridge has had its teething problems. The facility, which began operating in the spring of 1987, amalgamated the services previously offered by two smaller homes, the Frank Eliason Centre and the Saskatoon Sanatorium. It took a while for the two organizations to work together smoothly. Meantime, discrepancies in pay between employees who transferred from the two older homes created resentment that was erased only as new collective agreements were negotiated and the two pay streams were brought into line. Some employees also say they miss the intimacy of the two smaller institutions, though they acknowledge that architecturally speaking, Parkridge is a fine facility. In fact, the advice of people who would be working there was sought during design and construction, and many of the ideas from employees were incorporated.

While management is generally praised, employees criticize communications. While executives were approachable and friendly, they did not always communicate their ideas to the staff.

Because of a relatively high unemployment rate in Saskatchewan, Parkridge has no difficulty in recruiting people for jobs in laundry, food service or as nursing attendants. However, Human Resources Director Bill Ellis says he can see a looming problem in finding nurses (because of a national shortage). Already it is difficult for him to locate specialists in occupational therapy, physical therapy, recreational therapy and physiotherapy.

Much emphasis is placed on continuing education. In 1988,

there were 131 in-service educational seminars. Staff also have the opportunity to travel out of province for professional training. Each year, for example, a number of nurses are sent on a two-week gerontology course. One nurse says: "Those are valuable for us." The centre also has close training links with the University of Saskatchewan.

Employees say the program is run in a superior manner. The opportunity for professional development, they add, is much more important than promotion, the chances of which are limited.

Executive Director Tom Archibald says the quality of service that Parkridge provides is directly proportional to employee satisfaction. He says there is no perceived hierarchy, and managers are not given overtly preferential treatment.

As a manager, Archibald says: "Our bottom line is a bit different from a company that sells a product. But we still see it as the key that our customers are well served. In health care, the key issues are quality of service and recognizing the uniqueness of our clients' individuality and trying to ensure that they have the highest level of well-being. We put a major emphasis on dignity and quality-of-life issues."

Parkridge is concerned with "quality assurance" programs and outside volunteers conduct regular quality satisfaction surveys to ensure that clients are receiving good care. Clients' families are also asked to rate the centre's service.

As an example of the level of concern, when 190 clients were moved from the two older homes into Parkridge in the spring of 1987, a psychologist was brought in to work with patients and their families both before and after the move to minimize the effects of the disruption.

Says one employee: "We are acutely aware of the fact that this is the residents' home and we are, just by accident, in their home and trying to make their life enriched." A nurse adds: "I don't consider that there are 36 residents living on my unit. Basically, there are 36 families that we try to care for. You never look after one resident; you always deal with the family. For independent nursing practice, that is exactly where it's at." Another worker says: "A lot of our residents don't have anyone from outside coming in here. For them, *we* are their family."

For employees in the health-care field, Parkridge Centre offers great opportunities.

THE PERSONAL INSURANCE CO. OF CANADA

703 Evans Avenue
Toronto, Ontario
M9C 5A7
(416) 620-3970

Pay: **AVERAGE**	Atmosphere: **EXCELLENT**
Benefits: **GOOD**	Job Satisfaction: **VERY GOOD**
Promotion: **VERY GOOD**	Communication: **VERY GOOD**
Job Security: **GOOD**	Personal Development: **EXCELLENT**

★ *The Personal Insurance Co. of Canada sells group car and home insurance to employees of companies willing to deduct premiums from payroll. The Toronto-based insurer has 158 employees from coast to coast. The company was acquired in 1988 by Quebec-based La Capitale Cie d'Assurance Générale.*

THOSE WHO work for "The Personal" (as almost everyone calls it) think the company has been aptly named. "The number of new employees who tell me that they can't believe how wonderful this company is, is startling," says Director of Personnel Christina Keown. Other workers echo this refrain: "Everybody is relaxed, enormously friendly and considerate from the top to the bottom. It's just delightful."

What's equally surprising is that The Personal has been able to maintain this pleasant, people-oriented environment despite two changes of ownership in the 1980s. In the mid-1980s, the firm was acquired by the Laurentian Group, which then sold it to

La Capitale General Insurance Co. in 1988. Yet throughout, the work atmosphere has remained stable, cheerful and unstressful. "If anything, the atmosphere is even better since the last change," Keown explains.

The credit for much of this is due to the influence of Hans Johne, the firm's founder and former chief operating officer. His management style stemmed from his belief that *all* jobs at *all* levels of the company were important. "The way you treat your employees," he says, "is ultimately the way they act to each other." Although bad health forced Johne to retire early, he remains on the board of directors, and the impact of his style is still felt at the firm.

The result of his policies is an informal, first-name organization where people tend to stay (at least 40 of the 158 employees have been there for five years or longer) and those who leave for seemingly greener grass elsewhere in the insurance industry often ask for their jobs back. The pay is good in comparison to scales in other insurance companies (in an industry not known for big salaries). The benefits package is also good, and naturally includes a generous discount on general insurance.

In a move unusual in the insurance industry, President Patrick Moher has started a profit-sharing scheme. The first payout, amounting to 5% of the company's 1988 profit of $2 million, gave every employee a bonus that varied between $50 and $100, prorated according to salary level.

Communication is open. Got a problem? Forget the formal channels and give someone a call. The company encourages questions. The new president has made a conscious effort to improved his personal approach to communicating by going to each branch each quarter to explain what happened at board meetings. This is followed by a question-and-answer period and then a cocktail party.

The annual Christmas party reflects the company's attitude to its workers. One woman employee says: "No cost to any of the employees. Spouses and boyfriends can go. An open bar. Music . . . It's first class all the way."

The head-office environment makes it instantly clear that this company appreciates its employees. It's spacious, beautifully decorated, and everyone has access to a window. There are comfortably furnished "quiet rooms" where people can take breaks when they need them — not at appointed times. As one employee says, this is "a beautiful place to come to work. That in itself enhances how everyone performs and how they feel about their positions."

Because the small, highly specialized insurer is fully automated, almost 100% of The Personal's employees have computer terminals. The company has taken a number of measures — including scientifically designed workstations — to minimize the physical and emotional stress involved. This same type of environment exists at every branch office.

In a company where 80% of the employees are women, an encouraging 50% of managers are women, as well. Opportunties for advancement seem good, regardless of gender.

The Personal offers lots of opportunities for bright, team-oriented individuals who prefer to work in a small, caring environment.

Relcon

RELCON INC.

80 Walker Drive
Brampton, Ontario
L6T 4H6
(416) 458-1100

Pay: **GOOD**	Atmosphere: **GOOD**
Benefits: **GOOD**	Job Satisfaction: **VERY GOOD**
Promotion: **GOOD**	Communications: **GOOD**
Job Security: **GOOD**	Personal Development: **VERY GOOD**

★ *Relcon Inc. is a small but growing manufacturer and supplier of industrial drives, robotic welding systems and allied equipment. Headquarters are in Brampton, Ont., with additional offices across Canada. The firm is employee-owned, with 212 of 227 workers holding shares. Sales are close to $40 million annually.*

EMPLOYEES at this aggressive and dynamic firm don't mind working hard or for long hours. And they have an insatiable thirst for knowledge about the company's activities. That's because most Relcon employees work for themselves.

Relcon has been an employee-owned success story since 1962, when 16 employees banded together and made an offer to buy the company from the late founder's estate. Since then, the company has grown and prospered to become a world leader in industrial electronics and automation. Despite its dramatic growth, Relcon has managed to maintain a friendly, co-operative atmosphere.

Relcon's ownership structure is unique. No employee is allowed to own more than 24% of the shares, in effect preventing a takeover or majority situation. But all full-time employees are eligible and encouraged to make an investment in the company after three months' employment.

Relcon employees also benefit from a profit-sharing plan. Each year, 12% of net operating profits are put into this plan. Every employee is automatically a shareholder and receives two thirds cash, one third Relcon shares, based on years of service and salary level. In an average year, it amounts to four to six weeks' salary. At the annual shareholders' meeting, Relcon employees elect directors according to the number of shares held: one share, one vote.

The money employees have invested in their future has paid off. In 1986, Relcon shares split 10 for one. At 1989 prices, each share is worth $19.50. An investment of $1 in shares in 1963 would be worth $50, and have paid out an additional $50 in dividends and bonuses.

Relcon's daily operation is much the same as any other company. Roger Peart, president and CEO since 1985, manages Relcon's business activities. But the company's ownership structure gives executive accountability new meaning. "It's certainly unusual to have all the shareholders — who are essentially all my bosses — right here to keep an eye on me," Peart says. "But it's a happy situation."

Relcon provides several company-paid benefits, including a dental plan, to which it contributes 80% of the cost. There is also a separate money-purchase pension plan, in which the company matches employee contributions up to 5% of salary.

Salary levels have increased because the company is operating within a highly competitive technological industry. Relcon rewards its employees because it knows good people are hard to find. A walk through the company's Toronto-area plant reveals a dedicated and earnest workforce. Plant productivity at Relcon is believed to be double that of a union shop. "The employees do take a lot of pride in their work," one supervisor says. "They'll go that inch further to get the job done."

Relcon's owners have made an effort to promote team spirit, both on and off the job. Recreational activities for employees and their families are organized on a sports field behind the plant. The field is also home to the Relcon soccer team. At work, there is a strong sense of unity among people who enjoy working for their own firm. The atmosphere is congenial, with tremendous freedom to widen the scope of any job. Teamwork is important, as are suggestions on how to make improvements. Promotion opportunities are also wide open.

The company is trying to improve communications, an area Peart describes as "absolutely essential" at an employee-owned business. A monthly newsletter keeps employees abreast of business activities, company developments and personal milestones. The company is also experimenting with regular shareholder committee meetings, which unite department representatives and senior management to discuss concerns, questions and complaints.

Opportunities abound at Relcon as the company continues to grow. If the present crop of shareholders has anything to do with it, the company's work environment will only get better.

TANNEREYE LTD.

West Royalty Industrial Park
Charlottetown,
Prince Edward Island
C1E 1B0
(902) 892-0357

Pay: **AVERAGE**	Atmosphere: **VERY GOOD**
Benefits: **POOR**	Job Satisfaction: **VERY GOOD**
Promotion: **AVERAGE**	Communications: **VERY GOOD**
Job Security: **POOR**	Personal Development: **GOOD**

★ *Tannereye produces luxury leather goods at a small manufacturing facility in Charlottetown, with about 70 full-time employees. Sales average $3 million annually. The company is privately owned.*

PETER LEUNES was searching for the right small business opportunity when he came to Prince Edward Island in 1975. After a couple of false starts, Leunes, a trained leather craftsman, came up with the idea of covering eyeglass frames with leather.

The unusual concept soon found favor with companies such as Bausch & Lomb, one of the world's largest manufacturers of sunglasses. By the mid-1980s, Tannereye frames were on sale in carriage-trade shops around the world, and providing employment for more than 100 P.E.I. craftspeople.

An atmosphere of trust and individual responsibility is the hallmark of this unusual small business. Leunes deliberately maintains an informal and unfactorylike environment at Tannereye. Hours are flexible, and Friday work afternoons end at 2.30.

Trainees start on hourly pay, but go on to piecework when

they're qualified, allowing them to increase their earnings significantly. An unskilled trainee starts at $4.75 an hour. After nine months, the worker will be making $5.49 an hour, considered the base rate. After that, as long as he or she maintains a good productivity rate, the employee moves to the piecework system. "Some workers here make as much as $9-$10 an hour," says the office manager, Wendy Quinn.

Promotional opportunities are limited because of size and the relative youth of the stable managerial group, but the company has made a commitment to promotion from within. According to Quinn, "Workers on the floor get the first crack at any openings now."

Benefits include insurance, a medical and dental plan and long-term disability. Two gaps in coverage, however, are sick pay and a pension plan. There are other perks, such as a regular Christmas bonus, a week's holiday at Christmas and productivity bonuses. The company also pays a portion of an employee's membership in a local fitness spa, a benefit 80% have taken advantage of. All employees share in 30% of pre-tax profits.

"Owners who care about the people are what make the difference at Tannereye," explains Pat Vessey, floor supervisor. "Everyone pulls together to help one another."

There are no secrets at this plant. The owners are on the floor every month to give employees a financial update, and to congratulate those with high productivity records. Each month, a company steering committee gets together with a representative from each area to talk about the business and listen to any concerns.

At the time of writing, Tannereye was negotiating to purchase the building it rented. On completion of the sale, the firm said, it intended to put in a gym and games room for the employees.

There were also plans to open eight stores in the U.S. by early 1991 (one in South Carolina, two in Georgia, and five in Florida). And the company had spent $1.5 million on research and development over the previous three years.

Tannereye is in this book because it has created a compassionate and superior working environment in a province where employment opportunities are slim. The owners are responsive to the needs of the workers, and that's what really counts.

TSB
INTERNATIONAL INC.

5399 Eglinton Avenue West
Suite 115
Toronto, Ontario
M9C 5K6
(416) 622-7010

Pay: **AVERAGE**	Atmosphere: **EXCELLENT**
Benefits: **AVERAGE**	Job Satisfaction: **VERY GOOD**
Promotion: **VERY GOOD**	Communications: **GOOD**
Job Security: **VERY GOOD**	Personal Development: **EXCELLENT**

★ *TSB International designs, manufactures, sells and services telephone network management systems. Customers include Northern Telecom, IBM, Digital Equipment and North American Bell companies. The private company is 75% owned by eight partners, 20% by Helix and Accel (two venture-capital firms) and 5% by employees. The 110 employees work at head office in Mississauga, Ont. Revenue in 1989 was $9.1 million.*

EMPLOYEES consistently say TSB is a relaxed and comfortable place to work. Hours are flexible, management is sensitive to the needs of employees, and there is opportunity to advance in this young and growing company.

The atmosphere belies TSB's position as a leader in a small but rapidly expanding niche market within the telecommunications field. Founded in 1981 by eight partners, the company brought telecommunications consultants together with computer software programmers. TSB technology gives users the tools to manage their telecommunications resources.

TSB's success, according to Chairman and CEO Jeremy Purbrick, is based on specializing in this niche market, providing the best value service, emphasizing quality, forming strategic international distribution partnerships, and spending 12% of sales on product development.

Employees say the work is exciting and offers opportunity to develop. "You're allowed to become an integral part of the company," an engineer says. "You can take on new responsibilities. There are no restraints — you decide how to operate your department. It's great, the management is very supportive and willing to change."

"When you are given a job, you can do it any way you want to as long as you get it done," one manager says. "There is no one looking over your shoulder." And an employee of one year adds: "Management is open to help you. You can ask for guidance and help. It's okay to say I don't know how to do this."

Most jobs are filled internally, and employees are given the chance to grow. "I applied to go into accounts payable and I had never done the job before, and they let me," a happy employee says. "If you are a good worker and don't like the job you are doing, management will look for something else or create a position for you."

"Everyone helps each other," a worker with the company for two years says. Awards help foster that feeling of togetherness. Every four months, employees in all four divisions vote for one of their peers in recognition of outstanding service. Winners receive an engraved plaque and a gold Cross pen.

Salaries are competitive but employees feel they could be better. One employee took a cut in pay to move to TSB because of the "growth potential I saw and my own personal opportunities for advancement." Pay increases are based on performance but, with the company's growth, have averaged 10%-12% a year.

The atmosphere, flexibility and people make up for salary, employees say. "If my child is sick and I have to go home, there is no problem," a single mother says. "If I go on a school trip with my daughter, my boss is more interested in how it went [than the fact I took the day off]. The flexibility is great."

Employees work off-hour shifts to avoid rush-hour traffic. They keep track of their own time, making up what they take off. They have keys to the office, and people can often be found working evenings and on weekends. Several women have reduced their work to part-time and had their salaries pro-rated to balance family and work life, including one vice-president who works three days a week.

Standard benefits include health and dental coverage, insurance and tuition reimbursement. Employees get three weeks vacation after the first year, and can save a week's holiday every year. One new worker was shocked when, after only a month on the job, she was given a week off for a trip she had won in a contest. Other benefits include a $500 commission to an employee whose referral is hired by the company, and an option to buy company shares.

Employees feel there are, and will continue to be, many opportunities for advancement. But the transition from an entrepreneurial to an established company has caused some disruption. The company has reorganized four times in eight years. "I look at it as positive that they did change so many times because they didn't get it right," one employee in marketing says. But no one was laid off as a result of the restructuring.

Employees feel TSB is a great place to start working. "It gives you the opportunity to develop, put your ideas into action and challenge your own abilities."

WAINBEE LTD.

121 City View Drive
Rexdale, Ontario
M9W 5A9
(416) 243-1900

Pay: **GOOD**	Atmosphere: **GOOD**
Benefits: **GOOD**	Job Satisfaction: **VERY GOOD**
Promotion: **AVERAGE**	Communications: **AVERAGE**
Job Security: **VERY GOOD**	Personal Development: **AVERAGE**

★ *Wainbee is a national distributor of hydraulic products, production equipment, controls and automation components. Manufacturing and distribution centres are located in Vancouver, Toronto and Montreal, with sales offices in eight other locations. Revenue in 1988 exceeded $30 million. Head office is in Toronto.*

"WE ARE ALL working toward a common goal: profit sharing and customer service. We all depend on each other." This really sums up the philosophy at Wainbee. "If I have a problem," a computer operator says, "I have to have it fixed before everyone else arrives in the morning. No one says I have to, but I feel I do. They are relying on me and I don't want to let them down."

"I've worked at companies where people said: 'That's not my job, why should I do that?' " an employee says. "I was sick of hearing that. Here, everybody tries to help everyone else."

Employees have a great deal of pride in the company. "Our products are very, very good. When you sell General Motors a tool they are using in their production line, we don't want that tool to break down," says a supervisor.

"We only handle top quality products," a sales representative says. The philosophy carries over to dealing with customers. A supervisor: "we try to repay the customer with the best service we can."

These attitudes are fostered by profit sharing, which in recent years has averaged 20-28% of salary and is paid in two lump sums — in April and December. "The profit sharing gives you the initiative to work a bit harder, to put more into it because you get more out of it," an employee of 20 years says. Employees with two years service or more receive a full profit share, while those with less receive 1/24th of a share for every month employed.

Employees can buy company shares once a year. "It's a good company to invest in," a salesman says. The shares are locked in until the employee retires or leaves the company. An employee's investment of $1000 in shares in 1982 had grown in value to $5,650 as of December, 1989. Half the 182 employees own company shares — with managers controlling 75% of the stock and employees the remaining 25%.

But employees say salaries are below average, because they don't consider profit sharing to be part of their wage. "The pay is not the greatest. I've had lots of offers from other places but they were jobs," a sales rep says. "If I accepted, I'd be making more money but I wouldn't be happy. I enjoy Wainbee. I wake up in the morning and I'm happy to come to work. As long as I have that feeling, it doesn't matter what I get paid. To me, being happy is the most important thing." However, when you consider profit sharing, the pay is good.

Employees say opportunities for advancement are poor since the company spends little time training staff for new roles. Some feel their chances of promotion are better if they leave the company, gain experience elsewhere and then come back — something a number have done.

Benefits do not include a vision or dental plan, and employees have to be with the company two years before they are eligible for the pension plan. "But why," one supervisor says, "should company profits be contributed to a dental plan or vision plan when at the end of the year I get a nice lump sum of money? If I want to have dental work done, I can."

Employees receive $250 for every successful job applicant they refer to the company — a popular benefit with one employee of 20 years who has had three successful referrals.

Job security is very good. Even during the difficult times of the 1981-82 recession the company didn't let anyone go. Employees worked four days a week and collected UIC the fifth. And everyone still received a profit share equal to 16% of their salary — the lowest amount ever in the history of the company's profit sharing.

Profit sharing and employee ownership have created an interesting atmosphere:

- "Everyone is treated equally here. We're all on a first name basis — there are no barriers."

- "It is not one person who is thinking for the company. Even people on the order desk have input."

- "If you make a mistake, no one jumps down your throat."

- "Managers are actually owners too. So they have something at stake."

Wainbee offers employees a stake in the company, binding employees' fortunes to the company's and resulting in a tightly knit staff with a common purpose.

THE BEST PAYING COMPANIES

Apple Canada
Canadian Hunter
Esso Resources
Royal Bank
Syncrude
Ultramar

RUNNERS-UP

B. C. Building   Kodak
Du Pont   Labatt
Heinz   Lavalin
Hewlett-Packard   Scott Paper
Imperial Oil   Shoppers Drug Mart
Imperial Tobacco   Westcoast Energy
Jacobs Suchard   Xerox

These companies pay the best salaries in Canada. There may be other companies where an individual could do better with bonuses, profit-sharing and other incentives, but these organizations have generous salary structures for all staff, from junior clerks to senior managers.

Most of these companies also add on performance-based extras. The Royal Bank, for example, gives increases of up to 8% to employees whose work meets expectations, and awards 9%-12% increases for outstanding work.

Some of these companies pay an entry level clerk as much as $29,000 a year. At Lavalin, Apple Computer and Imperial Oil, senior secretaries make more than many executives in smaller companies. In general, salaries increase with the size of the company.

The best-paying companies believe the best pay attracts and retains the best talent. Most of them survey the competition annually to make sure their own salaries remain tops.

Pay isn't everything, but it certainly helps to oil the gears.

THE BEST COMPANIES FOR BENEFITS

Great-West Life
Hewlett-Packard
Husky
IBM
Labatt
London Life
Northern Telecom
Procter & Gamble
Syncrude
Royal Trust

Good benefits programs indicate to employees how much their companies value them. And 48 of the second 100 Best Companies provide very good to excellent benefit packages. Those listed above offer the best.

We have interpreted benefits broadly. At minimum, the first-class benefit packages contain comprehensive medical and dental plans (including orthodontics), life insurance, disability insurance, as well as superlative pension plans. But some offer additional perks, such as share-purchase plans, employee savings plans, mortgage and home/car insurance discounts, tuition assistance, computer purchase programs or special Toronto allowances (to compensate for the high cost of living there.)

A growing number of companies offer women employees enhanced maternity benefits. Among those in this book: Apple, CMHC, Digital Equipment, IBM, London Life, Lavalin, Manufacturers Life, Northern Telecom, Procter & Gamble and Ultramar. The Toronto Sun and McDonalds offer eight-week paid sabbaticals to employees after 10 and 20 years' employment. Some companies give extra weeks of vacation after specified periods of service.

THE BEST COMPANIES FOR WOMEN

B. C. Telephone   Procter & Gamble
Federal Express   Royal Trust
Manufacturers Life   VanCity
Pillsbury   Warner Lambert

RUNNERS-UP

Four Seasons Hotels   Great-West Life
The Personal   Royal Bank

Companies that offer superior opportunities for women to advance into management appear in the upper list. In them, remarkable numbers of women are in managerial positions and executive ranks. Federal Express, recognized as one of the top employers for women in the U.S., leads the pack with a remarkable 50% women managers and 35% female executives.

Companies in the runners-up list have strong numbers of women in managerial positions, but fewer in executive posts. These companies have the potential to make dramatic strides.

But numbers alone are not the only criterion for judging good companies for women. Attitudes toward women juggling careers and motherhood also play an important role. Many of these companies make life easier for their women employees through a variety of programs, such as flex-time, job sharing and day-care assistance. Others create new career paths to the top, or provide career counseling to help women advance upward. These are all factors we have taken in account when judging which companies are best for women.

In spite of the significant advances in overall numbers since the first edition of this book, there are still disappointingly few women presidents and vice-presidents. And the route to senior positions still seems to be stereotyped: either through human resources or public affairs.

THE BEST COMPANIES FOR INCENTIVES

Allen-Bradley	Husky
Burns Fry	IBM
Canadian Hunter	London Life
Canadian Tire	MacDonald Dettwiler
DMR Group	Royal Trust
Esso Resources	S. C. Johnson
Hayes-Dana	Steelcase
Hewlett-Packard	Tembec

These employers offer superior financial incentives for *all* employees to participate in the company's growth. The incentives range from productivity and performance bonuses to profit- and gain-sharing programs, as well as stock purchase plans. The companies on this list use a minimum of two of these programs to motivate their workforces.

More than 40% of the companies in the 100 Best offer profit-sharing schemes to all workers. Generally, the plans that seem to work best have a cash component, giving employees a clear link between performance and reward. However, it's also important that profit-sharing plans have a deferred or saving element.

These companies believe that an employee with a personal stake in the company achieves greater productivity. The feeling that each individual has a positive influence on the operations of the company, and thus the bottom line, can be a significant incentive.

Incentives come in many forms. IBM's suggestion plan has an award ceiling of $200,000. Sun Microsystems pays staff recruitment bonuses of up to $4,000 per new hiree.

London Life and Royal Trust have a myriad of plans. One, for example, gives employees Trilon shares whenever they purchase services from any company within the Trilon group. In addition to bonus pay schemes, both also offer attractive mortgage discounts and assisted stock purchase schemes. Those kinds of incentive packages are hard to beat.

THE BEST COMPANIES FOR SPIRIT

Apple
B.C. Tel
CAE Electronics
Canada Trust
Canadian Hunter
Canadian Pacific Hotels
Four Seasons Hotels
Hongkong Bank
J. W. Lindsay

MacDonald Dettwiler
McDonald's Restaurants
NovAtel
Parkridge Centre
The Personal
Shoppers Drug Mart
Steelcase
VanCity

Each of these companies has what can best be described as a superior esprit de corps — a working atmosphere of enthusiasm, enjoyment, amiability, co-operation and fun. This spirit permeates all ranks, not management alone.

In some cases, this spirit can be linked to the physical working environment. Some company offices, such as those at Steelcase (office experts), are ergonomically superior, clearly designed to enhance employee enjoyment and productivity.

Clearly, though, a good physical working environment alone cannot create a team spirit. Some of the most enthusiastic employees we met work in average, undistinguished factory environments.

Spirit stems from a complicated blend of excellent up-down communications, a sense of purpose and a genuine involvement in decision making. Good companies define a clear mission. They convince employees to share the vision and help to implement it.

Workers who feel they're putting a part of themselves into their jobs on a daily basis are the most likely to develop emthusiasm and a sense of well-being.

THE BEST COMPANIES FOR EDUCATION AND TRAINING

Bell Canada
B. C. Tel
Canada Trust
Du Pont
Esso Resources
Great-West Life
Imperial Oil
London Life
Manufacturers Life
New Brunswick Telephone

Parkridge Centre
Procter & Gamble
Raychem
Royal Bank
Royal Trust
Shoppers Drug Mart
Syncrude
VanCity
Zittrer, Siblin, Stein, Levine

These companies offer superior opportunities for employees to improve their personal knowledge and job skills, either by providing in-house programs (separate from job-specific training) or by financing outside education.

Many put employee re-education and continuous education high on their list of priorities. Canada Trust, Manufacturers Life and Zittrer, Siblin, Stein, Levine are among several companies that have set up their own in-house programs.

Royal Trust leads the pack by spending more than $1,700 per employee on training and development annually. And New Brunswick Telephone offers a back-to-university program to retrain employees whose skills need to be updated.Employess return to school full-time while continuing to earn 70% of their salaries.

Some companies offer scholarships to children of employees, although the number of scholarships is usually limited. Imperial Oil, however, is unique. It pays for the education of both its employees and their children. Imperial Oil employees or annuitants are eligible to receive grants covering the full cost of tuition at a university or community college, as long as they maintain a 70% average.

THE BEST COMPANIES FOR
CAREER DEVELOPMENT

Bell Canada
Bell-Northern Research
CAE Electronics
Canadian Hunter
DMR Group
Esso Resources
Merck Frosst
Parkridge Centre
Procter & Gamble
Royal Bank
Royal Trust
Shoppers Drug Mart
Warner Lambert

These companies offer superior facilities, in addition to opportunities, for employees to get ahead. They all encourage their people to advance. Some of them do detailed career planning for workers, either through annual evaluations or through a process like Royal Trust's self-assessment workbook career paths booklet. Some companies provide counseling, training and voluntary job-rotation programs.

Warner Lambert, for one, puts a great deal of effort into career development. Each employee helps to prepare his or her own performance evaluation, and identifies short-term as well as career-path goals. The human resources department then bases the coming year's training and development program on these assessments.

Career development is doubly beneficial — to both the employee and the company. Employees get a clear idea of the career goals they want to attain. The company gets an useful aid to manpower and succession planning.

THE BEST COMPANIES FOR
HIGH SCHOOL STARTERS

Bell Canada
CAE Electronics
Canadian Pacific Hotels
Four Seasons Hotels
H. J. Heinz
Hayes-Dana
Husky
McDonald's Restaurants
Moore
PCL
Relcon
Royal Bank
Russelsteel

These employers offer superior opportunities for inexperienced Canadians without postsecondary educations to "start at the bottom" and advance into management by ability and ambition. Lack of formal education is no bar.

At the Royal Bank, for example, more than a few top-level executives, including the president and chief executive officer, joined the institution from high school. Most of Hayes-Dana's managers and division heads routinely come up from the plant floor. And some managers at McDonald's started with the organization as teenagers, flipping hamburgers.

HOW TO PICK A GOOD EMPLOYER

JOB HUNTERS should carefully check out their prospective employers before accepting a position with the company.

If the company is publicly traded, get a copy of the annual report and read it carefully. Companies that value their employees make their commitment visible in the report, in a mission statement or through a list of goals. Some firms even publish a separate employee report.

Talk to the firm's employees. Visit the cafeteria, for example, and chat with workers. They're one of the best barometers of the work environment.

The first step in deciding which company to work for is to identify the charactersitics you are seeking in an employer. It's a bit like an arranged marriage. You have to be sure that your basic characteristics are compatible: Are you most at ease within an open, loosely structured environment, where you are expected to take the initiative, or do you feel more comfortable in a more formal setting, where the rules and limits are clear?

Once you've established your criteria, you'll be in a better position to recognize the signposts of an above-average employer. If your potential employer has half the characteristics listed in the job hunter's checklist on the next page, you can be sure it's an environment that highly values its workers.

JOB HUNTER'S CHECKLIST

The company . . .
- [ ] Maintains a physical training or recreation facility.
- [ ] Subsidizes visits to a physical-fitness centre
- [ ] Offers an employee-assistance program (to help with personal problems like debt, legal advice or drug dependency).
- [ ] Runs a subsidized company cafeteria.
- [ ] Pays some or all orthodontic and other dental costs.
- [ ] Subsidizes vision care.
- [ ] Has an affirmative-action program.
- [ ] Pays additional maternity benefits, on top of unemployment insurance benefits.
- [ ] Encourages the employment of physically or mentally disabled people.
- [ ] Encourages emloyment of minorities.
- [ ] Reimburses the cost of further education.
- [ ] Offers scholarships to employees' children.
- [ ] Makes special effort to offer summer work to employees' families.
- [ ] Promotes from within whenever possible.
- [ ] Encourages and rewards productivity/cost-saving ideas from employees.
- [ ] Encourages lateral movement even if there are no opportunities for promotion.
- [ ] Has profit-sharing or share-purchase plans.
- [ ] Annually conducts formal performance appraisals, indicating how well your boss thinks you're doing your job.
- [ ] Offers a flex-time option.
- [ ] Encourages suggestions and works to resolve problems. Is the boss willing to listen?
- [ ] Pays moving costs (including lawyers fees, new drapes, etc.).
- [ ] Has formal mechanisms to encourage two-way dialogue between employees and management.
- [ ] Offers annual salary reviews and pay for performance.

Index